Coopers & Lybrand

Centre for Excellence in Corporate Practice

THE

ADMINISTRATION

AND

CONDUCT

OF

CORPORATE MEETINGS

Coopers
& Lybrand

Centre for Excellence in Corporate Practice

THE
ADMINISTRATION
AND
CONDUCT
OF
CORPORATE
MEETINGS

WITH APPENDIXES, PRECEDENTS
AND SHAREHOLDERS' QUESTIONS

Grenville W. Phillips

F.C.I.S., F.S.C.A., F.I.Mgt., A.C.I.B., J.P.

Canoe Press University of the West Indies
BARBADOS ● JAMAICA ● TRINIDAD & TOBAGO

Canoe Press University of the West Indies
1a Aqueduct Flats   Mona
Kingston 7   Jamaica W I

00 99 98 97 96   5 4 3 2 1

CATALOGUING IN PUBLICATION DATA

Phillips, Grenville W.
  The administration and conduct of corporate
  meetings : with appendixes, precedents and
  shareholders' questions / by Grenville W.
  Phillips.

  p. cm.
  Includes bibliographical references and index.
  ISBN 976-8125-26-8 (cloth)
  ISBN 976-8125-27-6 (pbk)
  1. Corporate meetings - Handbooks, manuals,
  etc. 2. Corporate meetings - Law and legislation -
  Caribbean, English-speaking. 3. Corporation
  law - Caribbean, English-speaking. 4. Corporation
  law - Canada. I. Title.
  HD2743.P54 1996   346.06645   dc - 20

Book design Colybrand Company Services, Barbados
and Prodesign Ltd, Jamaica

Dedicated to the memory of all the people who have helped and encouraged me in my pursuit of a professional career

TO THEM I AM A DEBTOR

USING THE BOOK

The book is divided into a number of sections. The main text is followed by a table of comparative references to assist the user in the various Caribbean territories to make easy reference to applicable regional corporate legislation.

Following the table of comparative references is the section on precedents which the corporate practitioner will find useful. The precedents include a section on typical shareholders' questions which shareholders may ask at general meetings of the company. Familiarity with the questions will also assist directors and management staff of corporations in their preparation for the annual meeting.

The book also contains a compendium of the legal cases referred to in the main text, designed to assist the student and the practitioner to achieve a better and more detailed grasp of the legal issues and authorities presented.

The Administration and Conduct of Corporate Meetings concludes with a selection of questions for the student as an aid to course revision.

CONTENTS

FOREWORD

by the
Hon. H. de B. Forde, Q.C., M.A., LLB

The right of people to associate is one of the fundamental freedoms of a democracy.

When members of a body corporate meet in furtherance of their common interest and to transact the business of a corporate entity they do so in exercise of that fundamental right of association. They must, however, conduct their activities in accordance with rules and procedures which protect the rights of all members and permit the concerns of all segments of the group to be properly considered or divisiveness and conflict will emerge.

The forum, which for centuries has facilitated interaction between members of various organisations and the collective decision making process is the meeting.

Modern company law has enshrined the importance of meetings in the institutional life of corporate entities. The law, as is clearly reflected in a vast number of judicial decisions, has also established the principle that decisions made at meetings will only be given judicial recognition, and be considered effective, if the proper rules and procedures are meticulously adhered to and followed.

As regional governments enact laws to promote greater use of the Caribbean Basin as an attractive area and desirable jurisdiction for the development and expansion of regional and legitimate international business, there will be an increase in the use of corporate entities as vehicles for business transactions. The meeting will become the pre-eminent instrument for corporate decision making process.

The enactment of new company legislation in Barbados, Guyana, Trinidad and Tobago and a number of the countries of the Organisation of Eastern Caribbean States is part of the movement towards harmonisation of Company Law in the Caribbean area. Statutory changes to the substantive laws also require the adaptation of old rules and the adoption of new procedures in place of those which previously governed the conduct and administration of company meetings.

Updated by-laws and the facility to meet and conduct business by telephone, fax and video and the new telecommunication techniques place additional responsibilities on directors and corporate secretaries. Knowledge of the new laws, rules and procedures is a *sine qua non* for the proper functioning of the corporate entity and the satisfactory conduct of business.

The standard authorities on parliamentary practice are not readily applied to circumstances of companies and other private sector organisations since in large measure, such authorities only deal with the issues of formal deliberative bodies of a political character. The publication of this book is therefore very timely.

This book is primarily intended for those persons who are required to play an active role in the affairs of corporate entities.

The text will fall into that unique category of published works which not only deals with the topic from a theoretical perspective but also focuses the reader's attention on the practical application of the theory.

Chairmen, directors and company secretaries, all of whom must understand the proper process and procedures through which corporate decisions are made, will find the text to be a practitioner's handbook. Accountants, lawyers and other professionals who are required to advise clients on various aspects of corporate procedure will find it an indispensable source of reference, while shareholders who seek a better understanding of corporate procedure and the process through which their rights may be exercised will find the book user friendly. In this connection the appendix of typical questions most asked by shareholders will be of special interest and value.

Students pursuing a career in Corporate Law are another target group to whom the book is relevant. As we enter the twenty-first century such students must, among other areas, acquire a deeper understanding of the administration and conduct of corporate meetings — a topic which is only covered briefly in their study of company Law — if they are to meet the challenges and equip themselves to deal with the demands of a commercial law practice. For them the book is required reading.

It is a delight to be able to welcome this authoritative text as a worthy contribution to Caribbean business and professional literature.

I know personally that the author's experience is vast; as a financial adviser, a professional corporate consultant and as a chartered secretary in public practice who has, over many years, advised company directors and senior management on many delicate aspects of corporate governance and procedure.

Experience, however, as the Right Hon. Sir John Donaldson once observed, although an essential qualification is not enough; it is also necessary to be able to communicate that experience to others. My friend Mr Grenville Phillips has this ability in abundance. As a result he has been able to produce a work which gives the reader the full benefit of that experience in a form which is a rare amalgam of theory and practice and which should prove invaluable to all involved and concerned with the administration and conduct of corporate meetings. I strongly recommend this book as required reading for all those whose business is business.

In concluding this foreword, I could not resist the temptation of expressing the hope that, as the region continues the process of harmonisation of its commercial laws and practice, Mr Phillips may be persuaded to undertake the additional task of providing Caribbean corporate practitioners and business persons with a companion definitive work on corporate insolvency, an aspect of professional practice for which he is equally well known and eminently qualified.

Juris Chambers, Barbados
May 22, 1996

PREFACE

There is, to the best of my knowledge, no existing Caribbean text that deals with the administration and conduct of company meetings. To the extent therefore that I have entered into uncharted waters I have had to rely heavily upon my own research and draw on my experience as a chartered secretary in public practice.

While this book deals primarily with the conduct of company meetings, its contents are equally applicable to other types of corporate meetings and I hope those company chairmen, corporate secretaries, directors, shareholders and other persons concerned with the administration and conduct of business meetings will find it useful.

I trust however, that fellow practitioners and other experts who may refer to this book do follow the admonition that King David gave to his servants with respect to their dealings with his son Absolom and similarly deal gently with any shortcomings which they may discover in this text.

The law relied upon and cited is the Companies Act CAP 308 of the Laws of Barbados 1982-1991. I have however included a Table of comparative references to Canada Business Corporations Act 1985 and other Caribbean regional company legislation, commencing at page 171, in the hope that such will enhance the usefulness of the text to the wider Canadian and Caribbean communities.

My thanks are due to: The Hon. H. deB. Forde, Q.C., M.A., LL.B., whose wise counsel has always been a source of strength to me in my professional practice and who graciously consented to write the Foreword to this book; Mr. John Wickham, MBE, who proof-read the original manuscript; Sir Jack Dear, K.C.M.G.,CHB, Q.C., Mr. Harold Hoyte of The Nation Publishing Company Ltd, and Professor Elwin Griffith of the Caribbean Law Institute for their insightful observations; Mr. Kyffin Simpson of Simpson Corporation and my partners at Coopers & Lybrand who encouraged me to write this book; to my secretaries Mrs. Charmaine Blackman who patiently did the typing of the original manuscript and its several revisions and Ms. Judy Watson who assisted her with the first draft; Mr. Derek Ashby who assisted in the compilation of the Case Compendium; Ms. Delores Dottin who assisted with the indexing and checking of the cross references and the preparation of the pre-publication marketing brochure for the book; my publishers without whose assistance and guidance this work would not have been published and finally, but by no means least, my wife Grace, who on a holiday in 1993 forbore the silence of many long hours during which period the first draft of the manuscript of this book was written.

G.W.P.
Bridgetown, Barbados
18 June 1996

INTRODUCTION

A company is a creature of statute. The law imputes to the company its 'breath of life', clothes it with a legal personality and gives it the capacity of a person thus enabling it to enter into contracts, to hold and own property and to sue and be sued. There is, however, one deficiency in this artificial being: it has no mind of its own.

The mind and management of a company vest in its directors and in its members by whom and through whom the directors are appointed. The law, however, prescribes the method by which the mind and management of the body corporate (i.e. the company) must function in order to be legally effective. The method so prescribed is by way of resolutions and or meetings of the board of directors and members of the company.

Very often the statutes may be silent or vague in dealing with procedural matters concerning the conduct of meetings. One then naturally turns to the company's corporate instruments only to discover that there are almost as many versions of these as there are practitioners, and they may also fail to address the specific issue of concern.

In the English-speaking Caribbean, company law is the subject of widespread revision aimed at updating a body of legislation that has served the region well but which has lost much of its relevance to modern commercial needs and practices.

As part of that revision a serious attempt towards harmonisation of the law is also being made and a great deal of similarity is emerging between Canadian and Caribbean corporate law.

In addition to the foregoing, the current thinking is that any new company legislation must require greater accountability from directors, officers and those who manage companies and at the same time enhance the rights of shareholders.

In the past, many shareholders' meetings were characterised by an almost undue sense of deference to the chairman of the meeting. I expect that most meetings will continue to run smoothly but there will be greater challenges to chairmen and company secretaries and some meetings will prove turbulent or even acrimonious. In those situations much will depend upon the skill, knowledge and impartiality of those who chair and conduct company meetings, and the extent to which directors and company secretaries as well as shareholders understand the guidelines that govern the conduct and administration of such meetings.

This book is meant to fill that gap and also cater to the needs of Caribbean and Canadian students who desire a handbook to assist them in their study of the subject.

It is not intended to be a legal treatise but rather a practical guide to the administration, procedure and conduct of corporate meetings. It seeks as its primary objective to assist practitioners and shareholders who organise and participate in corporate and other business meetings to do so better, not by regimentation but through a proper understanding of the applicable rules and procedures so as to facilitate and expedite the business of the meeting and to minimise dilatory actions.

CHAPTER 1

You and your company

1   The law recognises each individual as a separate legal person and each individual on reaching the age of majority has the legal capacity to enter into contracts, to hold property, to deal with such property and, subject to any other regulatory requirements, to carry on a trade or business in his or her name.

2   Where the business is carried on by a single individual in a personal capacity that individual is called a sole trader or proprietor and he\she and his\her business are legally inseparable.

3   The sole trader owns the tools and other equipment used in the business and he is entitled to all of the income derived from the business activity but he is also personally liable for all of the debts incurred in carrying on such business. The proprietorship is the oldest form of business unit.

4   As trade and commerce developed, people began to realise that there were certain benefits and advantages to be gained by teaming up with others; thus we saw the emergence of partnerships.

5   Today these are found mainly in the professions such as law firms and accounting firms but there have been and there are still many trading or commercial partnerships. In this form of business venture two or more persons enter into an agreement to carry on business for their mutual benefit.

6   Usually all of the partners are involved in the affairs of the partnership or work in the business. In the absence of any agreement to the contrary, the profits and losses of the partnership are shared equally and all of the partners both individually and collectively are liable for the debts of the whole partnership.

7   It is a feature of partnerships that, technically speaking, on the death or retirement of any one of the partners the partnership is dissolved but the remaining partners may elect to carry on a similar partnership under the same name or style.

8   The expansion of trade and commerce during the 17th and 18th centuries required greater capital to finance business ventures which were becoming more costly, complex and risky. Out of this need the concept of the company was developed.

9   The legal status of a company is that it is a distinct legal entity quite separate and apart from its shareholders. That fundamental legal issue was clearly settled in the landmark decision *Salomon* v *Salomon & Co.*[1] That distinction more than anything else distinguishes a company from a proprietorship or partnership.

10   Since a company is a separate legal entity, the property of the company is therefore not the property of its shareholders but of the company itself.

11   The company carries on business and trade for and on its own account and shareholders are not liable for the debts incurred by the company. The latter is what is meant by the term 'a company with limited liability'. The liability of the shareholders, as such shareholders, is limited to the amount they have invested into the company or agreed to invest by purchasing shares.

---

[1]   (1897) A.C. 22 (see p. 288)

12   Notwithstanding what has been said, it is nevertheless correct to say that in a practical sense this artificial legal person called a company is however owned by its shareholders collectively through their ownership of shares in the company.

13   Much has been written concerning what a share is and what it is not. Many shareholders believe that ownership of shares means that they own part of the assets or property of the company. This view is far from correct. Shareholders are not owners of the company's assets or property. They are owners of the shares in the company held by them.

14   The Act defines a share as personal property and not of the nature of real property.[2] Perhaps it may best be defined as a bundle of transferable legal rights which constitutes an equitable interest of a shareholder in a company. These rights, which are in the nature of personal property will normally include and confer upon the holder of the shares; the right to attend meetings, the right to vote, the right to elect directors, the right to receive dividends of the company when so declared by its directors, and the right to share in the surplus assets of the company on its dissolution.

15   Under older company legislation it used to be that a company's authority to trade or do business was circumscribed and limited to the extent that the documents creating the company empowered it so to do. If it traded outside the scope of such powers such activity was deemed to be *ultra vires.*

16   In traditional company law the doctrine of *ultra vires* means that a company has the legal capacity to do only such acts as are expressly or by reasonable implication authorised by its objects as set out in its memorandum of association. Any act or thing done outside of such objects was totally void for want of legal capacity in the company, and not even the unanimous assent of all of the shareholders could have validated or cured such incapacity. Over the years this situation gave rise to much litigation.

17   The rule was originally established, it is alleged, for the protection of shareholders. However to avoid having transactions of a company rendered void for want of legal capacity, it became the practice to seek to

---

[2]   The Companies Act of Barbados Cap. 308 section 26 (1)

include every conceivable type and aspect of business activity in the objects clause of a company upon its formation so as to enable the company to carry on the widest possible range of business activity.

18   Most modern company legislation now confers upon a company the same legal capacity to enter into contracts and do business as a natural person. Consequently the documents of incorporation have been greatly simplified.

19   A company is formed by filing documents called Articles of Incorporation with the appropriate regulatory authority and comes into existence on the date shown on its Certificate of Incorporation.

20   Another practical distinguishing feature between companies and other forms of business units is that the shareholders of companies are not normally all employed in the business of the company. Twentieth century shareholders are to a large extent investors.

21   Since it would be impractical for all shareholders to run and manage the affairs of their company certain conventions and rules of conduct evolved over time, many of which have now become statutory.

22   The Companies Act Cap 308 of the laws of Barbados provides that, with the exception of lunatics, bankrupts or persons under age, one or more persons may incorporate a company. It then stipulates that the affairs and business of a company shall be managed by its directors and that such directors must be appointed by the shareholders.

23   Extensive provisions dealing with the rights of shareholders and directors and regulating the administration of a company's affairs are contained in the Act. In particular, shareholders must note that in the absence of any unanimous shareholders' agreement, their influence and authority on the management and affairs of the company may only be exercised through the medium of the meeting, in which forum decisions are made in the form of resolutions passed in accordance with certain rules and procedures.

24   Over time, these rules and procedures have been developed to enhance the orderliness, effectiveness and productivity of company meetings, as well as to curb potential abuse of authority by directors.

25   The purpose of a meeting is to conduct and deal expeditiously with the business before members. It is neither a forum for gamesmanship nor one for the mere rubber stamping of management's decisions.

26   Shareholders should have a vested interest in ensuring that company meetings are productive. Successful corporate meetings can be beneficial both to management, as well as to shareholders and their company, but they must all act and conduct the business in a manner that is in the best interest of the company.

CHAPTER 2

Discussion

A prerequisite for informed decision making

27   While the purpose of corporate and other business meetings is to make decisions, effective discussion contributes greatly to the whole process of informed decision making but most of us give little or no thought to the art of discussion.

28   This book is about the administration and conduct of corporate meetings for it is in that forum that decisions of the body corporate are made. It is however not enough that the decisions are made within the rules through a process that is procedurally correct, but that such decisions are also made on the basis of informed opinion. It is in pursuit of that later objective that this chapter is included.

29   I am indebted to the Royal Bank of Canada for much of the material included in this chapter which was originally published in one of their newsletters.[3] The author of that publication commenced with the bold assertion that effectiveness in discussion can have a vital bearing on our lives. He then further asserted that one of the reasons why discussions

---

[3]   See Royal Bank of Canada, *Newsletter,* Vol. 74, No. 5 (September/October 1993).

---

often fail to achieve results is because people mix them up with other forms of discourse. Because of this, said the writer, a discussion is perhaps best defined by what it is not.

30   First, a discussion is not a conversation.

31   "While a conversation may range over a variety of subjects, a discussion is focused on a specific topic or list of topics. When — as they would in a conversation — people talk about matters other than the question being discussed, they throw discussion off the track. A conversation generally has no particular purpose, but a discussion is aimed at a definite objective. It may be to solve a problem, to decide on a course of action, or to reconcile conflicting opinions. To discuss something is, by definition, to work towards resolving a question through mutual examination of facts, ideas, and views."

32   Secondly, a discussion is not an argument. An argument is a verbal dispute.

33   Thirdly, a discussion is not a debate. A debate is a contest in which one side strives to conquer the other through rhetoric. The parties to a debate are cast in the role of adversaries. The parties to a discussion are joined as it were in a partnership working and striving towards a conclusion acceptable to the collective will and for the common good.

34   "When we enter into a discussion, we should always keep in mind that we are aiming at reaching an understanding with the other party or parties. This is not to say that conflict should be avoided. On the contrary, it is usually best for people to speak frankly . . . if not so bluntly that they offend others and thereby blight the feeling of partnership . . . A discussion should embrace all points of view."

35   While we must admit that it is human nature to want to have one's own way, in a civilised society as well as in a properly ordered meeting the person who gets his or her way is expected to deserve it by objective standards. There is no room in the business meeting nor any place in a productive discussion for the rhetorical trickery employed in competitive debating.

36   People who take this combative approach are also prone to display considerable rudeness and inclined to contradict other speakers midway through the exposition of their cases. They may also try to 'win' by attrition seeking to make the same point over and over again or may resort to verbal sniping at opposing parties with scorn or sarcasm. A little comic relief is often welcomed in serious deliberations but there is a fine line between jest and jeer. Our opponents must always be respected.

37   "We all have a natural tendency to depart from the issue being discussed and pounce on the weak and sore spots in others' personalities. We should strive to keep this instinctive reaction in check . . . When a discussion gets personal, people will resort to unworthy devices like calling names, making accusations, reviving disputes from the past, rubbing it in ('I told you so'), ascribing malicious motives, wilfully misunderstanding what their interlocutors are saying, and throwing embarrassing facts in their faces."

38   "Many of the debating gambits condemned by ancient logicians as sophistry depend upon shifting the discussion away from the issues and on to personalities. These have imposing Latin names, but in modern terms, they might be stated as: bullying; blackmailing; trying to buy people out by preying on their vanity or appealing to their instinct to conform or holding them up to ridicule and making irrelevant comparisons."

39   "In the 1940s Professor Irvin Lee, the American author of *How to Talk with People*, conducted a systematic study of why discussions fail by monitoring fifty groups in various situations. At the top of his list of causes of 'discussion breakdown' was the shift from the issues to personalities. Many of the other causes stemmed from personal pride: . . . when a colloquy between factions is marked by such 'ego statements' as 'you are absolutely wrong' — 'I have had years of experience on this' — 'I know what I am talking about' — etc."

40   One of the basic rules of discussion is to try not to confuse assumptions with facts. A fact is something that is capable of verification by demonstration. If the truth of a notion cannot be demonstrated, it is merely being assumed. If you are not sure whether something is true or not say so. Never pretend to know something you actually don't know to serve

your vanity or to save yourself from embarrassment. If facts should not be assumed, neither should they be twisted to fit one's opinions. This is often done quite unconsciously.

41   No matter how objective we like to think we are, our convictions are bound to be subject to a degree of distortion arising out of our backgrounds and interests. We should make ample allowance for our prejudices and emotional hang-ups. Discussions give us a chance to test our own fallible beliefs against the facts and the logic of our interlocutors.

42   "Whether it is a one-on-one encounter or it takes place within a larger group, a discussion is a matter of alternately speaking and listening. Thus a prime qualification for being a good debater is to be a good listener."

43   "Listening is not as easy as it seems; a study of 'listening efficiency' some years ago estimated that people in North American industry understood only half of all that was said to them in their work. The starting point in any effort to listening properly is to train yourself to concentrate on what the other person is saying, and stop mentally rehearsing what you intend to say when your turn comes. By assiduously following what is being said, you can ensure that your own remarks are to the point when you are on the speaking side." [4]

44   **Discussion is an integral part of the meeting.** In the forum of the meeting a matter will usually be brought before members for deliberation framed in the form of a proposition or motion. After the motion is proposed and seconded, the presiding officer may then invite members to speak on the proposition. It is a period too valuable to be wasted, it is in fact, discussion time, an opportunity when hopefully the varied and diverse views of members will be transformed into informed opinions, to be collectively expressed through the voting process in the form of a resolution of the body corporate. It is a prerequisite for informed decision making.

---

[4]   The text in quotations are selected extracts from the newsletter referred to at footnote 3.

CHAPTER 3

The concept and theory
of corporate resolve

45   The concept of 'meetings', an issue with which this book is primarily
      concerned, is capable of many interpretations but the interpretation which
      interests us most is the concept of the meeting as 'an assembly of persons
      for a lawful and common purpose'.

46   Complex societies have made increasing use of assemblies and other
      organised forums for social, political and business intercourse and
      governance. The actual assembly or meeting may be casual or organised
      and its object may be to receive information or to participate in the
      management or administration of some public or private enterprise.

47   The question, 'Was there a meeting?' was one of the essential issues
      which the Court of Appeal had to determine in the case of *Byng* v *London
      Life Association,* which is referred to later in this book. Counsel for the
      plaintiff had alleged on the facts before the court that there was no
      meeting and in support of his submission relied on the definition of the
      word 'meet' in the *Shorter Oxford Dictionary*, viz. "to come face to face or
      in the company of another person". The Court did not accept the

submission. The learned judge opined that the rationale behind the requirement for meetings in the (UK) 1985 Act is that the members should be able to attend in person so as to debate and vote on matters affecting the company.

48   Until recently this could only be achieved by every one being physically present in the same room face to face. Given modern technological advances, the same result can now be achieved without all the members coming face to face, without being physically in the same room they can be electronically be in each other's presence so as to hear and be heard and to see and be seen.

49   The fact that such a 'meeting' could not have been foreseen at the time the first statutory requirements for meetings were laid down, does not require us to hold that such a meeting is not within the meaning of the word 'meeting' in the 1985 Act.

50   The learned judge went on to express the view, that he had no doubt that valid meetings of a company can be properly held using overflow rooms provided, first, that all steps are taken to direct to the overflow rooms those unable to get into the main meeting hall and, second that there are adequate audiovisual links to enable those in all the rooms to see and hear what is going on in the other rooms. Were the law otherwise, he concluded, with the present tendency towards companies with very large number of shareholders and corresponding uncertainty as to how many shareholders would attend meetings, the organisation of such meetings might prove to be impossible.

51   The term 'corporate resolve' may best be defined as the collective corporate will or collective corporate decision of the assembly or meeting when constituted as such.

52   To properly appreciate the theory and concept of 'corporate resolve' it must first be recognised that corporate bodies generally and more specifically those created or governed pursuant to company law are democratic institutions. Here a fine line of distinction must be drawn between democratic institutions and egalitarian institutions. Companies are constitutionally democratic but they are not egalitarian.

53   They are democratic in the sense that, except for those matters which are prescribed by law, the internal affairs and management of companies are regulated though a form of government and administrative procedure in which ultimate sovereign power resides in the shareholders and is exercised either directly by them through meetings of the company or by directors elected by them.

54   In this sense, companies and similar corporate bodies are said to be democratic institutions as distinct from egalitarian since all members of the body corporate are not necessarily equal in standing, but often exercise an influence on the affairs of the body corporate in proportion to their respective financial interest in the corporation.

55   In chapter 1 we observed that a corporation was a creature of statute. Its fundamental characteristics were outlined and we concluded that having no mind of its own, its mind and management was therefore the collective mind and management of its shareholders and/or directors when exercised at properly constituted meetings.

56   Sometimes difficulty is encountered when one tries to distinguish when persons are acting in their collective capacity and when acting as individuals especially in circumstances when the interest is not fully compatible. For this reason a proper understanding of the theory of corporate resolve is therefore an essential prerequisite for meaningful participation by the wider community in commercial enterprises in developing societies.

57   If it is accepted that companies are theoretically democratic institutions, then it ought to follow that some method must be provided for ascertaining, 'the corporate resolve' or democratic will of such institutions.

58   The Act prescribes the forum and method to be used. It is the formal assembly which we commonly call shareholders meetings. That is the forum where the democratic masses i.e. 'the shareholders' may meet.

59   When meeting as a formally constituted assembly in what the Act calls 'a meeting of shareholders' or 'a meeting of members' they constitute a special assembly which is referred to as 'the company in general meeting'.

60   That meeting or assembly is the repository of the ultimate authority of the company. That authority is however not vested fragmentarily in the several shareholders, but is vested collectively in them when meeting as a proper and validly constituted meeting of members.

61   When shareholders meet in the forum of such an assembly they enjoy the most important of all their rights; namely the right of the shareholders of a company by majority vote to order its affairs; for it is a cardinal principle of corporation law, as it is of political government, that the will of the majority of the members, duly formulated, must be taken to be the will of the whole body corporate and must prevail.[5] See *Australian Auxiliary Steam Clipper Co.* v *Mounsey*[6] and *Cie de Navigation Union* v *Christen*.[7]

62   A meeting must be carefully defined. The question, 'What constitutes a meeting?' is therefore one that requires careful explanation. It must be noted that the mere assembly of all the necessary parties by chance cannot be converted to a meeting by fiat of one of the parties, neither can an instant meeting be forced upon the group without unanimous consent.

63   So fundamental is the issue of the collective corporate resolve as distinct from personal expressions of opinion that the Act has established certain provisions which must be complied with in order to have a validly constituted meeting which, with limited exception, is the only forum through which the 'corporate resolve' or collective will of members may be ascertained.

64   That resolve flows from the authority of the meeting and is expressed in the form of resolutions of the meeting, and such resolutions must be the product of the stipulated voting process.

65   In the chapters that follow, you will discover that the voting process is the means of ascertaining the wills of the majority of members present and voting. It is the expression of that majority's preference in general meeting which constitutes the corporate resolve of the company, and which binds the collective membership of the company despite the fact that a minority of members may have voted against the resolution.

5   See Wegenast, *The Law of Canadian Companies,* p. 315.
6   (1958) 4 K & J 733 (see p. 289)
7   (1880) 4 L N 162

66   The rules and procedures prescribed by the Act and a company's corporate instruments for determining the mind of the meeting i.e. its corporate resolve, must therefore be strictly observed as failure to do so may invalidate the meeting or the resolutions passed thereat. Within the pages of this book you will find guidance on those rules and procedures.

67   The meeting is an important event not only as a place where eligible persons may meet and express their preference by voting, thereby helping to shape the collective corporate will, but also as a forum for communication. In this forum members' comprehension of the subject matter, upon which the meeting is asked to make a decision, may be enhanced through the process of dialogue and discussion, all of which, if done sincerely and within the rules and in the spirit of seeking to determine that which is in the best interest of the company, can only enhance the democratic process and ensure that decisions are made on the basis of informed opinion. "It is, perhaps," opined Professor Welling,[8] "for this reason that democratic political societies protect and encourage free speech, while autocratic governments prefer informative monologues delivered to silent, subservient listeners."

68   Welling further opined that in *MacDougall* v *Gardiner.*[9] The English Court of Appeal response betrayed a misguided judicial view in underestimating the importance of the general meeting. There Lord Justice James said: "Has a particular individual the right to have [the meeting held strictly in accordance with the articles] for the purpose of using his power of eloquence to induce the others to listen to him and to take his view? This is an equity which I have never yet heard of in this court . . . That this Court is to entertain a bill for the purpose of enabling one particular member of the company to have an opportunity of expressing his opinions *viva voce* at a meeting of the shareholders. If so, I do not know why we should not go further, and say, not only must the meeting be held, but the shareholders must stay there to listen to him and to be convinced by him".

69   Welling concluded by stating: "If the views of James L. J. were to prevail, there would seem little point in gathering the shareholders together for a general meeting at all. Management propaganda by post and mail-in

---

[8]   B. Welling, *Corporate Law in Canada*, pp. 457-58.
[9]   (1875) 1 Ch D 13 (see p. 292)

votes by shareholders would accomplish the same purpose if the law does not actively encourage the raising and discussion of dissenting opinions."

70   The author concurs fully with the views expressed by Welling. Indeed meetings are important not only as a forum for ascertaining the corporate resolve, but also as a forum where management can be called to account.

71   Shareholders in North America are desperately seeking to establish greater control over their companies. In many cases the delegation of substantially all authority to directors has virtually reduced shareholders' influence to a mere rubber stamp, and now the directors are discovering that their own powers are being usurped by hired management.

72   In very large companies these 'non-proprietary mandarins'[10] have virtually made themselves dictators and have hijacked the process of the corporate resolve from the grasp of directors and stockholders. It is an evil to be guarded against in developing societies. I believe that a better understanding of the administration and conduct of corporate meetings will assist in maintaining an equitable balance of power between directors, shareholders and their company.

---

[10]   B. Welling, *Corporate Law in Canada*, pp. 457-58.

CHAPTER 4

The legal framework applicable to company meetings

TYPES OF MEETINGS

73   There are several types of meetings. The main types we generally encounter include:

> **Public meetings:** These are some of the oldest form of meetings from which the private meeting derived some of its features and characteristics. Any meeting in a public place and/or any meeting which the public is permitted to attend whether on payment or otherwise will normally be classified as a public meeting. Persons concerned with the conduct and management of public meetings should acquaint themselves with the Public Order Act or such similar legislation and the issues relating to disorder at public meetings, disorderly conduct, breaches of the peace, and the role and functions of the police.

♦   **Meetings of elected members of government**: These types of meetings are usually governed by specific rules of procedure known as standing orders.

♦   **Meetings of unincorporated bodies:** Unincorporated bodies include social clubs and other common interest societies and groups. These bodies usually have a constitution which generally includes rules for meetings. The rules are however not usually extensive or elaborate.

♦   **Meetings of registered corporate entities:** Such meetings are usually regulated by statute, the corporate instruments of the body corporate, case law and common law, all of which have combined to impose very detailed procedures on the conduct and administration of corporate meetings.

These corporate meetings include general and class meetings of members, meetings of the directors or management body, and special or extraordinary meetings of members. It is these types of meetings with which this text is concerned.

There is a widely held view in the Caribbean that accountants and lawyers are best equipped to conduct meetings. The truth is that people who have a proper grasp of business, especially that of their organisation, and of the rules governing the conduct of meetings are the ones best equipped to chair and conduct corporate meetings.

LEGAL FRAMEWORK

74   Dennis Roberts in his book *The Administration of Company Meetings* made a rather profound statement which is worth quoting: "The company secretary or chairman need not be a lawyer, but he needs to know where to find the answers to legal problems as they arise. Often there will not be time to consult legal advisors during the urgent pressures of a meeting, and so he will turn to the Companies Act without finding what he is seeking. Often he would do better to turn to the company's own Articles of Association, but even the Act and the articles together will not provide a

complete guide to the law." He concluded by posing the question: "Where, then, is the law of company meetings to be found?"[11]

75   It is that question which is addressed in this chapter.

76   There are three main sources from which the law on company meetings may be found and four basic rules by which company secretaries and presiding officers must be guided.

Sources of Applicable Law

77   **The companies acts:** These are of paramount importance. It should be pointed out, however, that only relatively small portions of these Acts are concerned with the administration and conduct of company meetings.

In the Caribbean, we face a special problem in that almost every territory has its own company legislation, some, more ancient than others. Throughout this book the Barbados Companies Act CAP 308 1982-1991 is used as the source of reference since at the date of writing it is probably the most up to date body of company legislation on the statute book in the English-speaking Caribbean.

There is also in existence a draft Companies Bill which has been prepared under the auspices of the Caribbean Law Institute (CLI). This bill is modelled after the Barbados legislation and mirrors closely the Barbados Companies Act CAP 308. It is anticipated that this Bill will be adopted by most of the English-speaking territories. Practitioners however will need to consult the relevant legislation which, for the time being, is applicable to their respective territory.

A further problem also confronts Caribbean practitioners. As these territories seek to enhance their own economic well being, several regional governments have introduced special legislation in order to attract foreign investment or to develop their territories as offshore financial centres. While in some territories, such as Barbados, there is, with the exception of banking, a single Act under which companies may

---

[11]   D. Roberts, *The Administration of Company Meetings*, p. 3.

be incorporated this is not necessarily the case in all territories of the region.

Some such territories provide that international business companies may be incorporated under special international business companies legislation and not under their respective companies acts which then only apply for the incorporation and regulation of domestic companies.

In Barbados, while formations are generally done under the Companies Act CAP 308, other legislation such as the International Business Companies Act, the Foreign Sales Corporation Act and the Exempt Insurance Companies Act may provide exemptions from compliance with certain provisions of the Companies Act CAP 308.

Practitioners will therefore need to familiarise themselves with the applicable provisions of such other enactments in appropriate circumstances. In addition, not only must the main body of the other enactments be consulted but also the regulations made under such legislation.

78 **The company's corporate instruments:** Throughout this book I have elected to use the term 'corporate instruments' in preference to the 'Memorandum and Articles of Association'. The Barbados Companies Act and the draft CLI Companies Bill mirror closely Canadian corporate law and practice and there are differences of interpretation to some of the terms previously used as well as new terms which have been or are now being introduced into the region's corporate vocabulary.

Modern company law has introduced the concept of Articles of Incorporation and by-laws. The first is akin to the former Memorandum of Association while the latter is comparable to the former Articles of Association. It is these documents which I sometimes refer to either singly and/or collectively as 'the company's corporate instruments'.

It is often the case that, in matters relating to the administration and conduct of company meetings, the company's corporate instruments, especially the by-laws, are of greater immediate relevance to the problems which presiding officers may encounter than the Act itself.

The by-laws should, and would normally, make provision for such matters as the giving of notices, the quorum required for a valid meeting, the voting rights of members, the right to demand a poll and the person entitled to take the chair and preside over meetings.

79   **The common law:** Very often company secretaries and chairmen find themselves in positions where, on some matters such as rules of order, the conduct of debates and dealing with disorderly conduct, neither the Act nor the company's corporate instruments will give the answers or guidance that they seek. In such circumstances they must rely upon common law practice and custom which have been established over many years, in some cases, with the sanction or guidance of the courts through various legal decisions handed down.

80   In dire circumstances when neither the Act, the company's corporate instruments nor the common law speak clearly to the matter under consideration, practitioners will have to rely upon four basic rules, namely the rule of *ultra vires*, the majority rule, the rule against oppression and the rule of natural justice by whose precepts, in any event, they should always be guided.

Basic Rules

81   **The rule of *ultra vires*:** Under the provisions of older company law the extent of the company's legal capacity was set out in its Memorandum of Association. Modern company legislation seeks to amend this practice by providing that a company shall have the rights, powers and privileges of an individual but notwithstanding the foregoing provision, a company shall not carry on any business nor exercise any power that it is restricted by its articles from carrying on or exercising. The *ultra vires* rule is therefore still very relevant and where any action of the company is outside of its powers, that action is null and void.

Directors, company secretaries and those who manage the corporate affairs of companies should note that where directors act within the powers of the company but exceed their own powers as officers under the by-laws, their action may be made valid through the process of ratification by the company in general meeting.

However, if the action of the directors was such so that the matters done by them were outside the powers of the company, i.e. *ultra vires* the company itself, such cannot be cured merely through the process of ratification by members of the company in general meeting. Furthermore, if third parties were adversely affected the directors may find themselves in a position where neither they nor the company may be able to rely upon their own acts of *ultra vires* as a shield or any protection against such third parties who may have acted in good faith.

The rule which underscores this principle is known as the rule in the Turquand case or the Turquand rule.[12] Simply put the rule emanating from the judgment is that a person dealing with a company is entitled to assume that its internal procedures have been complied with. The rule seems to make good sense, for if a person dealing with a company was bound to satisfy himself or herself that all of the formalities required by the company's documents have been satisfied, the efficient conduct of business would be severely impeded.

Much case law has developed around the rule, and there are of course many exceptions. The Act by section 21 provides, for example, that where a person has, or ought to have by virtue of his position with the company, knowledge of any non-compliance such person may not rely on the relief granted in the Turquand rule.

Practitioners must therefore ensure that resolutions and contracts which the company is asked to pass or adopt are properly within the power of the company.

82   **The majority rule:** It has often been said that the voice of the majority is the voice of God. The foregoing is merely a partial statement of truth. While a company is owned by its shareholders and such shareholders exercise their power and influence through the process of a majority vote in general meetings, they may only act within the law and not *ultra vires* the company, neither must they act in an oppressive manner towards minorities. In other words shareholders must act equitably, legally and

---

12   *Royal British Bank* v *Turquand* (1856) — 6 E & B 327 (see p. 294).

within the confines of the company's own powers through the majority voting process.

While on the subject of the majority rule let me caution against a common fallacy held by some shareholders who believe that just because the company is collectively owned by its shareholders, they can, at any time and in any manner, through a majority vote in general meeting, usurp the powers of the directors or, as some have put it, 'do as they please'.

Shareholders may be able, through the proper corporate process, to remove the directors and appoint others in their place or amend the corporate instruments of the company to restrict the powers of the directors or to enter into a unanimous shareholders' agreement to accomplish the foregoing; but until either of those actions has been accomplished, shareholders cannot vote to overrule the powers and actions of directors in so far as they relate to the management of the business of the company.

It is perhaps appropriate under this caption to make mention of the famous rule in *Foss* v *Harbottle*[13] which for many years was the underpinning of the doctrine of majority rule. Simply put, the doctrine emanating from the case *Foss* v *Harbottle* was that where a wrong was done to the company, an individual shareholder of the company could not maintain an action in the name of the company to rectify the matter if a majority of the shareholders of the company had or could ratify the wrong. There were some exceptions to this rule. Essentially those exceptions fell into one or more of the following categories:

(a) an act that was *ultra vires* the company or otherwise illegal

(b) an act that constituted a fraud against the minority where the wrongdoers were themselves in control of the company

(c) an irregularity in the passing of a resolution that required a qualified majority

(d) an act that infringed the personal rights of an individual shareholder

---

[13]   (1843) 2 Hare 461 (see p. 296)

The Courts had apparently adopted the view that it was not their role and function to manage and regulate the affairs of a company. It believed that business decisions were to be made by the directors and where a sanction was required the voice of the majority was sufficient.

The facts of the case were as follows. Harbottle and other directors had sold land to the company for development at inflated prices. The directors mismanaged the company and matters deteriorated to an unsatisfactory state. Foss, representing a group of shareholders, tried to get a general meeting held so that the directors may be called to account. He was unsuccessful in having the meeting held and therefore applied to the Court, holding himself out as a shareholder who had suffered loss, in order to assert the company's rights against the directors.

The Court dismissed the action and held that only the company was competent to sue to assert its rights. Individual shareholders, said the Court, should bring their complaint before a general meeting with a view to obtaining a majority decision for the company to take the necessary action.

83 **The rule against oppression:** Because of the impact of the *Foss* v *Harbottle* rule and the developing awareness as to what constituted good corporate governance, law reformers in England developed the concept of the derivative action and the remedy against oppression of minorities.

Modern company law has now modified the *Foss* v *Harbottle* rule through the introduction of the concept of the derivative action and statutory provisions dealing with the oppression of minorities which counterbalances and modifies the application of the majority rule in certain circumstances.

Most actions on the issue of oppression revolve around the question of whether the pecuniary interest of individual shareholders has been affected.[14]

With leave of the court minorities may now bring an action or defend an action in the name of and on behalf of the company to cure an abuse or rectify a situation which the directors or the majority ought properly to

---

14   See "CCH Corporate Brief " 2 (October 1994).

have attended to, but which for one reason or another they neglected or refused to do. It should be noted that derivative actions must be for the benefit of the company.

The restraint against oppression is somewhat personal and is intended for the relief of minorities in that a person may apply to the court for an order of relief if it can be shown that the business or affairs of the company have or are being carried on or the powers of the directors are being exercised in a manner that is oppressive or unfairly prejudicial or unfairly disregards the interest of any shareholder, creditor, director or officer of the company.

The remedy against oppression has been referred to as the broadest, most comprehensive and most open-ended shareholder remedy in the common law world.

Like any new remedy it may itself be subject to abuse. Mr Justice Farley of the Ontario Court of Justice made the following observation in *Blair* v *Consolidated Enfield Corporation:* "We must guard against debasing the nature of the oppression remedy by attempting to employ it to address the most trivial of complaints."[15]

Further observations of Mr Justice Farley on the subject in an unreported judgement of the Ontario Court of Justice are also worthy of note.[16] The learned judge made the following insightful comment: "The purpose of the oppression section (remedy) is not to reward either side in a game of 'corporate chicken'. Indeed a proper remedy in an oppression application is not to reward any party but rather to bring the relationship back to normal (or if an even keel is not possible, then to allow a disengagement on neutral terms)."

In an article under the caption 'Perspectives on Corporate Law' which appeared in CCH Corporate Brief[17] the author opined that "nothing comes out of the Court quicker these days than a decision on a derivative action or oppression application . . . but shareholder remedies may not be

---

[15] Ontario Court of Justice (General Division) August 11, 1994. File No. G13156, p.12

[16] *Borsook* v *Broder* in the Ontario Court of Justice (General Division) November 4, 1994. Court File No. B294/94

[17] "CCH Corporate Brief" 9 (May 1995).

available to all shareholders". He points out that to apply for leave to commence a derivative action or to apply for relief from oppression the applicant must fall within the statutory definition of 'a complainant'.

The position is not dissimilar in our own companies legislation, but recent litigation in Canada has interpreted this matter in a variety of ways. (See for example *Richardson Greenfields of Canada Limited* v *Kalmacoff*[18] and *Royal Trust Corporation of Canada* v *Hordo*[19].)

The issues are complex and are really outside of the scope of this book but one of the interesting views expressed by the Court of first instance was that a person who acquired shares after the facts which were the subject of the complaint were known should not be treated as a 'complainant'. The Court of Appeal objected to the conclusion of the Court of first instance stating that the law did not impose a condition of share ownership contemporaneous with occurrence of the acts complained of.

I do not believe that we have heard the last of this matter. The issue will no doubt reach the Supreme Court of Canada in due course, for there is powerful logic in the reasoning of the Judge in the Court of first instance. He said ". . . a sale of the shares from the holder who may have been oppressed did not carry with it the right to collect damages for such oppression. The value of those shares in the market would have decreased to compensate for the amount of the oppression; so in effect the purchaser would have received the benefit of purchasing the shares at a reduced value and the benefit of being compensated for the oppressive conduct." In the words of the learned Judge, "that benefit should generally remain with the person who is actually oppressed".[20]

---

[18]   Ontario Court of Appeal decision released April 7, 1995

[19]   (1993) 10 B.L.R. (3d) 86

[20]   In the "Directors Briefing" 2 (July 1995) by CCH Canadian Limited Mr Robert W. Beattie, a member of the editorial board, made the following comments in an article captioned "The Oppression Remedy — Some Welcome Guidance for Corporate Directors":

> The oppression remedy provisions in the federal and provincial business corporations statutes give broad discretion to the courts in determining appropriate remedies. Two recent high court decisions in the case of *Naneff* v *Concrete Holdings Limited* et al. have reinforced that principle, and have also provided some useful guidance as to the limits of the judicial discretion in oppression remedy cases.

> In the case cited, Alex one of Mr Naneff's sons brought an action under the oppression remedy provisions of the Ontario Business Corporation Act. The

This therefore leads us into the fourth rule.

84   **The rule of natural justice:** This is an elusive concept. It is possible to convene meetings which were properly summoned, a quorum being present throughout, the votes cast were checked by scrutineers, but somehow one left the meeting feeling that justice was not done.

> trial judge found that various acts of the corporation, the directors and the controlling shareholders were oppressive of Alex's interest. Those findings were not disturbed by the higher courts but the decisions in both the Divisional Court and the Court of Appeal varied certain of the remedies ordered by the trial judge.
>
> The thrust of the Divisional Court's decision ((1994) 19 O.R. (3rd) 691) is that, since the discretion given to the courts under the oppression remedy provisions is so broad, appellate courts should be reluctant to substitute their decisions for that of the trial judge.
>
> The trial judge had ordered that the entire business should be sold and that Mr Naneff's sons would be entitled to bid for it. He had rejected the alternative option of requiring that Alex's interest in the business be purchased by the others since, according to the trial judge, such would allow Mr Naneff to accomplished the very objective which he had sought through his oppressive conduct to achieve.
>
> The Divisional Court allowed the order of the trial judge to stand, but the Court of Appeal overturned the trial judge's order and in fact substituted the alternative option which the trial judge had rejected.
>
> The Court of Appeal reiterated the principle that the oppression remedy provisions give broad discretion to the courts in fashioning appropriate remedies, and also the corollary, that where such broad discretion is given to a court of first instance, "an appellate court's power to review is quite limited". However in giving the judgement for the Court of Appeal, Galligan J.A. then went on to set out what he described as two important limitations on the discretionary powers of the courts in determining appropriate remedies under the oppression remedy provisions.
>
> > 1. The remedies must only rectify oppressive conduct.
> > 2. The remedies must protect only the person's interest as a shareholder, director of officer as such.
>
> Galligan J.A. enunciated a principle which he stated was rooted in an English House of Lords decision. Said he, "Any remedy must be just having regard to the rights, expectations and obligations which actually exist between the individuals in the particular circumstances." Applying that principle the Court of Appeal concluded that the order to sell the entire business would then be unjust to Mr Naneff.
>
> *Author's note: The derivative action and the statutory provision dealing with the oppression against minorities are new and developing aspects of corporate law and practice. In dealing with the administration and conduct of meetings, being the forum at which decisions are made, directors and officers need constantly to bear these new provisions in mind when relying upon the majority rule.*

What then is this rule of natural justice? Perhaps it may best be described by citing the following principles by which all directors and company officers should be guided:

i. No person shall be judge in his own case. For example, if the chairman is an interested party in a contentious contract which is being debated he should not only declare his interest but prudence should dictate, even if the company's corporate instruments do not so require, that a disinterested person should take the chair while the item is being considered.

ii. No person shall be condemned unheard. This provision is especially relevant when it involves disciplinary matters or the status of individuals such as the company's auditors etc.

iii. Corporate decisions or the passing of resolutions must not be obtained by trick.

iv. Finally, presiding officers must not only conduct the proceedings fairly and impartially, but they must be seen to have so conducted the meeting.

CHAPTER 5

The types and purpose of company meetings

85   A company is a creature of statute. We previously observed that its persona is that given to it by or under the legislation through which it was incorporated and thus brought into being. We acknowledge however that a company has no mind of its own. Its mind and management are derived through the minds of its directors and members.

86   A general meeting of the members (i.e. shareholders) of the company represents the source of ultimate and final authority within the corporate structure of a company. It is the means through which the corporate resolve is ascertained.

87   The term general meeting must not be too narrowly interpreted to mean only the annual meeting or the annual general meeting, but rather to encompass all general meetings of members as distinct from class meetings or a committee meeting etc.

88   It is to the general meeting to whom directors must give an account of their stewardship and to which the auditors must report and from whom authority must be obtained before the directors may enter into extraordinary transactions on behalf of the company.

89   Again, it is this meeting that must approve changes in the corporate instruments of the company and whose sanction must or should be obtained before the directors are empowered to sell, lease or exchange all or substantially all of the property of the company other than in the ordinary course of business.

90   The general meeting is also the repository of all or any powers of the company which have not, by the Act or the corporate instruments of the company, been given or bestowed upon the directors of the company; consequently, the general meeting of the company has an inherent authority to cure acts done by the directors which was within the powers of the company but *ultra vires* the authority of the directors.

91   In the case of *Bamford* v *Bamford* [21] the directors were alleged to have acted without proper authority or in bad faith by issuing shares to certain friendly persons during a take-over bid situation. Their action was however confirmed by the company in general meeting and so the attempt to reverse or void the allotment of the shares failed on the grounds that, even if the directors' action was outside the scope of their authority, the allotment per se was not void since it was not *ultra vires* the company and it had been confirmed by the company in general meeting, which meeting possessed the power and authority to remedy any want of authority on the part of the directors.

92   There are several kinds of company or general meetings. The term company or general meeting is used to distinguish meetings of members (i.e. shareholders) from meetings of directors; however there is one special directors' meeting to which reference may be appropriate under this caption.

93   **The organisational meeting:** Section 62 of the Act provides that after obtaining a Certificate of Incorporation a meeting of the directors of the company must be held. At this meeting the directors may:

(a)   Receive the corporate instruments from the incorporator;

(b)   Make by-laws;

(c)   Appoint the company secretary;

[21]   (1970) 1 Ch 212 (see p. 297)

(d) Adopt forms of share certificates and corporate records;

(e) Authorise the issue of shares;

(f) Appoint other officers;

(g) Appoint an auditor to hold office until the first annual meeting of shareholders;

(h) Consider any draft business plan;

(i) Make banking arrangements; and

(j) Transact any other business.

94 The organisational meeting may be called by the incorporator of the company or any director named in the corporate instruments of the company. Specimen organisation minutes are shown in Appendix II Precedent A.

95 **Annual meeting or annual general meeting:** This meeting is commonly referred to as the AGM. Section 105 of the Act prescribes that each company must in each year hold an annual meeting not later that 18 months after the date the company came into existence and subsequently not later that 15 months after holding the last preceding annual meeting.

96 The business to be transacted at the annual meeting is governed by the Act and the by-laws of the company and will usually consist of:

(a) Receipt of the auditors' report;

(b) Consideration of the financial statements;

(c) The election of directors;

(d) The re-appointment of the incumbent auditor;

(e) Any special business.

97 Company secretaries and presiding officers should note however that if any special business is to be transacted, notice of the nature of that business in sufficient detail must be given so as to permit members to form a reasoned judgement thereon and the text of any special resolution

to be submitted to the meeting must also be given with the notice. (See section 110.)

98   **Special or extraordinary meetings:** In addition to the annual meeting of members, the directors of a company may at any time convene a special meeting of shareholders. Neither the Act nor the company's by-laws will prescribe the nature of business to be dealt with at special meetings, but the Act does stipulate that all business transacted at a special meeting of shareholders is special business and, as such, the requirements and provisions applicable to any special business to be transacted at annual meetings, as noted above, will apply to any business to be transacted at special or extraordinary meetings.

99   **Class meetings:** Where the issued capital of the company is divided into shares of several classes with different rights attached thereto, class meetings will be necessary if it is proposed to vary the rights attached to one or more classes of shares. Indeed the Act makes it mandatory for the holders of shares of a class or of a series to vote separately upon certain specific proposals which are set out in sections 201 and 202 of the Act. It is to be noted that voting on certain of these provisions by class holders is mandatory whether or not shares of that class or series otherwise carry the right to vote.

100   **Requisitioned shareholders meetings:** It is a provision in the Act (see section 129) that holders of not less than five percent of the issued shares of a company, that carry the right to vote at a meeting sought to be held by them, may requisition the directors to call a meeting of shareholders for the purposes stated in the requisition notice.

101   The requisition must state the business to be transacted at the meeting and must be sent to each director and to the registered office of the company. (See section 129 (2).) Upon receiving a requisition the directors must call a meeting of shareholders within 21 days to transact the business stated in the requisition. If the directors do not call the meeting within the 21 days, any shareholder who signed the requisition may call the meeting. (See section 129 (4).)

102   There are limited circumstances under which the directorate may refuse to comply but directors must exercise considerable caution if they elect to

ignore a legitimate request from shareholders to convene a meeting. (See Section 129 (3) and the references made therein to section 115 of the Act).

103   Requisitioned meetings will normally only occur when there is strong disagreement between some shareholders of the company and the board of directors. The atmosphere is therefore likely to be charged with tension and it is important for the company secretary and the board of directors to ensure that everything is done correctly. Very often the directors will look to the company secretary for advice. He or she should therefore note that:

   •   The power to call the meeting is vested in the board. The requisitioners have no authority to instruct the secretary to convene the meeting.

   •   The directors, unless for good reason they elect not to convene the meeting, must call the meeting within 21 days. This does not mean that the meeting must be held within 21 days but rather that notice of the meeting must be given within 21 days of receipt of the requisition.

   •   The meeting must be called as nearly as possible in the manner in which meetings are to be called pursuant to the provisions of the Act and the company's corporate instruments. Therefore the requirements applicable to notice, quorum and the chairmanship of meetings of the company will continue to apply.

   •   If the directors do not send a notice to convene the meeting within 21 days after receiving a requisition, any shareholder who signed the requisition may call the meeting and, unless the shareholders at that meeting resolve otherwise, the company must reimburse the shareholders who requisitioned the meeting the expenses reasonably incurred by them in requisitioning, calling and holding the meeting.

   •   It is not permissible to discuss at a meeting convened by requisition any matter not covered by the terms of the requisition. The Act clearly states that the requisition must state the business to be transacted. (See section 129 (2); see also *Ball* v *Metal Industries Ltd.*[22])

104 **Resolution in lieu of meeting:** The purpose of a meeting is to ascertain the corporate resolve of the company on any matter which requires determination by its members. Section 128 of the Act provides an alternative method in limited circumstances for ascertaining that corporate resolve. It is the resolution in lieu of a meeting.

105 Except for consideration and determination of matters arising out of any written statement made by a director or an auditor on the question of his or her removal or resignation, a resolution made in writing and signed by all the shareholders entitled to vote on that resolution at a meeting of shareholders is as valid as if it had been passed at a meeting of the shareholders.

106 Furthermore a resolution in writing dealing with matters required by the Act to be dealt with at a meeting of shareholders and signed by all the shareholders entitled to vote at that meeting satisfies all the requirements of the Act relating to meetings of shareholders.

107 Copies of all such resolutions in writing must be kept with the minutes of the meetings of shareholders. Company secretaries should note however that the resolutions must be signed by all shareholders entitled to vote on the matter, failing which the resolution will not be valid.

---

[22]   (1957) SLT 124 (see p. 299)

CHAPTER 6

Persons entitled to attend company meetings

108   To pose the question: 'Who may attend company meetings?' may at first appear simplistic. After all, who else but shareholders? Yet at times the answer may be as complex as answering that Biblical question: Who is thy neighbour?

109   The Act adds to the complexity by making the provision (in section 111) that a shareholder and any other person who is entitled to attend a meeting of shareholders may . . . etc. Hence we may legitimately and with justification make enquiry as to the persons who are entitled to attend company meetings.

110   A proper determination of this question is important for two reasons. First, attendance is often linked to the issue of voting, which in turn affects or determines the corporate resolve of the company; and secondly, the admission of persons not entitled to attend the meeting or the exclusion of persons entitled to attend may render the meeting or its proceedings void.

111   Perhaps the problem may best be addressed by considering the entitlement of a number of persons in various capacities.

112   **Members:** All members of a company are, as a general rule, entitled to attend meetings of the company.

113   In jurisdictions where the law provides for the incorporation of companies by filing a Memorandum of Association, the subscribers to the Memorandum of the company are deemed to have agreed to become members of the company and on the filing or registration of the company's corporate documents the names of such subscribers must be entered in the register of members. Thus the subscribers become members upon the incorporation of the company.

114   In other cases persons become members when shares have been allotted to them in response to an application for an allotment of shares or when shares have been transferred to them. In both cases membership occurs when their names have been entered in the register of members.

115   **Deemed membership:** The Act by section 448(u) provides that in relation to a company, the word or term 'shareholder' includes:

   i.   The personal representative of a deceased shareholder.

   ii.   The trustee in bankruptcy of a bankrupt shareholder.

   iii. A person in whose favour a transfer of shares has been executed but whose name has not been entered in the register of members.

   Therein lies part of the complexity of the question which at first appeared to be a simple matter.

116   **Representatives of deceased members:** On the death of a sole shareholder the personal representative, upon giving notice to the company and producing the evidence required by the directors such as letters testamentary, would become entitled to receive any dividends paid by the company on the shares registered in the name of the

deceased. In this sense and for similar purposes the personal representative is, by the Act, deemed a member.

117   Most corporate instruments of companies will permit personal representatives of deceased members a choice of leaving the deceased's name on the register of members until such time as the personal representative elects to transfer the shares to the beneficiaries entitled thereto, or to have his or her name entered on the register in place of the deceased member.

118   Where personal representatives elect to have their names entered on the register they will of course become entitled to the full rights of membership. They will also become liable for any calls outstanding on such shares or other liabilities attached to such shares. For this reason as well as the complex process of adjudicating share transfers in the Caribbean and the uncertainty of the law in some jurisdictions on the question of the payment or double payment of stamp duties and other transfer taxes, personal representatives often find it more convenient to adopt the former course of action.

119   Having due regard to the peculiarities of the circumstances outlined, it is my view that personal representatives of deceased members should be admitted to the meeting, but unless their names have been entered on the register in place of the deceased members or the corporate instruments stipulate otherwise, such personal representatives may not be entitled to speak or vote.[23]

120   There are two situations of importance to the company secretary when dealing with matters connected with shares remaining in the names of the deceased members and by extension their legal representatives.

121   The first situation relates to a member who had received notice of the meeting and executed a valid proxy but died before the meeting was convened. Both the Act and the company's corporate instruments may be silent on this point; however, the common law rule is that the member's death revokes the proxy.

---

[23]   See p. 99, section 366

122   The second situation is one where the deceased member was a joint holder and the proxy was signed by all joint holders. The Act or the company's corporate instruments will usually provide that on the death of a joint holder, ownership of the shares will be vested in the other joint holders. If the deceased member was the first named person on the register, the surviving joint holder, or if more than one then in order of precedence as their names appear on the register of members, will become the eligible senior member who is entitled to vote and in such circumstances the proxy will remain alive unless revoked.

123   **Trustees in bankruptcy:** Trustees in bankruptcy of bankrupt members have the legal right to be registered as the holder of the shares registered in the name of the bankrupt member. Technically this registration is not a transfer of shares and may be effected by a letter of request from the trustee accompanied by evidence of his/her appointment, i.e. a certified copy of the court order.

124   Company secretaries and registrars should encourage trustees in bankruptcy to request that the shares be registered in their names. After registration the trustee will then become entitled to full rights as a shareholder. Before registration the trustee will be entitled to receive any dividend paid on the shares held by the bankrupt member and should be permitted to attend meetings but not to vote thereat.

125   **Joint shareholders:** The issues of attendance and voting must be kept separate and it is for this reason they are dealt with separately in this book. Both joint holders, and if there are more than two then all such joint holders, are members of the company and as such are entitled to attend meetings of the company. The difficulties which may arise on voting are dealt with in chapter 12.

126   **Representatives of corporate shareholders:** A body corporate acts through the corporate resolve of its board of directors or management. Corporate shareholders have two options available to them to attend meetings. They may elect to appoint a representative or to appoint a proxy. Generally speaking, a representative has greater standing than a proxy in that his appointment remains valid until revoked.

127   In jurisdictions where older company legislation is still applicable, the old rule which stipulates that a proxy may attend and vote but may not speak, may still apply. In such circumstances unless the Act or the corporate instruments conferred authority upon a proxy to demand a poll, if no one else demanded a poll, a proxy holder could not make such a demand and as such would be deprived of exercising the right to vote. For this reason the appointment of a representative under resolution of the board of directors is to be preferred since such representative would have the right to attend, speak and vote and of course join in demanding a poll.

128   Under the Act, differences between the two methods have been substantially eliminated. The Act now provides that the power given to a proxy holder is that authorised and conferred by the proxy itself. However, a proxy is valid only at the meeting in respect of which it is given or any adjournment of that meeting whereas the appointment of a representative remains valid until revoked.

129   **Proxies:** Proxy holders are entitled to attend meetings, but company secretaries and registrars must check both the Act and the company's corporate instruments applicable to the specific company to ensure that only those persons capable of being appointed as proxy holders are admitted to the meeting.

130   In some jurisdictions, for example, a proxy holder must himself be a shareholder while in others, such as those to which the Act and other recent legislation applies, a proxy holder need not be a shareholder of the company.

131   **Auditors:** Although auditors are not members of the company, they are by law entitled to receive notice of general meetings and to attend and answer questions relating to their duties as auditors. (See sections 161 to 163.)

132   **Other persons:** The right of other persons to attend must be viewed against the background of the law with respect to meetings on private property which is summarised below.

133   The ownership or lease of property carries with it the right to the sole, exclusive and peaceful possession of that property. Any unlawful violation

of that right constitutes a trespass and the rightful occupier may assert those legal remedies which are available to him or her and which include an action for damages against the trespasser and/or ejection of the trespasser.

134   A person is therefore only entitled to remain upon premises in the lawful occupation of another by the licence and permission of the lawful occupier.

135   It follows therefore that persons not entitled by the Act or the company's corporate instruments to be present at meetings of the company may only do so by permission of the chairman of the meeting but, notwithstanding the discretion vested in the chairman to grant or refuse permission of the press or of other persons not entitled to attend the meeting, the chairman ought not to admit persons not entitled to be present if the sense of the meeting is against the admission of such persons.

CHAPTER 7

Planning the company meeting

136   All meetings must be carefully planned if they are to be productive. The business of unplanned meetings is often not completed and such meetings may deteriorate into crosstalk and a state of confusion. Even when this is not the case, unplanned meetings may leave a bad impression in the minds of participants and do not inspire the confidence of members in the ability of those elected to manage the affairs of the corporation.

137   While the type of planning and the method of preparation will vary for meetings of members and those of directors, in this book we will use the annual general meeting as the model to illustrate the planning process.

138   For public or large companies it is a good practice for the company secretary to meet with the chairman to go through or develop a check list and settle a provisional timetable. The purpose of the check list is to ensure that essential matters are not overlooked and that all matters to be dealt with are brought to the attention of the board in a proper and timely manner. A draft check list is given in Appendix II Precedent B.

139   In fixing the dates of the annual meeting of the members and the meeting
       of the directors which should precede the AGM, due regard must be
       given to both the requirements of the Act and the company's corporate
       instruments with respect to certain prescribed formalities and the period
       of notice that is required.

140   Strict attention must also be given to the provisions relating to documents,
       papers, reports and other information which is required to be sent to
       shareholders before the meeting. If the company is a public listed
       company on any stock exchange, the rules of the exchange and other
       listing requirements must also be taken into account.

141   **Selecting the venue for the meeting:** The venue of the meeting is of
       prime importance and when selecting, the following matters must be
       taken into account:

       ◆   Convenience and easy access to members.

       ◆   Number of persons expected to attend.

       ◆   Expected length of the meeting.

       ◆   Lighting, acoustics, ventilation, toilet facilities, and security of the
              premises.

142   Shareholders have a right to attend and participate in the proceedings of
       their meetings. It is the duty and obligation of the board to ensure that
       adequate accommodation is available and it is far better to err on the side
       of too large a meeting room than too small, otherwise it may be necessary
       to adjourn the meeting to another place if members are unable to gain
       sufficient access to the meeting room to hear the proceedings and to
       participate therein.

       Notwithstanding the foregoing, conference or meeting hall facilities
       available in the region to accommodate large private meetings are
       limited. Therefore as the number of shareholders increase in Caribbean
       companies, regional company law may need to be amended in order to
       permit companies with, say, more than 1,000 shareholders to include in
       their corporate instruments a provision which would enable the company

to determine, prior to the date of the meeting, the number of shareholders who are desirous of attending and to issue admission cards to such shareholders.

143   It is regrettable that directors often miss the opportunity which the annual meeting affords to foster and enhance the goodwill between management and members of the company. Simple things can be done to foster and enhance that spirit of goodwill. The following are a few observations:

- Ensure that the meeting room is well lit, that there are adequate public address facilities and seating arrangements.

- A display of the company's products or photographs or short video presentation could create a good atmosphere.

- Pay attention to the presentation of the annual report and accounts. Too often the annual report and accounts are compiled in a sparse and somewhat unattractive manner to reveal the least information possible, merely to satisfy the minimum requirements of the Act. This is unfortunate and springs from a somewhat perverse view of some boards that they 'cannot let shareholders know too much'.

- The attitude of directors must convey to members the board's recognition that the company belongs to its shareholders and, subject to certain information which for competitive or other valid reasons it would be inappropriate to put in the public domain, they are entitled to receive sufficient details concerning the management and business of their company so as to enable them to form a reasonable judgement on its operation, financial results and the effectiveness of its management.

- Notwithstanding the foregoing observation it must also be stated that shareholders should not seek to extract and thereby put in the public domain sensitive corporate data.

- It is a good gesture to offer refreshments at the end of the meeting.

144 **The pre-AGM board meeting:** Some two months or thereabouts before the annual meeting of members a meeting of the directors will be required to deal with certain legal and formal requirements. The company's auditors should be requested to attend this meeting and to sign their report after the formal accounts have been approved and signed on behalf of the board. A draft agenda and minutes of this board meeting are given as Appendix II Precedents C and D.

145 It should be noted that section 150 of the Act stipulates that a company shall not issue, publish or circulate copies of its financial statements unless they are approved and signed by one or more directors and accompanied by a report of the auditors of the company.

146 It is general practice that most public or large companies now print their accounts and report. Where this is the case it will be necessary to settle the accounts with the auditors before the formal meeting of the board and to have available at that meeting three copies of 'final proofs' for signature on behalf of the board and by the auditors. One copy will be retained by the auditors, one by the company and the other returned to the printers with the print order.

147 The contents of the annual report prescribed by section 147 of the Act to be laid before members of the company in general meeting is stated below. It is mandatory that the directors of a company must place before the shareholders at every annual meeting of the shareholders of the company:

(a) Comparative financial statements, as prescribed, relating separately to:

  i. the period that began on the date the company came into existence and ended not more than 12 months after that date, or, if the company has completed a financial year, the period that began immediately after the end of the last period for which financial statements were prepared and ended not more than 12 months after the beginning of that period, and

  ii. the immediately preceding financial year.

(b)   The report of the auditor, if any; and

i.   Any further information respecting the financial position of the company and the results of its operations required by the articles of the company, its by-laws, or any unanimous shareholder agreement.

148   In addition thereto for companies having more than 15 shareholders the directors must also send a management proxy circular. This will be dealt with more fully in the following chapter.

149   The Act does not make it mandatory that a directors' report and/or a chairman's review should be sent to members, but it is good corporate practice to do so. In jurisdictions which require that a directors' report should be sent, its contents may be prescribed and it will usually therefore be a formal document.

150   At annual meetings chairmen have traditionally delivered speeches. In more recent times formal speeches have been practically replaced by the chairman's written review or report. Today this medium is used mainly as an avenue and opportunity for the company to review its progress and prospects and to comment on a wide range of national, economic and social issues.

151   Where it is intended to produce a wide ranging report, care must be exercised to ensure the authenticity and credibility of the report. This may best be achieved by making the report a cooperative effort involving the company's technical and marketing managers, the financial controller, the chief executive officer, the company secretary and the chairman of the board. The company secretary will often have to act as coordinator.

152   Some presiding officers are of the view that the chairman's report affords them the opportunity to express personal views and opinions. This tendency must be resisted. The chairman should see himself as the spokesman of the board and in his review of wider issues as speaking on the company's behalf. It is therefore good corporate governance for the chairman to discuss his report with the board before its publication.

153   **Class meetings:** Not many Caribbean companies have different classes of shares, but there are some and the holding of class meetings, although infrequent, will at times occur. When they do take place there are always practical difficulties to be settled. For example, should all the meetings be held on the same date and at the same place? What is the minimum time required between meetings? Is it possible to have a joint session for certain items common to all of the meetings? Many of these issues were addressed in the case *Carruth* v *Imperial Chemical Industries Ltd*[24] which went before the House of Lords. The judgement is instructive.

154   In 1935 Imperial Chemical Industries Ltd, a company which had several classes of shares, sought to reorganise its capital structure and convened a series of meetings to follow the annual general meeting.

155   After the annual general meeting, the chairman stated that that meeting would be followed by the other class meetings. He said, as the issues were common to all such meetings, he proposed to make one speech and then take the vote at each meeting separately without any further speeches.

156   The procedure was challenged subsequently in the courts. The House of Lords held that the conduct of the meeting rests in the hands of the chairman. It observed that no objection had been made to the chairman's procedural ruling at the time, and the presence of other shareholders at a separate meeting of another class of shareholders did not invalidate the meeting.

157   Practitioners must be careful in interpreting the House of Lords' decision too liberally. They should refer to the text of the decision, the salient points of which are summarised below.

158   Lord Maugham observed that the decision was based partly on matters of convenience and the better and wiser course is to make provision for truly separate meetings in the ordinary way. Nevertheless where circumstances constrain companies to hold similar class meetings, the lessons and principles of the decision must be carefully observed. These are as follows:

---

[24]   (1937) Ac 707 (see p. 300)

- Unless an objection is made at the time of the ruling, the chairman of the meeting has authority to decide on procedural matters of the meeting.

- If an objection is made, the chairman should seek the mind of the meeting and abide by its resolve.

- If no objection is made at the meeting, it cannot be subsequently made.

- The chairman should be explicit at each stage of the proceedings.

- Careful and detailed arrangements must be made for the administration and conduct of the meeting so as to ensure that the class meeting vote is confined to members of that class.

- If the meeting is held in a single unpartitioned room, the use of colour coded voting cards or such other satisfactory procedure should be considered.

CHAPTER 8

Convening the meeting

Notice and agenda

NOTICE

159   Company law imposes stringent requirements for the convening of a general meeting. The Act requires that notice of the time and place of a meeting of shareholders must be given not less than 21 days nor more than 50 days before the meeting. It has been said that the purpose of these rules is to ensure that members are given sufficient advance notice of the meeting and of the business which it will transact so as to enable them:

- To decide whether to attend the meeting.

- To make arrangements to attend.

- To appoint proxies to represent them in their absence.

- To consult with other members to formulate an opinion or common approach to the business of the meeting; or

- If the company is a public company whose affairs may attract some comment in the public media, then to consider the views expressed by business and financial analyst.

160 The notice must be sent to each shareholder of the company entitled to vote at the meeting whose name is recorded in the register of members on the record date. (See section 109.)

161 If a meeting of shareholders is adjourned for less than 30 days it is not necessary, unless the company's corporate instruments otherwise require, to give notice of the adjourned meeting other than by announcement at the earliest meeting that is adjourned.

162 If however a meeting is adjourned by one or more adjournments for an aggregate of 30 days or more, notice of the adjourned meeting must be given as for an original meeting. Company secretaries should also note that if the meeting is adjourned by one or more adjournments for an aggregate of more than 90 days, it will also be necessary to send a new form of proxy with the notice. (See section 109(4).)

163 It is important that the formalities applicable to notices which are prescribed by the Act as well as the company's corporate instruments be fully complied with since a meeting that is improperly called may be invalid.

164 **A valid notice:** For a notice to be valid it must contain the following essential characteristics and meet the prescribed conditions:

- It must state clearly the date, time and place of the meeting.

- It must also state the purpose of the meeting and the business to be transacted.

- If special business is to be transacted, the nature of that business must be stated in sufficient detail so as to permit the shareholders of the company to form a reasoned judgement thereon. The text of any special resolution to be submitted to the meeting must also be given.

- It must be issued on proper authority, except for meetings which are requisitioned and convened by members.[25] Some corporate instruments may delegate that authority to the chairman, but when so acting he is acting as agent of the board of directors.

- The company secretary is the person under whose signature notices are issued but he should state his authority for summoning the meeting by adding before or after his signature the words 'By Order of the Board'. See draft notice in Appendix II Precedent E.

- It must allow the prescribed period to elapse between service and the date of the meeting. Where the Act or the company's corporate instruments specify that a specific period of notice must be given both the requirements of the Act as well as those stipulated in corporate instruments must be fulfilled or the meeting may be an invalid meeting.

  By way of example, the regulations made under the Act may state that notice is deemed to be given 24 hours after service. On the other hand company A's corporate instruments may prescribe that notice is deemed to be given three days after posting. It follows therefore that notice of the annual general meeting for company A should be posted not later than the 25th day before the date of the annual general meeting so as to put the adequacy of notice beyond any question of doubt.

- The prescribed elapse time should always be 'clear days', which means days exclusive of the day of service and of the meeting.[26] (See *Railway Sleepers Supply Co.*[27]) The model by-law given in

---

[25] A notice of a requisitioned meeting given by requisitionists should be signed by one or more of the requisitionists. See Section 129. The notice should also be accompanied by an explanatory letter or proxy circular from the requisitionists and a form of proxy in their favour.

[26] Curry & Sykes, *The Conduct of Meetings*, p.12

[27] (1885) 29 Ch. D 204 (see p. 304)

the companies regulations[28] as well as that included in this text as Appendix II Precedent T underscores this principle.[29]

- It must be sent to every person entitled to receive it.

165 The notice convening a meeting of members must contain sufficient details or descriptions of the business to be transacted in order that members may make informed decisions concerning the meeting and the business to be dealt with thereat.

166 If the notice does not contain sufficient details and the matter is challenged, the court may rule that any resolutions passed are without effect. In *Young* v *Ladies' Imperial Club Ltd* [30] the principle is well illustrated. In that matter notice was issued that a meeting will be held to discuss matters concerning two members. The notice did not indicate that the meeting would consider the expulsion of one of the members. The court appeal ruled that the expulsion was ineffective.

167 **Who is entitled to receive notice:** The Act requires that notice of shareholders' meetings must be sent to:

- Each director of the company

- The auditor of the company, and

- Each shareholder entitled to vote at the meeting.

168 The foregoing may at first appear free of ambiguity but this is not always the case. The company secretary will need to consult the company's corporate instruments and be fully conversant with the provisions relating to notice and voting especially in the case of companies having more than one class of shares.

169 Let us assume that the issued and outstanding capital of company A consisted of two classes of shares namely common shares carrying the right to vote at meetings of shareholders and Class B 6 percent

---

[28] The Companies Regulations of Barbados, S.I.1984, No 29, p. 159, paragraph 13.3
[29] See Appendix II Precedent T, paragraphs 12.3 and 18.8
[30] (1920) 2 KB 523. (see p. 306)

cumulative preferred shares which do not carry the right to vote except if payment of the dividend is in arrears for a period in excess of two years.

170 If it is further assumed that dividends on the preferred shares are normally paid within 30 days of the date of the annual meeting (which is held in March each year), then in circumstances when at the time notice is despatched payment of the preference dividend is in arrears for a period in excess of two years, notice of the annual meeting of members must also be given to the preference shareholders upon whom, by the terms of the issue of the preference shares, the right of voting is conferred, in the prevailing circumstances.

171 **The position of deceased and bankrupt members:** This is a special situation which must be considered against the background of the relevant legislation governing the conduct of company meetings as well as the corporate instruments of the company. Where the legislation is silent and the company's corporate instruments do not contain provisions dealing with the matter of notice to deceased and bankrupt members, then notice should be sent by post addressed to registered members at their address as recorded in the books of the company. In these circumstances notice is not required to be given to the personal representatives of a deceased member since they are not members and are not therefore entitled to vote.

172 Corporate instruments of companies or 'Table A' of some Companies Acts may require that notice be also given to every person upon whom a share devolves by reason of the death or bankruptcy of a member. In such circumstances notice should be sent to such personal representatives and trustees in bankruptcy at the addresses supplied by them.

173 Under the Act and jurisdictions covered by similar legislation there is a provision which states that 'shareholder' in relation to a company includes the personal representative of a deceased member and the trustee in bankruptcy of a bankrupt shareholder. Company secretaries should not be perplexed by this provision. There are rights and benefits other than voting which accrue to shareholders and it is appropriate that those rights and benefits, such as the right to receive dividends and the right to share in the surplus assets of the company upon a winding up, should devolve

upon the person standing in the shoes of the deceased or bankrupt member. The question of voting entitlement is dealt with in chapter 12.

174   The avoidance of notice giving to shareholders residing abroad is an exemption usually permitted by the corporate instruments of companies incorporated under older company legislation; it is however good corporate practice to ensure that notice is sent to all eligible shareholders notwithstanding that the corporate instruments may have permitted the company not to send notices to overseas shareholders.

175   **In the case of joint holders:** The notice should be sent to the first named of the joint holders as appears in the register of members.

176   **Mandatees:** Where a shareholder has mandated that dividends due to him be paid to another person such mandate has no effect upon the requirements of the Act or the corporate instruments in so far as the provisions relate to the giving of notice. The notice must be sent to the shareholder not the mandatee.

177   **Record date:** For the purpose of determining shareholders who are entitled to receive notice of a meeting of shareholders of the company (note that the words '*and to vote thereat*', have been omitted in this case) the Act permits the directors of the company to fix in advance a date as the record date for the determination of such shareholders.

178   This provision is for administrative convenience in recognition of the fact that there must be a 'cut off' period in order to permit the corporate secretary to temporarily close the register in order to extract a list of members. Such record date must not be more than 50 days nor less than 21 days before the date of the meeting. If no record date is fixed, the date for determining the shareholders who are entitled to receive notice of a meeting of shareholders is the close of business on the date immediately preceding the day on which the notice is given.

179   **The position of transferor and transferee:** This is a very delicate matter and must be examined and dealt with in the light of the foregoing administrative procedures flowing from the fixing of a record date. Unrecorded transfers are always a matter of concern both to the transferee and the corporate practitioner. The issue is greatly simplified if

it is clearly understood that only persons on the register are entitled to notice. The company should always endeavour to record all transfers in hand before closing the register.

180   If the name of a transferee is entered on the register after the record date or after notice has been given, but before the meeting is convened, such transferee is still not entitled to receive a notice. However, since at the date of the meeting the transferee would have been registered as a member, he would be entitled to attend the meeting and to enjoy all of the benefits rights and privileges of a member, despite the fact that he had not received a notice from the company.

181   **The accidental omission to give notice:** '*Mr Chairman, I have not received my notice*' is a protest often heard at shareholders' meetings. Very often it is a matter of the member changing his address and not notifying the company. Sometimes the notice is delayed in the post or gone astray. On other occasions it may be an accidental omission.

182   The accidental omission to give notice to a member entitled thereto will not invalidate the proceedings of the meeting. This saving grace is found in the model by-law contained in the Companies Regulations made under the Act and is also usually incorporated in the company's corporate instruments. However, in order for the company to avail itself of the saving provision, the omission must be accidental and not a matter of wilful or negligent default on the part of the company. (See *Re West Canadian Collieries Ltd.*[31])

183   **Waiver of notice:** This is a right conferred on shareholders by the Act. Section 111 provides that a shareholder and any other person who is entitled to attend a meeting of shareholders may in any manner waive notice of the meeting; and the attendance of any person at a meeting of shareholders is a waiver of notice of the meeting by that person, unless she/he attends the meeting for the express purpose of objecting to the transaction of any business on the grounds that the meeting is not lawfully called.

---

[31]   (1962) Ch 370 (see p. 308)

It is to be noted that this is not a right conferred on the company and as such no shareholder may waive the company's statutory obligation to give notice of a meeting of members.

184   Where the company desires to convene a meeting by giving less than the statutory period of notice required to convene the meeting, a waiver of the minimum statutory period of notice must be obtained from all persons entitled to notice of the meeting. Some enactments provide that waiver of the prescribed period may be made by 90 or 95 percent of members entitled to attend and vote at the meeting.

185   Company secretaries must therefore consult the applicable statutory provisions. They should note however that in the absence of any statutory provision the majority cannot waive the right to notice on behalf of the minority.

186   The right to notice and to waive notice, like the right to vote, is a personal individual right of shareholders and not a corporate right which may be waived by the company in general meeting unless statute so provides. As such, shareholders attending a meeting cannot waive the right to adequate notice on behalf of those not in attendance. (See Appendix II Precedent I.)

187   Finally, although members may agree to accept short notice, they cannot agree to relieve the company of its obligation to give a written notice. The articles of the company cannot override the Act.

THE AGENDA

188   The agenda ought to be an integral part of the notice. It is that portion of the notice that sets out the business to be transacted at the meeting and the sequence in which it will be dealt with. It has been held that the business of the meeting must be fairly stated. It must not be stated so as to mislead.[32] By implication the Act has to a large extent settled the agenda of annual meetings.

---

[32]   Kaye v Croydon Tramways Co. (1898) 1 Ch 358 (see p. 310)

189   Section 110 of the Act provides that all business transacted at a special
        meeting of shareholders, and all business transacted at an annual meeting
        of the shareholders, is special business, except:

    (a)   The consideration of the financial statements,

    (b)   The auditor's report,

    (c)   The election of directors, and

    (d)   The reappointment of the incumbent auditor.

190   The foregoing may be therefore be described as ordinary business. See
        Appendix II Precedent E for a specimen notice and agenda for an annual
        general meeting and Appendix II Precedent F for the chairman's
        extended agenda.

        Some corporate instruments may confer a power on directors to appoint a
        person to fill a casual vacancy in their number either to hold office until
        the next meeting of shareholders or for the unexpired period of the
        predecessor. It is the paramount right of shareholders to appoint
        directors. The power given to fill a casual vacancy is intended to facilitate
        the proper functioning of the corporate entity, should vacancies arise on
        the board between meetings of members. It is not an alternative to the
        right of shareholders.

        It therefore follows that, except in extenuating circumstances, it would be
        an improper exercise of directors' authority to seek to fill a casual
        vacancy after the date of a meeting of shareholders had been fixed. The
        better corporate practice would be to permit members to exercise their
        paramount right to make such appointment, especially in circumstances
        where the filling of the casual vacancy is for the unexpired period of the
        term of the predecessor.

191   As a general rule a meeting is not competent to deal with or consider
        matters which are not within the scope of the notice unless all of the
        persons entitled to attend the meeting are present and agree that such
        other matters may be considered. See (*Rex* v *Wake* [33] and *Machell* v
        Nevinson [34].)

---

[33]   (1728) 1 Barn KB 80 (see p. 311)
[34]   (1724) 11 East 84 (see p. 312)

192   Note however that consideration of business which is outside the scope of the meeting will not necessarily render the whole meeting invalid, but only that portion of business which was improperly considered. (See *British Sugar Refining Co.*[35])

193   Listening, learning and asking questions were not items on the formal agenda at Twentieth Century's annual meeting of shareholders on July 29, 1994 but some four hundred investors went to the meeting in Kansas City to do exactly that. There they heard members of Twentieth Century's executive committee deal with a number of issues and answered questions on matters which were of general concern to investors (shareholders).[36]

194   In the draft notices for annual meetings of members provision has been made for a question and answer period. Sometimes this item is titled 'Any other business'. This writer believes that a question and answer period is desirable and could provide the opportunity for a period of useful interaction between members and the management of their companies.

195   Regrettably, however, there are some individuals who, unless properly controlled, often regard it as an opportunity for them to introduce all manner of items under this heading irrespective of whether or not it is within the competence of the meeting to deal with such items.[37] Matters dealt with under this agenda head are for general information and discussion purposes only.

196   No motions may be introduced under this head, except a vote of thanks, and no resolutions may be voted upon in respect of any matter brought before the meeting under this agenda head except proper notice thereof had been given in the notice concerning the meeting.

197   **Documents to be sent with notice:** The Act by sections 151, 139 and 140 requires that not less than 21 days before each annual meeting of the shareholders of a company, the company must send a copy of the following documents to each shareholder unless the shareholder informed the company in writing not to send the documents:

---

[35]   (1875) 3 K & J 408 (see p. 313)
[36]   See "Twentieth Century Investor" *Advantage* (Fall 1994): 2.
[37]   See Chant, "Any Other Business", Corporation of Secretaries, p. 9

(a) Comparative financial statements.

(b) The report of the auditor.

(c) Any further financial information required by the corporate instruments of the company or any unanimous shareholders' agreement.

(d) Form of proxy.

(e) A management proxy circular.

198 The documents listed as (a) (b) and (c) above must be sent to all shareholders of the company and are not, like the notice, limited to shareholders entitled to vote at the meeting. Hence persons holding non-voting shares as well as noted personal representatives and trustees in bankruptcy of deceased and bankrupt members respectively are also entitled to receive these documents. In addition a copy of these documents must, in appropriate circumstances, be sent to the Registrar of Companies at the time they are despatched to shareholders. (See Section 152.) The documents referred to as (d) and (e) are only required to be sent to shareholders entitled to receive notice of the meeting.[38]

199 The form and content of the financial statements will be reviewed and approved by the auditors and it is therefore not proposed that such be dealt with in this book. Attention is however drawn to the prescribed contents of the annual report.

200 The form of proxy will usually be prescribed in the company's corporate instruments but examples are given in Appendix II Precedent G. The Act requires that a proxy form must be sent to each shareholder if the company has 15 or more shareholders.

201 Management proxy circulars are a new feature in Caribbean corporate law and practice. It is a means of enforcing greater corporate accountability upon directors and greater dissemination of information to shareholders with respect to proposals to be put before them or for which there is direct or indirect solicitation of the vote of shareholders to such proposals or resolutions. Provision is also made in the Act for other interest groups or dissatisfied shareholders to challenge certain policies

---

[38] The Companies Act Cap 308, section 139

of a board through the means of a dissident proxy solicitation. Sample proxy circulars are given in Appendix II Precedent H.

CHAPTER 9

Commencing and conducting the meeting

Stewards, scrutineers, quorum, chairmanship

202   In chapter 7 we discussed the planning arrangements which should precede the meeting. In this chapter attention is focused on some managerial aspects which will contribute to the smooth conduct of meetings. There are certain practical aspects which apply to the management of meetings which ought not to be overlooked, although they seldom receive the attention which they deserve.

STEWARDS AND SCRUTINEERS

203   Before commencement of the meeting, arrangements should have been made for the appointment of a number of persons to be stewards. The number of stewards to be appointed will depend upon both the size of the meeting and the nature of business to be dealt with at the meeting.

204   The personal qualities of persons to be selected as stewards should be carefully evaluated. Colton Bennett, a clergyman who, previous to assuming ecclesiastical duties spent many years as a tutor in psychiatry,

recalled an observation made by one of his own lecturers when he was a student in London. Said the psychologist, "When I visit a new place or attend a meeting at some unfamiliar venue for the first time, I can feel the tone of the place when I meet the man at the gate."[39] This experience may be equally true of a number of shareholders when they attend company meetings. The tone of the proceedings may very well be influenced by the steward they meet at the door.

205   Stewards should be courteous, polite, helpful and physically fit. They should be persons of sound mind and good judgement. Their duty is not only to eject persons on instructions of the chairman, but mainly to assist those attending the meeting in their seating, access and use of any public address system during debate, and generally to assist in the preservation of order.

206   It is good practice for the stewards to welcome persons attending the meeting and direct them to the appropriate point for the completion of formalities such as signing the attendance sheet or register and thereafter direct them to the meeting hall.

207   The duty of the scrutineer is to distribute polling cards or voting papers if required, collect them after the voting process, tally the votes and prepare a scrutineer's report or certificate on the voting and hand such to the company secretary or the chairman.

208   **Attendance register:** Persons attending the meeting should sign an attendance register or bring with them an attendance admission card which should be deposited at the entrance to the meeting hall.

QUORUM

209   A quorum is the stipulated minimum number of persons required to be present in order for a meeting to be validly convened. The Act states that unless the by-laws otherwise provide, a quorum of shareholders is present at a meeting of shareholders if the holders of a majority of the

---

[39]   Quotation from a sermon by Colton Bennet at James St Methodist Church, Bridgetown, Barbados, August 22, 1993.

---

shares entitled to vote at the meeting are present in person or represented by proxy. (See section 123.)

210   Most corporate instruments will fix the quorum for meetings of shareholders. In jurisdictions where the applicable law is different to the provisions as contained in the Act, the company secretary must familiarise himself with the requirements of the relevant legislation and corporate instruments of the company so that he may properly advise the chairman.

211   Where the corporate instruments provide that *two members personally present* shall constitute a quorum, a meeting in which there was one shareholder present and two other individuals not being shareholders, but representing other shareholders by proxy is invalid for want of a quorum. Note there should have been *two members present in person* as distinct from being represented by proxy.

212   Where the articles permit two members present in person or by proxy to constitute a quorum, the requirement will be met by the presence of two persons whether they be members or proxy holders. It does not permit however one person to constitute the quorum notwithstanding the fact that he may have held proxies for several shareholders.

213   A representative of a company which is a shareholder must be counted as a person present in person.

214   Where no quorum is present any business transacted at the meeting or any resolution passed is invalid. Before commencing the business of the meeting the chairman should therefore enquire from the secretary or the registrar if a quorum is present. Upon being advised in the affirmative he should, as a matter of courtesy, so advise the meeting and proceed with the business of the meeting.

215   The Act further provides that if a quorum is not present within 30 minutes of the time appointed for a meeting of shareholders, the meeting stands adjourned to the same day two weeks thereafter, at the same time, and place; and, if at the adjourned meeting, a quorum is not present within 30 minutes of the appointed time, the shareholders present constitute a quorum. (See section 123.)

CHAIRMANSHIP

216   Having completed the pre-commencement formalities the meeting should then be formally convened. A meeting cannot however be held without a chairman since every meeting must have a presiding officer or chairman to conduct and order its affairs.

217   The company's corporate instruments will generally regulate matters relating to the appointment of the chairman. It is usual for the chairman of the board of directors to be chairman of all meetings of the company.

In the unlikely event that the company's corporate instruments are silent on this matter or where the chairman refuses or is incapable of acting, the meeting itself must, as its first business, elect a chairman or presiding officer for the meeting.

218   The chairman may be appointed for a fixed term or he may be appointed to hold office indefinitely until he is removed. If the chairman has been appointed under the regulations or corporate instruments, he can only be removed under the regulations. The meeting cannot normally vote him out of the chair. However, if he has been appointed by the meeting he may also be removed by the meeting.

219   The functions, duties, powers and authority of a chairman may be summarised as follows:

It is the duty of the chairman, and his functions, to preserve order, and to take care that the proceedings are conducted in a proper manner, and that the sense of the meeting is properly ascertained with regard to any question which is properly before the meeting. [*National Dwellings Society Ltd* v *Sykes* (1894) 3 Ch 159 at p 162 per Chitty J.[40]]

220   The chairman of the meeting must possess such qualities as fairness and confidence. He should be able to express with clarity the decisions and mind of the meeting. It is his duty to guide the meeting into discussions that will best facilitate the successful completion of the business before the meeting, but he must avoid undue foisting of his personal views upon the meeting.

---

[40]   S. Shaw and D. Smith, *The Law of Meetings*, p. 46 (see p. 315)

---

221 Persons attending the meeting have an obligation, in making their contributions to the debate, to be civil and courteous to the chair; the chairman must not presume however that only those expressions of opinion which accord with his personal views or the views of the majority are worthy of note. He ought to be sufficiently magnanimous to appreciate that great philosophical truth uttered by Colton when in 1825 he opined: "We owe almost all our knowledge not to those who have agreed, but to those who have differed."[41]

222 The preservation of order is one of the greatest challenges to every chairman. He must nip in the bud any attempt to disrupt the meeting. He would need to be tactful rather than autocratic, but in the final analysis he must bring his authority to bear upon the meeting to ensure that order is preserved.

223 In most meetings one is likely to encounter a member who wishes to speak on several occasions upon the same item of business. Members are entitled to speak and be heard but no member is entitled to attempt to monopolise the meeting. It is the duty of the chair to regulate the discussion so that as many persons as possible may be heard.

224 Not only must a good chairman be capable of preserving order but he must conduct the meeting with impartiality. He must give both those who are supportive of any motion before the meeting as well as those who are against such motion ample opportunity to express their views and to ensure that speakers are heard without disruption from other members.

He should encourage members at all times to address the chair. Speakers who ramble into a subject area extraneous to the motion under discussion should be stopped.

The chairman must also conduct the meeting in a timely manner: unless something new is being added to the debate by speakers there is no need to permit repetitive speeches.

225 One of the attributes of a good chairman is his ability to deduce the sense of the meeting and to ensure that it is accurately recorded.

---

[41] "Dissent", *International Thesaurus of Quotations,* p. 253.

After debate on any motion, the chairman should sum up the issues clearly and if there is any uncertainty he should ask the secretary to read aloud the motion upon which members will be asked to vote. This is good corporate practice which should usually be followed.

226   During the course of the debate the chairman may be called upon to rule upon various points of order. He must be alert to the guise of some members who may attempt to raise points of substance under the privilege of points of order. The chairman should promptly disallow such tactics.

227   Finally, the chairman must have a sense of humour. Difficult situations are often better dealt with by a keen sense of humour than by force.

228   Dennis Roberts in his book, *The Administration of Company Meetings*, illustrates the point admirably. He states that "A wise chairman will always seek to avoid conflict. In this he may well find a sense of humour, or even gently irony to be his most potent weapon".

229   Roberts gives the following example taken from the annual general meeting of a company whose articles restricted attendance to those who had held at least 100 shares for at least one month.

230   "After one speaker had been criticising the company and the board fiercely for sometime, the secretary noticed the registrar at the back of the hall waving frantically. Receiving a sign from the secretary to write, the registrar passed him a note to the effect that the speaker was a Mr X who held 100 shares but had possessed them for only two weeks. He was therefore not entitled to be present, let alone speak and vote."

The secretary handed the note to the chairman and sat back to await the explosion.

"The chairman read the note and rose to his feet, saying: 'I am sorry to interrupt, but I have just received a message. Is there a Mr X in the hall?' When the speaker, after a pause, admitted that was his name, the chairman asked. 'Are you the Mr X who only holds 100 shares and has only held them for two weeks?' Roars of laughter negated all criticism and the speaker realised he could not continue. Humour and quick wit can turn an uncomfortable situation into a successful meeting."[42]

---

[42]   D. Roberts, *The Administration of Company Meetings*, p. 78.

CHAPTER 10

The basic rules of order

231   All societies require a degree of coordination among its members. Such coordination is seldom automatic. "Rules are control mechanisms for governing human behaviour. Human societies have a wide variety of such rules, including the rules of etiquette, moral prescriptions and the important body of rules commonly known as law."[43] This chapter is concerned with the basic rules of order which govern the administration and conduct of corporate meetings.

232   In his treatise on company meetings J. M. Wainberg, Q.C., observed that: "The preservation of the majority rule and the protection of minority rights is the paramount purpose of rules of order."[44]

233   This text is not intended to be an exhaustive treatment of all of the rules of order but rather to highlight and draw attention to the more frequently used rules with which presiding officers will need to be acquainted so that they may efficiently conduct the meetings over which they preside.

---

[43]   S. T. Seitz, *Bureaucracy, Policy and the Public*, p. 45.
[44]   J. Wainberg, *Company Meetings*, p. 3.

These rules will relate mainly to the treatment of motions and the following are in order of generally accepted precedence.

(a)   Motions to Adjourn or Close the Meeting

234   These have the highest priority of all motions. However there are a few basic rules that should be followed:

*   Motions to adjourn or terminate the meeting cannot be moved when someone has the floor or while a point of order is being considered.

*   Motions to adjourn have the effect of interrupting the business of the meeting and therefore require seconding.

*   Motions to adjourn or terminate the meeting may not be amended or debated except as to time, date or place of the adjourned meeting and should be voted upon immediately.

*   If the motion to terminate or adjourn is defeated it cannot be repeated until other business of the meeting has intervened.

(b)   Procedural Motions

235   Procedural motions carry the second highest priority. Presiding officers will usually encounter these under the form of motions on points of order or information, questions of privilege, and count quorum.

236   Once a meeting has commenced or proceeded to business, especially if the business includes binding decisions or financial implications, it is essential to ensure that the proceedings are procedurally correct and valid and that the members are protected from manipulation or undue influence. This is why observance of the regulations is so important.

237   If any member finds or suspects some irregularity in the convening, constitution or conduct of the meeting he can raise an objection to the chairman. This is done through a procedural motion. The rules applicable to procedural motions are as follows:

- A speaker or any discussion in progress may be interrupted.

- Procedural motions do not require seconding.

- They are not debatable nor amendable.

- No vote is required on a procedural motion except when such is in the nature of an enabling motion such as to elect multiple directors by a single resolution.

- The chairman settles the issue by making a ruling on the point raised.

238   The chairman should not permit any lengthy introduction to a procedural motion. The person proposing the motion should state succinctly and clearly the point being raised.

The decision on any question of irregularity rests with the chairman whose ruling should be immediate and should be accepted by the meeting.

239   Sometimes legal proceedings are instituted to have the ruling of the chair set aside, but usually such proceedings are only successful if it can be shown that the chair was not acting in good faith, or that his or her action was in breach of the rules or that hardship was caused by the ruling.

(c)   Subsidiary Motions

240   In this category we find such motions as to those to postpone discussion, vote immediately, to postpone, refer back, or shelve the matter. The general rules applicable to subsidiary motions are as follows:

- The motion may not be put while a speaker has the floor.

- These motions are not amendable.

- They require seconding.

- The business of the meeting may be interrupted in order that these motions be considered.

- With the exception of a motion to postpone the matter under consideration indefinitely (i.e. to shelve the matter) subsidiary motions are not debatable.

- They must be voted on and the voting majority required (other than for a motion to vote immediately or to close discussion, both of which require a simple majority) is the same as the main motion under discussion requires for passing.

(d)   Miscellaneous Motions

241   The most commonly used motions in this category are motions to nominate and to close nominations. Neither speakers who have the floor nor discussions of the meeting may be interrupted in order that these motions be put. They are neither amendable nor debatable. A motion to close nominations requires a seconder and the meeting must vote in favour for it to be effective.

(e)   Debate and Discussion

242   Debate commences when a matter has been put before the meeting for discussion and until a matter is before the meeting no debate can ensue.[45]

243   A matter is put before the meeting in the form of a motion or proposition. This is done by a person addressing the chair and proposing '*That etc*'. At that point in time the motion is technically not yet before the meeting. The chairman is in possession of the motion.

---

[45]   The word debate is used in a general sense and not as defined in chapter 2.

---

244   Unless the substance of the motion is regulated by statute or the company's corporate instruments as constituting a matter which must be put before members in general meeting, the chairman should enquire if there is a seconder to the motion. The purpose of having motions seconded is to determine if there is interest among members in having the matter brought before them for discussion.

245   On having the motion seconded the chairman should state the motion and may do so as follows: '*It is proposed that . . . etc*'. At that point when the proposition is stated it moves from the chair's possession and the meeting is then in possession of the motion.

246   Kerr and King's observations on the above point are worth noting. They opine as follows: the mover of a motion has no proprietary claim on such motion even though it stands in his name for purposes of identification. Once it is moved and seconded or stated by the chair it becomes the property of the meeting.[46]

247   All motions must be framed in positive terms except in circumstances where the company had already committed itself to a course of action which members now wish to reverse. Very often the fine distinction between a motion and a resolution is ignored. Despite that fact, the distinction is logical and practitioners will find it useful to bear the distinction in mind.

248   A motion is a proposition or proposal and is referred to as a motion because someone has moved a matter before the meeting. When it is finally considered and passed it becomes a resolution of the meeting, because the meeting has resolved or decided on the matter brought before it.

249   It is the chairman's right and duty to decide in what order persons should be permitted to speak; nevertheless the meeting has the overriding authority to resolve at any time that a particular person should be heard.

250   No person is entitled to speak more than once to the same motion except the proposer who normally has a right of reply to the debate.

---

[46]   M. K. Kerr and H. W. King, *Procedures for Meetings and Organisations*, p. 83, section 69.

It has been pointed out that "this rule is designed to keep debate within limits, but the chairman may, in his discretion, relax it when necessary to permit explanation of the comment of a speaker who had concluded his contribution to the discussion".[47]

(f)   Main and Substantive Motions

These are considered in chapter 11.

---

[47]   S. Shaw and D. Smith, *The Law of Meetings*, p. 63.

CHAPTER 11

Transacting the business of the meeting

Motions, discussion, amendments, resolutions, rules of debate, etc.

251   This chapter deals with the procedures relating to motions and propositions, the conduct of discussions, tabling of amendments, ruling on points of order and finally stating the proposition in the form of a motion prior to voting thereon. This process is influenced greatly by generally accepted rules of debate.

252   In using the terms 'rules of debate' it ought to be appreciated that these are not statutory rules. They will not be found in the Companies Act nor is it usual to find them in any company's corporate instruments. They are rules and procedures which have been developed over time and which have proven satisfactory for the conduct of business meetings.

253   With reference to meetings of shareholders the Act makes reference to the business to be transacted at such meetings. The Act separates the business into ordinary business and special business and defines special business as any other business except the ordinary business of annual

meetings which consists of consideration of the financial statements, the auditor's report, the election of directors and the reappointment of the incumbent auditor.

254   The annual meeting of members or any special or extraordinary meeting of shareholders conducts its business by having propositions or motions placed before it, discussing the merits of the various matters and finally members making a decision upon such motions through the process of voting.

255   Most meetings are conducted, and will no doubt continue to be conducted, on a rather informal basis but it must always be remembered that it is the right and duty of the chairman to ensure that the business of the meeting is conducted in an orderly manner and, notwithstanding the rather informal manner in which small meetings are usually conducted, the chairman has the inherent authority to insist upon strict observance of the rules of procedure. Indeed in larger meetings the insistence on such rules often prevents confusion.

256   **Reading the notice:** The chairman, after ascertaining that a quorum is present and having called the meeting to order, should then proceed with the first item of business and instruct the secretary to read the notice convening the meeting.

257   **Minutes:** For many years, in most of the Caribbean territories, it was the practice at annual meetings of members to read the minutes of the previous annual meeting and any intervening extraordinary meetings and to have such minutes 'approved' or 'confirmed' by the meeting. To a large extent this practice has changed, in that it is now accepted that minutes are not required to be held in suspense pending 'approval' or 'confirmation' by members. The accuracy of the minutes are confirmed by the chairman of the meeting or by the board of directors at their next meeting following the members' meeting.

258   There is no requirement in the Act, nor is it usually a requirement in companies' corporate instruments that the reading of the previous minutes should be an agenda item at any annual meeting. It is entirely a matter of personal preference. I believe that in appropriate circumstances a useful purpose may be served by having the reading of previous

minutes as an agenda item. It may be that in the course of a previous extra-ordinary or special meeting management may have given certain assurances to members. If these were recorded, the reading of the minutes should refresh the minds of members and facilitate a review of such assurances in the light of subsequent events.

259   If however, the 'reading of the minutes' is included on the agenda it should be clearly understood by all concerned that it is only an information item. As such, it should follow immediately after the notice is read. Note that since both of these items are matters of information they are not debatable. A member who wishes to ask a question on a matter arising out of the minutes will have to seek to do so under some relevant head of discussion during the course of the meeting. The agenda of shareholders' meetings should, as a rule, not contain any item such as 'matters arising out of the minutes'.

260   **Reports and financial statements:** The auditors' report and consideration of the directors' report and financial statements will normally be the next item of business at the annual meeting.

261   The auditor's report is the report to members on the financial statements of the company which were prepared by, or under the auspices of the board of directors.

262   For many years it was the practice to have the auditors' report read at the annual meeting. Some older enactments required the auditors' report to be read before the company in general meeting. The reading of such a report is no longer a statutory requirement and it is sometimes argued that since the report is attached to each copy of the financial statements sent to members the auditors have fulfilled their obligation in reporting to members of the company and there is therefore no need to have the report read at the meeting.

263   I believe however that it is good corporate practice for the reading of the report to find a formal place on the agenda of any annual meeting. This is particularly desirable in circumstances where the auditor has expressed any reservation on the financial statements. Indeed members may even wish to hear the auditor speak thereon.

264   The report should preferably be read immediately preceding the motion to adopt the directors' report and the financial statements of the company.

265   The Act provides that the remuneration of the auditors may be fixed by ordinary resolution of the shareholders, or if not so fixed, it may be fixed by the directors.

266   Fixing the remuneration of auditors by directors is a convenient method since shareholders are not very often aware of the extent of the auditors' time and involvement in carrying out the audit.

        It is however a default mechanism and the preference is clearly by way of shareholders resolution although the chairman of the board should, for the reasons stated, make a recommendation to members.

        This may be done either by a motion from the chair to the effect that the directors recommend that the remuneration payable to the auditors be fixed at $; or that the directors request that they be authorised to fix the auditors' remuneration at such fee as may be agreed.

267   In the Caribbean, auditors are often required to render additional professional services over and above those required for the statutory audit. The fee for such additional and ancillary services is usually not a matter required to be submitted to shareholders for approval and should therefore not be lumped together with the audit fee.

268   Adoption of the directors' report and the audited financial statements for the year under consideration is therefore likely to be the first formal motion requiring a vote to be put before the meeting.

269   It is good planning procedure to arrange for someone to move and second this motion prior to the commencement of the meeting. The method of so doing may be as follows:

Proposer addressing chair: *"Mr Chairman (or Madam Chairman as the case may be), I propose that the report of the directors and the audited financial statements of the company for the year ending be adopted."*

Seconder addressing chair: *"Mr Chairman, I second the motion."*

The chairman may then address the meeting as follows: *"It has been proposed that the directors' report and audited financial statements of the company for the year ended be adopted and I now invite members who wish to speak on the motion to so indicate."*

270   It may appear curious to some that the motion to adopt the directors' report and financial statements should be made before discussion on these items are invited. Indeed I was present at an annual meeting when a member, a lawyer by profession and speaking with some authority, challenged the chair on a point of order and informed the chairman that having a motion to adopt the directors' report and financial statements before members had the opportunity to speak thereon was tantamount to putting the cart before the horse. The chairman, not sure of the rules of debate, yielded. The member was wrong for the simple reason that until a motion is before the meeting, there is nothing to which members can speak.

271   Some presiding officers like to read the chairman's report or give an oral presentation. Where this is the case it should be done immediately following the reading of the auditors' report and before the motion is made to adopt the directors' report and financial statements.

272   Members who wish to speak or ask any question relating to the reports of the auditors or directors or on any matter relating to the financial affairs of the company should, following the chairman's invitation to members to make their contributions, signal to the chair their intention to speak.

273   The chairman, with the assistance of the secretary, should make a note of the members who have signalled their request and invite such persons by name or other indication to speak on the motion.

274   One regrets that in large measure annual meetings of some public companies are becoming something of a staged affair to be completed in the shortest possible time. Indeed a certain chairman has boasted that he has been able to complete an annual meeting in less than eight minutes.

While not subscribing to the view that annual meetings should be long and tedious affairs, one wonders if the trend towards the state of affairs as described is not the result of a combination of a touch of management's arrogance and a dose of shareholders' lethargy.

275   It is a good practice, where the members are not known to each other, for speakers to commence their presentation by stating their names.

276   After permitting a reasonable number of persons to speak and having ascertained the sense of the meeting the chairman should formally state the motion and ask members to vote thereon.

277   **Auditors:** The chairman should then announce the next item on the agenda which is usually the reappointment of the incumbent auditors. The Act stipulates that part of the ordinary business of the annual meeting of members is the reappointment of the incumbent auditors. Shareholders cannot, on the spur of the moment, decide at an annual meeting to appoint another set of auditors.

278   If shareholders are not satisfied with the auditors they may by ordinary resolution at a special meeting remove the auditors and appoint other auditors in their place. However, remember that the auditors of the company are entitled to receive notice of every meeting of shareholders of the company and at the expense of the company to attend and be heard at the meeting on matters relating to their duties as auditors.

279   The motion for the auditors' reappointment may be put as follows: *"that Messrs   the incumbent auditors be reappointed auditors of the company for a further year at a fee of $ "* or alternatively the motion may be made *"that Messrs   the incumbent auditors be re-appointed auditors of the Company for the ensuing year and that the directors be authorised to fix their remuneration".*

280   **Payment of dividends:** Distribution of the profits of a company among its shareholders in respect of the shares held by them are described as dividend payments.

Such distributions are usually made by the directors by resolution declaring a dividend as a certain sum per share, or in the case of shares having a par value, at a rate percent upon the shares. In addition the resolution should state that the dividend should be payable on a certain date to shareholders of record as of a specified date, preferably subsequent to the date when the resolution is passed.

281   Under the provisions of the Act payment of a dividend is usually no longer an agenda item for the general meeting. The Act and most corporate instruments now place the authority for payment of dividends within the management discretion of the board.

This is however not the case in all jurisdictions, nor even for all companies registered under the Act and directors and company secretaries should note that any special regulations as to dividends embodied in the corporate instruments of the company must be observed.

282   Some older corporate instruments still require that the annual meeting must confirm payment of the dividends recommended by the directors before such may be paid. In those circumstances there should be an agenda item "To approve payment of the dividend of $ per share as recommended by the directors" and accordingly an item of business would be a motion: "*that the dividend of $ per share as recommended by the directors be confirmed and declared payable on   to shareholders of record on the close of business on the   *".

283   The normal rules of debate will apply. The motion could be subject to amendment to declare a smaller dividend than that recommended or to vary the method or time of payment but it is usual and certainly good corporate practice for the company's corporate instruments to contain a provision to restrict shareholders from declaring a dividend exceeding the amount recommended by the directors.

It must also be noted that where the law vests the authority to declare dividends in the directors, the general meeting cannot interfere in the directors' exercise of that power. See *Scott* v *Scott*.[48]

284   It is interesting to note that directors of a company may appoint a managing director or a committee of directors and delegate to him or them any of the powers of the directors but there are certain exceptions and among the powers that are not capable of being delegated is the power to declare dividends. This is a reasonable provision since there are tests of solvency which a company must meet before a dividend may be properly paid, and directors who authorise improper payments may be personally liable.

285   **Directors:** The appointment of directors is one of the items which sometimes evokes lively discussion at annual meetings of companies and which often requires a more complex voting process. Voting procedures will be dealt with in the following chapter but it is appropriate to settle some of the preliminary issues at this point. One of the problems often faced by presiding officers is how to deal with nominations from the floor of the meeting of persons for election to the office of director.

286   The Act treats the election of directors at an annual meeting as ordinary business. The Act also requires that the shareholders of a company must by ordinary resolution at the first meeting of the company and at each following annual meeting at which an election of directors is required, elect directors to hold office for a term expiring not later than the close of the third annual meeting of shareholders although it is not necessary that all directors elected at the meeting should hold office for the same term. (See section 66.)

287   In the absence of extenuating circumstances, accepting ad hoc nominations from the floor or changing the entire board of directors at the same time may not be in the best interest of the company but, if there are no specific provisions in the company's corporate instruments, the chairman will have to accept nomination of persons for election to the office of director if such is made from the floor at the meeting.

---

[48]   (1942)1 All ER 582 (see p. 317)

288   In such circumstances a poll may be demanded and the chairman should, unless a substantial majority of the members are present or represented at the meeting, fix a date, place and time for the conduct of such poll so as to give as many members as possible the opportunity to vote on the matter.

289   Some companies have sought to avoid the practice of receiving nominations of persons from the floor of the meeting for election to the office of director by amending their by-laws. See Appendix II Precedent J.

290   It is the duty of both the chairman and the company secretary to ensure that persons nominated for the office of director are properly qualified as required by the Act and the company's corporate instruments. For example:

- Is there a shareholding requirement, and if so has the nominee satisfied such requirement?

- Is there an age limitation?

- Are the persons nominated or any one of them debarred by statute from holding the office of director?

- Will the nominee cause an infringement of the Act which stipulates that a public company must have at least two directors who are not officers or employees of the company or any of its affiliates? (See section 59.)

- Is there any unanimous shareholders' agreement, and if so have the provisions, if any, dealing with the appointment of directors been satisfied?

- Has the company issued more than one class of shares, and if so does any class carry special rights relating to the appointment of directors?

291   With reference to the motion for election of directors, section 183 of the United Kingdom 1948 Companies Act contained a provision to the effect that at a general meeting of a public company a motion for the

appointment of two or more persons as directors by a single resolution shall not be made, unless a resolution that it shall be so made has first been agreed to by the meeting without any dissenting vote.

292   An exact provision may not be found in all Companies Acts, yet later legislation like the Companies Act CAP 308 of Barbados contains an indication as to what is regarded as good corporate practice and has even gone the extra mile to promote shareholders' democracy.

Attention is drawn to the provision for cumulative voting in the Act which requires that a separate vote of shareholders must be taken with respect to each candidate nominated for election to the office of director, unless a resolution is passed unanimously permitting two or more persons to be elected by a single resolution.

293   The spirit of the law is therefore quite clear. Good corporate governance therefore requires that each person nominated for election as a director should be voted on separately. See Appendix II Precedent K.

294   If it is desired to elect two or more persons by a single resolution a suitable procedural motion, must first be made and passed unanimously. See Appendix II Precedent L.

295   If it is necessary to take nominations from the floor, the chairman may invite nominations by informing members *"that the meeting is now open for nomination of persons to stand for election to the office of directors to fill   vacancies".*

296   Members wishing to nominate persons may make their nominations as follows: *"Mr Chairman, I nominate   and   for election as directors of the company."*

297   The management proxy circular or the notice convening the meeting should contain a statement to the effect that "unless persons nominated for election are present, the proposers should table a written consent from the nominee to serve as a director if elected." See Appendix II Precedent M.

298   It may argue that if a person who has been nominated is present at the meeting, he is deemed to have agreed to serve if elected unless he had declined the nomination at the time that it was made. My own preference however is for written consents in all cases.

299   There is a school of thought that nominations do not require seconding. Indeed, in *Re Horbury Bridge Coal Co.*[49] it was stated: "There is no law of the land which says that a motion cannot be put without a seconder, and the objection that the motion was not seconded cannot prevail."

Subsequent to this ruling however, many institutions such as local government authorities and others have adopted the general practice modelled on standing orders which require a seconder for nominating motions and amendments. I prefer this later approach and recommend that presiding officers do adopt such form of rules and advise the meeting accordingly.

300   It should be noted however, that a motion to nominate is neither debatable nor amendable. Furthermore, notwithstanding the preferred model of standing orders which requires all motions to be seconded, it is a general convention that motions made from the chair do not require seconding.

301   After a reasonable period has elapsed or a sufficient number of persons have been nominated, a motion to close nominations may be made. This may be done by a member stating "*Mr Chairman, I move that nominations be closed*". Such a motion requires seconding but is not debatable.

If the chairman is satisfied that members have been given ample opportunity to make their nominations, the chairman may put the matter to the vote by stating: "*It has been proposed that nominations be closed. Those in favour please indicate by a show of hands, those against? I declare the motion . . .*" (Indicate carried or defeated.)

302   Chairmen should be alert to certain tactics which organised groups, having a vested interest in the election, may attempt to use in order to limit nominations after they have nominated their own candidates.

---

[49]   (1879) 11 Ch D 109 (see p. 319)

---

303   An example of the foregoing is as follows: working as a tag team, a member of a given organised group may nominate three persons for election to fill three vacancies on the board. As soon as this proposal is made and seconded another member of the said group may move that nominations be closed while a third member immediately seconds the closing motion.

304   The chairman has a duty to ensure that members have been given a fair and reasonable opportunity to make their nominations and he should tactfully resist any attempt by an obvious interest group to hijack the due process of the meeting.

In a situation as that highlighted above the chairman may wish to address the meeting as follows:

"A motion has been made to close nominations. Before consideration of this motion is there any other member who desires to make [50] *a nomination? [Pause] If not, would those in favour of the motion please indicate by a show of hands?"*

If members indicate a desire to make further nominations, the chairman may then wish to further address the meeting as follows:

"Ladies and gentlemen, you have before you a motion to close nominations. There are however other members who have indicated a desire to make further nominations. The chair is of the view that the meeting was not given adequate opportunity for members to make their nominations and I would therefore ask you to vote against the motion of closure. The proposition before you is that nominations be now closed. Those in favour please indicate by a show of hands. Those against? I declare the motion to close nominations   ." (Indicate carried or lost.)

---

[50]   Note, the chair must make it plain that he is not calling for additional nominations nor initiating a debate on the motion but merely seeking an indication as to whether or not there are other members who desire to make additional nominations. The acceptance of nominations after the motion to close nominations would be inappropriate without members first having voted upon the motion. Although the chair has the right to guide the meeting he cannot withhold the motion to close nominations from the meeting if it is properly moved and seconded.

305   It should be emphasised that the chairman does not have a discretion to withhold the motion to close nominations from the meeting, but in the interest of equity he/she may seek to guide the mind of the meeting on this procedural matter. Finally, note that a motion to close nomination is not a motion on a point of order, therefore a speaker who has the floor may not be interrupted by another member who desires to propose the motion to close nominations.

306   If more persons have been nominated for election to the office of director than there are vacancies a poll should be held. The chairman should therefore advise the meeting that *"X number of persons have been nominated for election as directors to fill   vacancies. I therefore declare that a poll shall be held on this matter such poll to take place on   the   day of   , 19 at between the hours of   and   ."*

307   If the number of persons nominated is equal to the vacancies to be filled, there is a school of thought that the chairman may declare the persons nominated to be elected. I have some difficulty with this practice.

308   Unless otherwise provided for, the election of directors is a right vested in members to be exercised by them in general meeting and members may only exercise that right when the matter has been properly put before them.

309   The chairman of the meeting must not presume that members will automatically vote in the affirmative in such circumstances. Additionally, some corporate instruments may require or specify that the election of directors shall be by ballot.

If the corporate instruments are silent on the point, the preferred course of action would be for the chairman to address the meeting as follows:

"Ladies and gentlemen three persons have been nominated for election as directors to fill the three vacancies on the board. May I put the three names before you in a single motion? [Pause for acquiescence — see voting by acquiescence.] *I therefore move that the persons nominated be elected directors of the company by acclamation and that they should hold office for a period expiring on the   etc. Are there any*

against [pause for acquiescence], *I therefore declare Messrs*   *duly elected directors of the company as proposed.*"

310   If there are any dissenting voices, the motion should be put to a vote by a show of hands in the usual manner.

311   I am aware that some of my professional colleagues differ with me on this procedure and may regard my treatment of the matter to be too pedantic. Such may be the case, but the election could never be challenged, in the light of the Act or the company's corporate instruments, for want of a shareholders' vote.

SPECIAL BUSINESS, SPECIAL RESOLUTIONS, AMENDMENTS

312   A resolution is the means through which the meeting expresses its corporate resolve. As such, resolutions must be carefully worded so that the meaning and intention is unambiguous. Clarity and preciseness are the hallmarks of good resolutions.

313   A resolution which is inconsistent with the by-laws of the company but otherwise within the authority of the company's articles and the Act will be invalid unless it is proposed and passed as a special resolution; and a resolution which conflicts with the articles of the company is invalid unless it is passed in pursuance and in conformity with the provisions of the Act for the amendment or modification of the Articles of Incorporation. (See the inference in *Quin & Axten Ltd* v *Salmon.*[51])

314   If an invalid resolution is combined as part of a transaction with a resolution that is otherwise valid, the whole transaction is vitiated. See *Re Imperial Bank of China, India & Japan,*[52] but where the resolutions are distinct and independent, the invalidity of one will not affect the other, although both are put to the vote together.[53] See also *Thompson* v *Henderson's Transvaal Estates Ltd*[54] and *Cleve* v *Financial Corporation.*[55]

---

[51] (1909) Ac 442 (see p. 320)
[52] (1866) 1 Ch App 339 (see p. 322)
[53] S. Shaw and D. Smith, *The Law of Meetings,* p. 143.
[54] (1908) 1 Ch 765 (see p. 324)
[55] (1873) Lr 16 363 (see p. 327)

---

315   I have heard the view expressed by some shareholders who disagree with certain resolutions passed by a company in general meeting that they do not consider themselves to be bound thereby because they were absent and/or did not participate in the meeting. This is a fallacy.

316   Members not present at a meeting are nevertheless bound by its decisions and affected by any information disclosed at the meeting provided the matters dealt with were within the competence of the meeting and the proceedings of the meeting were in strict compliance with the company's corporate instruments and the Act. See *Re Norwich Yarn Co. Ex Parte Bignold.*[56]

317   The notice of the meeting states the business to be transacted but the meeting itself has the right through its members to propose amendments, providing the amended motions remain within the scope of the notice convening the meeting. The point is well illustrated in *Betts & Co. Ltd* v *MacNaghten.*[57]

318   The Act requires that the text of any special resolution to be submitted to members must be set out in the notice. It is for this reason that such resolutions are more likely to be subject of proposed amendments when they are being considered at a meeting of members.

319   There are however different rules which the court will apply if the motion is a resolution to be passed or adopted at a special or extra-ordinary meeting or if it constitutes special business at a general meeting. In those circumstances the precise terms of the resolution to be put before members must be embodied in the notice convening the meeting.

320   In *Re Mooregate Mercantile Holdings Ltd* [58] the principle is re-enforced that the exact text of the resolution to be proposed must appear in the notice and consequently it cannot therefore be altered by amendment in substance although minor corrections would be permitted.[59] Until this decision is modified or overturned I recommend that Caribbean practitioners be guided thereby.

---

[56]   (1856) 22 Beavan 143 at page 165 (see p. 329)
[57]   (1910) 1 Ch 430 (see p. 330)
[58]   (1980) 1 WLR 227 (see p. 332)
[59]   See M. T Lazarides, "General Meetings and Notices, etc." *The Administrator* (August 1994) : 28.

321   **An amendment** is a proposition to alter the terms of the motion currently before the meeting and under discussion. It is also possible to move an amendment to an amendment of the original motion under discussion.

322   Amendment is a procedure for permitting members, whose views and position on the substance of the motion being discussed would not be reflected or satisfied either by accepting or rejecting the motion as proposed, to propose a variation to the original motion.

323   Presiding officers must however be on the alert to the ploy of some members who may attempt to introduce counter motions under the guise of an amendment. Counter motions, or for that matter any motion or amendment, should be refused if:

- It is outside the scope of the meeting to decide the matter and therefore *ultra vires* at the meeting.

- It bears no relation to the original motion and its subject matter and is consequently irrelevant.

- It proposes something already resolved by the meeting and is therefore redundant.

- It is incompatible with a decision previously made and is therefore inconsistent.

- It is vexatious in that it is only intended to impede the transaction of the business of the meeting.

324   The following are some basic rules applicable to amendments with which presiding officers and company secretaries must be familiar:

- An amendment may not be proposed to a resolution that has already been passed.

- Generally speaking a person may move only one amendment to any one motion.

- An amendment may take the form of omitting certain words, adding certain words at the end of the motion, inserting certain words in the body of the motion, substituting or rearranging certain words to the text of the motion.

- An amendment must not be in terms as would constitute a direct negative of the main motion. That result may be achieved by voting against the main motion.

  Thus for example if the main motion was "that X be elected a director of the company to hold office for a period of three years" an amendment which seeks to add the word 'not' after 'be' and before 'elected' so that the amended motion reads that Mr X be not elected a director . . . etc, is not acceptable; but an amendment which proposes the deletion of the word 'three' and the substitution of the word 'two' in its place so that X would hold office for two years instead of three years would be in order.

- An amendment should be within the scope of the main motion and must not alter the original motion to such an extent as would make the original motion so materially different as would bring it outside the scope of the proposal contained in the notice convening the meeting.

325   As earlier observed, the main motion before the meeting may be subject to amendment. Consequently, when a proposition has been made to amend the main motion, debate on the amendment takes precedence over the main motion and discussion must then be confined to the proposed amendment.

326   The amendment must be voted on first. If the motion of amendment is lost, the main motion remains unaffected and discussion thereon resumes. If the motion to amend is passed the amendment is incorporated into the main or original motion which then becomes the substantive motion. The chairman may then permit debate to continue upon the motion as amended, i.e. the substantive motion.

327   The skill of the chairman may be tested when a sub-amendment has been proposed to the amendment before it is voted upon. It is the privilege of members to propose amendments to an amendment under discussion.

When this occurs the sub-amendment should usually be dealt with first. However when there is more than one amendment before the meeting matters tend to become blurred. It is therefore better, whenever possible, to seek to make such sub-amendments, amendments in their own right so that one amendment may be dealt with at a time.

328   If the foregoing procedure is followed, the main amendment would be debated and voted upon first. If passed it is then incorporated into the main motion. The sub-amendment which was proposed to the amendment may then be proposed as an amendment to the substantive motion. The following example may illustrate the point:

329   *Main motion:*   *"Resolved that X be appointed president for a period of four years at an annual remuneration of $50,000."*

330   *Amendments:*   *1.*   To insert the words 'of the company' after the word 'president'

                          2.   To delete the word 'four' and substitute the word 'three' before the word years.

                          3.   To delete the figure '$50,000' and substitute the figure '$40,000'.

        Sub-amendment: *4.*   To amend Amendment number 3 by adding the words 'Not more than' immediately before the figure '$40,000'.

331   A convenient method of dealing with these proposed amendments may be as follows:

    ♦   To vote upon Amendment 1 first.

    ♦   Secondly to vote upon Amendment 2.

    ♦   (If carried, Amendments 1 and 2 would have been incorporated in the main motion so that it becomes a substantive motion reading as follows "That Mr X be appointed president of the company for a period of three years at an annual remuneration of $50,000".)

- Amendment 4 being a sub-amendment to Amendment 3 should be tabled when Amendment 3 is being debated. As such, sub-amendment 4 should be voted on before Amendment 3, since if passed the sub-amendment 4 will have the effect of amending Amendment 3.

- Finally, Amendment 3 should be voted on.

332   If sub-amendment 4 is passed, Amendment 3 would then be put to the vote in its amended terms, i.e. 'To delete the figure $50,000' and substitute the following in its place 'not more than $40,000' but if Amendment 3 is then defeated the text of the substantive motion would remain unaffected and the motion would then be put in its substantive form (as amended by Amendments 1 and 2) to members for voting.

333   You should note that despite the fact that the sub-amendment 4 may have been passed it will have no effect upon the motion if Amendment 3 is defeated since it was a sub-amendment, i.e. an amendment to Amendment 3 which was defeated.

334   **Withdrawal of a motion:** A motion or amendment may be withdrawn or modified with leave of the chair before it has been seconded or stated by the chair. Some authorities hold the view that a motion if seconded, but not yet stated by the chair, may also be withdrawn by the proposer with leave of the seconder and the chair, while others believe that the chair should not permit a motion to be withdrawn after it has been seconded.

335   It is my opinion that the purpose of having a motion seconded is to ascertain from the meeting whether it is desirous of have the matter brought before it for discussion. If that be the case, then I am inclined to the view that a motion once seconded may not be withdrawn except with the consent of the meeting.

336   There is a school of thought that the consent to withdraw must be unanimous, but I am of the view that a majority vote is sufficient.

It should be noted however that there is a strong presumption that members once in possession of a proposition or motion are entitled to discuss the matter, even if for no other reason than to 'kill' the proposition by voting against it so that it be not brought before them again. In view of the foregoing, if there is strong objection from the floor to the withdrawal of any motion it would be prudent for the chair to permit the matter to be debated and voted upon.

TERMINATION OF DISCUSSION

337   When contentious matters are being discussed it is sometimes difficult to control the length of debate. The chairman may curtail debate on any issue after a reasonable period and may even take a vote of the meeting on the question of cessation of debate. He must be aware however of the fine line which separates controlling the meeting and stifling debate.

338   There are certain legitimate methods of interrupting discussion on a motion. These consist of the following subsidiary motions:

- That the question be now put. (This is commonly called the closure.)

- That debate on the question be now terminated.

- That the meeting do proceed to the next business.

- That the question be not now put. (This is commonly called the previous question.)

339   The previous question or the closure may be moved while the motion or substantive motion is before the meeting but not while an amendment is under discussion. It may be moved by any member who has not spoken on the main motion but a speaker may not be interrupted in order that the motion be put. Subject to the foregoing, motions to terminate discussion which are not debatable nor amendable must be put to the meeting before any other business is discussed.

340 **If the motion is one of closure i.e. "that the question be now put"** is passed then debate on the substantive motion is curtailed and the substantive motion is put to the vote immediately. If a motion of closure is defeated then debate continues and such motion may not be entertained again until a reasonable period has elapsed. Half an hour is deemed a reasonable period of time.

341 **A motion to adjourn debate on the question** must not be confused with a motion to adjourn the meeting. Discussion on a particular motion may be deferred or adjourned until later in the meeting or otherwise in accordance with the terms of the motion to adjourn debate. It may not be moved by any person who has spoken upon the main motion or any amendment thereto. If no period is fixed in the resolution to adjourn debate the matter should be brought back to members at the next available meeting under an agenda item of 'adjourned business'.

342 **The motion "to proceed to the next business"** may be moved at the end of any speech. If it is lost the main motion is however not put to the vote immediately, discussion continues thereon and the motion may not be entertained again until a reasonable period has elapsed. If it is passed the effect is the same as the motion of the previous question.

343 There is a school of thought that a motion to proceed may be moved by any member whether or not he has spoken on the main motion. I do not share this view. Since the effect of this motion is to curtail discussion it should not be proposed by persons who have already spoken on the main or substantive motion.

344 **If the motion "that the question be not now put" (i.e. the previous question)** is passed the original proposition which was under discussion is removed from further consideration by the meeting and may only be brought back to members by a proposal at a subsequent meeting. It is in effect as if the item was deleted from the agenda of the current meeting. If the motion "that the question be not now put" is lost then the substantive motion which was under discussion must be put to the meeting for voting thereon forthwith without any further debate.

345   It may seem a little surprising that there must be an immediate vote on the substantive motion if the motion on the previous question, i.e. "that the question be not now put", is lost.

346   The apparent ambiguity may be resolved if we examine closely the language of the motion. It is framed in the negative.

Generally speaking, if a proposition to do a certain act or to adopt a certain course of action is lost, then what the meeting has in fact decided is that that certain act or course of action as proposed be not done.

In the case of the previous question the motion being framed in the negative is that the question be not now put. If the reasoning of the foregoing example is applied, then, by voting against the previous question what the meeting has implicitly decided is that the question should be now put.[60]

347   The motion of the previous question is one of the most potent weapons in the armoury of the skilled debater. It is also a useful tool against the objectionable practices of 'filibustering' and 'stonewalling' and a remedy for the fribble of the devout egotist. Yet it must be used sparingly for it has the effect of forcing the meeting to either remove the item from the agenda or in the alternative to vote upon the matter under consideration immediately without further discussion.

348   In many institutions the standing orders or rules require a two-thirds vote for ordering the previous question. This they consider important in order to protect the democratic process. Roberts opined that if this two-thirds rule was not observed, a temporary majority of only one vote could deny the remaining members all opportunity to discuss any measure that such a majority wished to adopt or kill.[61]

349   Most corporate instruments will not have any regulation dealing with the majority required to pass a motion on the previous question. In such circumstances the rule of the simple majority will apply, unless at the commencement of the meeting it was proposed and agreed that any motion on the closure would require a two-thirds majority for passing.

---

60   *Roberts' Rules of Order*, p. 195
61   *Roberts' Rules of Order*, p. 198.

---

350   It is a convention that a motion on the previous question may not be proposed at a meeting of a committee.

Discussion

351   The following rules are those which usually apply to debates at company meetings.

- A person should normally only be permitted to speak once on any one motion.

- Speakers must at all times address the chair.

- If there is a proposition to amend a motion, a person who had spoken on the main motion is also entitled to speak on the motion to amend.

- When a motion to amend is being considered speakers may only speak on the amendment — not to the terms of the main motion.

- A seconder who has spoken has no right of reply to a motion; only a proposer has that right.

- A seconder may make his contribution at the time he seconds the motion but his interest may be better served if he merely seconds the motion as follows: "*Mr Chairman, I second the motion but reserve my right to speak thereon.*"

- The rules of common courtesy must apply at all times. Members should rise to speak, but if the chairman rises a member who has the floor should yield and resume his seat. Members should avoid interrupting other speakers.

- Persons participating in the meeting must not overlook their duty to be civil. Civility means a great deal more than just being nice to one another. Our democratic systems and institutions presuppose civil conduct. Civility calls upon us to make an effort to see the other person's point of view. It allows us to engage in dialogue with those whose ideas we oppose in a non-aggressive fashion.

- Speeches should be kept as short as possible. This will of course depend upon the complexity of the subject matter under discussion.

- If speakers are unduly lengthy the chairman should remind speakers that there are others who may wish to make a contribution. The chairman may then ask a particular person to sum up, allowing, say, two minutes for the speaker to do so. If the speaker persists the chairman can interrupt and seek the mind of the meeting; alternatively the chairman may propose a motion of closure.

- Points of order may, subject to the proper procedure, be raised at anytime by members during the course of the meeting and must be ruled upon promptly by the chairman.

CHAPTER 12

The rules and methods
of voting

352   The corporate resolve of the meeting is ascertained through the medium of voting. After the various propositions have been discussed by members the chairman of the meeting must determine the mind of the meeting. This is achieved by stating the motion and putting it to the vote.

353   J. M. Wainberg, Q.C. of the Ontario Bar states that "it is the duty of the chair to ascertain the sense and/or consensus of the meeting with regard to all questions properly brought before it, and to decide all emergent questions which require decision at the time . . . Unless there are provisions to the contrary in the governing statute or the by-laws, all ordinary questions are decided by a majority of votes. Certain resolutions require a larger majority".[62]

354   The Act stipulates that unless the articles of the company otherwise provide, on a show of hands a shareholder or proxy holder has one vote, and upon a poll a shareholder or proxy holder has one vote for every share held. (See section 124.) The right to vote is therefore largely influenced by the company's corporate instruments although there are certain overriding statutory provisions to which attention must be paid.

---

[62]   J. M. Wainberg, *Company Meetings*, pp. 65-66.

---

355 A company has practically no influence over how its members vote or use their votes. Voting is a right attached to shares and the company, being restricted from taking any notice of trusts is also, unless specifically ordered by any court, not entitled to look behind the bare fact of registered legal ownership of the shares as per its register of members. There are however certain exceptional circumstances, particularly in cases of fraud or manipulation, when voting will be scrutinised or even disallowed but these belongs to the supervisory realm of the court.

356 Generally speaking, the freedom of a shareholder to vote according to his own interest extends even to a shareholder who is also a director, except where the director is in breach of his fiduciary duty. However to say that a person is in a fiduciary position only commences an analytical process. It begs the question: To whom is he a fiduciary?

An eminent law lord is reported to have said that to describe a person as a fiduciary without saying more is meaningless.

This writer is of the view that a person may be in a fiduciary position in respect of a part of his activities and not in respect of other parts. Such I believe is the position of a director who is also a shareholder; thus a director, acting as such, owes a fiduciary duty to his company but while exercising his right as a shareholder he does not owe any fiduciary duty in respect of his voting power as such shareholder, except that it cannot be used to perpetuate a fraud on the minority shareholders. [63]

357 A director was even held to be entitled to vote as a shareholder although his interest in the subject matter was opposed to the interest of the company. See *North-West Transportation Co.* v *Beatty.*[64] Moreover, even where the articles prohibited a director from voting in respect of any matter in which he had an interest, such a prohibition did not preclude him from voting as a shareholder in general meeting in respect of any such matter. See also *East Pant Mining Co.* v *Merryweather.*[65]

---

[63] For an extensive treatment of the subject of fiduciary relationships see Underhill and Hayton, *Law of Trust and Trustees;* Hayton and Marshall, *Cases and Commentary on the Law of Trust;* and *Maudsley and Burns' Trust & Trustees Cases and Materials.* The relatively recent case of *New Zealand Netherlands Society Oranje Inc* v *Kuys* (1973) 2 ALL ER 1222 is also instructive.

[64] (1887) 12 App Las 589 (see p. 334)

[65] (1864) 2 H & M 254 (see p. 337)

---

358   In an earlier chapter, I pointed out that the right to attend meetings must not be confused with the right to vote, for although there is a great deal of similarity between the two there are nevertheless some fundamental differences. It is therefore appropriate, before considering methods of voting, to determine in general terms who may vote.

PERSONS ENTITLED TO VOTE

359   Except when a company has only one class of shares, in which case the rights of the holders are equal in all respects and include the right to vote at any meeting of shareholders, one must examine the articles of the company which may provide for varying classes of shares to have different rights and privileges, including the right to vote or a restriction on voting rights.

360   To determine those entitled to vote, the company secretary must therefore consult not only the Act but also the company's corporate instruments and the resolutions creating and issuing the several classes of shares. Subject to the foregoing the general rules governing the entitlement to vote may be summarised as follows:

(a) It is not unusual to find that holders of preference shares which have no general voting rights may nonetheless be entitled to vote if payment of the preference dividend is in arrears.

(b) The Act by section 202 confers upon the holders of the shares of a class or series the right to vote upon certain specific proposals as set out in the Act whether or not the shares had otherwise carried voting rights.

361   The proposals upon which the holders of such shares are given a statutory entitlement to vote are set out in section 202 and include any proposal

i.   To change or remove the rights, privileges, restrictions or conditions attached to the shares of that class;

ii. To increase the rights or privileges of any class of shares having rights or privileges equal or superior to the shares of that class;

iii. To create a new class of shares equal or superior to the shares of that class;

iv. To make any class of shares having rights or privileges inferior to the shares of that class equal or superior to the shares of that class;

v. To effect an exchange or to create a right of exchange of all or part of the shares of another class into the shares of that class;

vi. To constrain the issue or transfer of the shares of that class, or extend or remove the constraint.

362   Unless the corporate instruments of the company otherwise provide, holders are entitled to vote separately as a class or series upon a proposal to amend the corporate instruments or to increase or decrease any maximum number of authorised shares of that class, or increase any maximum number of authorised shares of a class having rights or privileges equal or superior to the shares of that class; or to effect an exchange reclassification or cancellation of all or part of the shares of that class.

363   In addition to the foregoing, sections 134 and 208 of the Act also confer upon holders of all shares in a company the right to vote upon certain extra-ordinary transactions, such as the sale of substantially all of the property of a company and proposals for any amalgamation of a company, both of which require the approval of all shareholders by vote whether or not all shares had otherwise carried the right to vote.

364   **Joint holders:** All joint shareholders are members and are entitled to vote but usually only the first named of the joint holders as recorded in the register of members may cast the vote. If the first named person appointed a proxy to attend and vote but the second named person attended the meeting in person, entitlement to vote in the absence of any specific provision in the company's corporate instruments, would vest in the second named person since a vote in person has precedence over a vote by proxy.

If, however, the corporate instruments contained a provision which stipulated that the vote of the first named, whether in person or by proxy, shall be accepted to the exclusion of the votes of the other joint holders, then the holder of the proxy will have priority.

365 Generally speaking, voting difficulties between joint shareholders only arise where there are personal differences in the relationship between the two parties. The company should not bend its regulations to accommodate nor become involved in such personal matters.

If the differences between joint holders are so acute, they have the option of dividing their shares so that instead of being joint holders they become registered as separate shareholders for such portion of the shares as they may among themselves determine, or, alternatively, a poll may be demanded.

366 **Deceased members:** On the death of a sole shareholder, the personal representatives of such deceased member are the only persons entitled to deal with the shares of the deceased. As such they are entitled to transfer the shares or to be registered as the holders of such shares.

Although the Act in relationship to shareholders includes: the personal representative of a deceased member, a trustee in bankruptcy of a bankrupt member and a person in whose favour a transfer of shares has been executed but whose name has not been entered in the register of shareholders, the Act by several other references makes a distinction between shareholders entitled to receive notice and those entitled to vote and this distinction must be understood as well as enforced.[66]

367 Only shareholders whose names are on the register of members are entitled to vote.

368 Section 121 of the Act provides that a company must not later than 10 days after the record date is fixed under section 106 or, if no record date is fixed, then at the close of business on the date immediately preceding the day on which notice is given for a meeting, or if no notice is given, then as of the day on which the meeting is held, prepare a list of its shareholders

---

[66] See chapter 6 — Representatives of deceased members. (p. 35, section 116)

who are entitled to receive notice of a meeting arranged in alphabetical order and showing the number of shares held by each shareholder.

The Act further states that the persons named in the list are entitled at the meeting to which the list relates to vote the shares shown opposite their names.

369   A personal representative who has not elected to be registered as the holder of the shares held in the name of the deceased may not vote such shares since the shares would have remained registered in the name of the deceased and any notation of the personal representatives in such circumstances only serves to indicate to the company the address to which notice and other communication from the company to the deceased member, such as dividends etc., should be sent.

370   When shares are held jointly and one of the joint holders dies the survivor is entitled to vote all of the shares.

371   Where a deceased member had, prior to his demise, given a valid proxy to another, that proxy must be disallowed since death operates as revocation of any proxy previously given.

372   **Unregistered transferees:** The above view is buttressed by the Act when its provisions in relation to the treatment of a person ('shareholder') to whom shares had been transferred but whose name had not been entered in the register are considered.

The Act provides that such person may produce the properly endorsed share certificates to the company or otherwise establish to the company that he owns the shares and may demand, not later than 10 days before the meeting of the shareholders that his name be included in the lists of shareholders before the meeting and in those circumstances the transferee may vote his shares because his name was added to the list, i.e. he had become a registered member and by reason of such 'late' registration was therefore entitled to vote.

Note carefully that the pre-requisite to voting is the addition of the transferee's name to the list of shareholders pursuant to the transfer of the shares in his favour.

373 An alternative procedure would be for the transferor to give a proxy to the transferee in respect of the shares transferred so as to enable the transferee to vote if the transfer had occurred less than 10 days before the meeting.

This alternative method is however not available to personal representatives, since unless there is specific empowering provision in the company's corporate instruments, a personal representative may not appoint a proxy in respect of shares still remaining registered in the name of the deceased.

374 The power to appoint a proxy is governed by sections 135 and 136 of the Act, which defines a proxy as a written or printed form signed by or on behalf of a shareholder who is entitled to vote at a meeting. Such proxy must be executed by the shareholder or his attorney, authorised in writing. A personal representative does not fall into this category. He is not deemed an attorney of the deceased, and any power of attorney which the deceased member may have given lapses on his death.

375 **Bankrupt members:** The position of bankrupt members and trustees in bankruptcy is somewhat different, although there is a school of thought that the trustee in bankruptcy of the bankrupt member should be treated in a similar position as personal representatives.

376 Until the company has received formal notice it may continue to recognise the vote of the bankrupt member but on receipt of formal notice from the trustee in bankruptcy, accompanied with a certified copy of the relevant court order, the vote of the trustee in bankruptcy should be recognised whether or not the trustee in bankruptcy had elected to have his name entered in the register as the registered holder of the shares held by the bankrupt member.

This writer takes this view because the trustee in bankruptcy, in relation to the company, is exercising his authority pursuant to an order of the court and his position may be more akin to the holder of a power of attorney.

377 **Corporate entities:** Other companies or legal entities which are shareholders of companies may either appoint a proxy or a representative and such appointed persons are entitled to attend, speak

and vote at meetings of shareholders on behalf of the corporate entity which they represent.

It may be found that in companies which are governed by older legislation a representative will have greater authority than a proxy holder in that the right of a proxy holder may be restricted to voting whereas a representative may exercise all of the powers as if the representative were the registered shareholder. See Appendix II Precedent N for notice and resolution appointing a corporate representative.

378 **Company's own shares:** The Act permits a company, in certain circumstances, to repurchase its own shares. Section 43 stipulates that a company holding shares in itself or its holding body corporate shall not vote or permit those shares to be voted unless the company holds the shares in the capacity of a legal representative and has complied with section 144 of the Act. That section imposes certain duties and restrictions upon the company in respect of those shares.

379 **Nominees:** Nominee shareholders are a growing feature in modern corporate practice. Very often requests are received from nominee shareholders to split dividends or to accept multiple proxies, etc.

Computerisation of corporate records have made these requests more manageable but there is a fine line as to whether some of these requests border on the question of taking notice of trusts by the company; yet it must be recognised that a person is entitled to split his vote on a poll and vote some of his shares in favour of a proposal and some against. When this is done some members attempt to cast a single net vote. This practice should be discouraged. When members desire to split their votes they should vote shares for and shares against the motion.

380 Splitting the vote of nominee shareholders or the appointment by a nominee shareholder of multiple representatives does not however entitle such representatives to speak separately on a proposition.

381 The general rule is that a member is entitled to speak once on any proposition and all such representatives are representatives of the same one member.

Where such nominee shareholder desires that each representative shall have the right to speak on a given proposal, then the shareholding will have to be split into separate designated account holdings (e.g. Smith Banking Corporation A/C ZA001, Smith Banking Corporation A/C ZA002, etc.). The disadvantage to the nominee holder is that changes of beneficial interest between accounts may then necessitate execution of transfer instruments.

382   **Bearer shares:** Holders of bearer shares or of share warrants to bearer are entitled to receive notices of general meetings and to vote thereat if the corporate instruments or the terms of the issue of such shares so specify.

383   Notices are usually given by advertisement in one or more newspapers. The notice should follow the wording of that given to registered members and in addition should contain instructions as to how holders may vote in person or by proxy.

384   Usually the holder will be required to deposit the warrant or bearer certificate with the company at least three days before the date and time of the meeting, but if the corporate instruments so provide, a certificate of a bank or other financial institution or safe deposit company of good repute certifying that such agent holds the warrants in safe custody, may be accepted by the company in lieu of the deposit of the warrants themselves.[67]

385   When the share warrant is deposited the company must give to the person depositing the share warrant a certificate (not a share certificate) stating his name, address, and the number of shares represented by such share warrant and that certificate shall entitle him to attend and vote at a meeting in respect of the shares specified therein as if he were a registered member.

After the meeting, upon surrender of such certificate to the company the share warrant in respect whereof it was given shall be returned.

---

[67]   *Company Secretarial Practice,* 9th Supplement, pp. 4/18 and 4/81.

PROXIES

386   Following the review of those entitled to vote it may be helpful to consider some aspects of the administrative procedures applicable to proxies. These procedures are neither prescribed by the Act nor is it usual to find them embodied in the company's corporate instruments. It is rather a practical matter which must be dealt with as may be appropriate to specific individual circumstances. The method described herein should therefore be taken as a guide.

387   The company's corporate instruments will normally require that forms of proxy should be completed and returned to the office of the company not later than 48 hours before the meeting.

    The company's authority to make this stipulation is conferred by section 138 of the Act which provides that the directors of a company may specify in a notice calling a meeting of shareholders of the company a time not exceeding 48 hours preceding the meeting or an adjournment of the meeting before which time proxies to be used at the meeting must be deposited with the company or its agent and in the calculation of time for the aforementioned purposes Saturdays and holidays are to be excluded.

388   The general rule is that proxies deposited prior to the original meeting are, in the absence of any revocation by the shareholder, valid for any adjourned meeting since an adjourned meeting is a continuation of the original meeting.

389   Companies which were incorporated under older legislation may continue to rely upon the rule in *McLaren* v *Thompson* [68] in which it was held that proxies could not be deposited after the original meeting to be used at an adjournment thereof.

390   By the wording of sections 137 and 138 of the Act the judgement in *McLaren* v *Thompson* as referred to above is no longer relevant to companies incorporated under the Act or similar legislation since the Act implies that proxies may be deposited at any time up to 48 hours before the meeting or any adjourned meeting.

---

[68]   (1917) 2 Ch 261 (see p. 338)

---

391   On the question of polls, adjournment and deposit of proxies etc., it should be noted that the suspension of business merely for the purposes of taking a poll does not constitute an adjournment. The authority for this interpretation is found in *Shaw v Tati Concessions Ltd.*[69]

"A poll demanded at a company meeting was directed to be taken at a future date, but the meeting itself was not adjourned. Held, that the mere postponement for the poll was not an adjournment of the meeting within the meaning of an article allowing for the lodgement of proxies before the meeting 'or adjourned meeting', the original meeting continued for the purpose of taking a poll and no fresh proxies could be lodged between the two dates."[70]

392   I strongly recommend that companies avail themselves of the facility afforded by the Act and require the deposit of proxy forms 48 hours before the meeting or any adjournment thereof. This will allow the company secretary or registrar to list the proxies in alphabetical order and the shares represented by such proxies.

393   The above procedure will assist the chairman to determine whether or not a quorum is present and, where the proxy form used is one in which the shareholder has directed the proxy holder to vote in a certain manner upon specific resolutions, it would also assist the chairman in dealing expeditiously with a demand for a poll.

394   On receipt of the proxy forms these should be date stamped on arrival. If members send in multiple proxies the general rule is that the later will prevail since it would be deemed to have revoked the earlier proxy.

395   Unless the standard proxy form or card is very elaborately worded, it cannot anticipate all of the proposed amendments that may be tabled to the resolutions (motions) set out in the notice convening the meeting. If a substantial amendment is carried, the proxy's authority to vote is unaffected but he may no longer have valid instructions as to how he should vote. The holder of the proxy should therefore exercise his discretion in a manner which he honestly believes is likely to reflect the wishes of his appointer.

[69]   (1913) 1 Ch 292 (see p. 339)
[70]   I. Shearman, *Shackleton on the Law and Practice of Meetings*, p. 183.

396   An instrument of proxy is in effect a power of attorney and is revocable at will pursuant to the provisions of section 137 of the Act. The improper rejection of valid proxies may be a ground for setting aside an election of directors or other resolutions.

If a shareholder, after appointing a proxy, attends the meeting in person such shareholder can vote in person as the right of the shareholder to vote in person is paramount to the right of the proxy.

It is a mute point however if, in the absence of specific provisions in the company's corporate instruments, the presence of the shareholder revokes the proxy or merely suspends its use. There are conflicting views on this issue.

The better opinion seems to be that a proxy cannot be exercised, thought it may not strictly be revoked, if the person who had given the proxy attends the meeting in person, but if the shareholder votes before his proxy had voted on his behalf, it would seem, impliedly that the proxy had been revoked. (For further research see *Cousins v International Brick Co. Ltd* [71] and *Knight v Bulkeley.* [72]

397   The company secretary should have the form of proxy carefully examined to ensure that the person giving the proxy is a shareholder entitled to vote and that the proxy holder is a person qualified to be such under the applicable legislation and corporate instruments.

In this regard it must be noted that companies to which the Act applies may no longer require that a proxy must be a member of the company in that it is now stipulated that a shareholder who is entitled to vote at a meeting of shareholders may appoint a proxy holder and such proxy holder need not be a shareholder. (See section 136.)

Care must however be taken to ensure that a vote is not received and counted from both the proxy holder and the shareholder.

On attendance by the shareholder the proxy holder should be excluded from the meeting unless he holds proxies for other non-attending

---

[71]   (1931) 2 Ch 90 (see p. 340)
[72]   (1859) 5 Jur (N.S.) 817 (see p. 346)

members or is him/herself entitled to attend the meeting in his/her own right as a shareholder.

398   Finally, it is recommended that all rejected proxies should be carefully retained for a period of at least three months in case any matter arising out of the meeting is challenged.

399   A past president of the Institute of Chartered Secretaries and Administrators opined that: "On a highly contentious question, thought should be given to the merits of asking a professional firm such as the company's auditors (unless they are the source of the contention!) to act as tellers, checking and counting all votes in the poll. The objective is not so much to help the company's registrar at a time of great pressure (indeed experience suggests that bringing in the auditors will only add to that pressure) but to present the results of the poll in a form which should satisfy even the most suspicious opposition." He further stated that "if this course is adopted, the auditors should be given precise instructions by the secretary before they start work . . . these might include an instruction to refer to the company's solicitors (or attorneys) any doubtful proxies and any the auditors believe they should reject".[73]

VOTING METHODS

400   Shareholders entitled to vote may do so either by acquiescence, acclamation, a show of hands or on a poll. In some organisations, or in particular circumstances, a roll call vote may be used. Before any vote is called for it is the duty of the chairman to put the motion, either in its original form or as amended during the course of discussion, in clear and precise terms to the meeting and invite members to vote thereon. Once the motion is so stated and members are invited to vote thereon the meeting may not be interrupted for further debate on the matter.

401   **Acquiescence** is a method of voting on non-contentious issues where the chairman feels that members are unanimous in their view on the question before the meeting.

---

[73]   D. Roberts, *The Administration of Company Meetings.* p. 35.

It may for example be used when dealing with the minutes of a previous committee meeting; these having been read the chairman may ask *"Are there any corrections to the minutes?"* After a brief pause and no objection is raised to the minutes the chairman may then state *"There being no suggested corrections, the minutes will stand verified as read".* The principle in this situation is that silence from the floor is an indication of assent or agreement with the chair.

402   **Acclamation** is a midway method of voting between acquiescence and a show of hands. This method is sometimes referred to as a voice vote.

It is an imperfect method of voting and should only be used where the chairman senses that the meeting is overwhelmingly committed in its support on the question before it. In such circumstances the chairman may ask *"All in favour say 'aye', those against say 'no'".* On the basis of the response he may then declare the motion carried or lost. If the chairman is in doubt he should ask for a show of hands.

403   **Voting by a show of hands** is one of two recognised methods of voting prescribed by the Act.

It is an easy and effective way of determining the general consensus of persons present and voting. The chairman should make sure that the hands are properly counted, in this task he should seek the assistance of tellers or scrutineers. When the count has been communicated to him he should then declare the motion carried or lost. Again care should be exercised to ensure that only those entitled to vote do in fact vote.

404   In *Horbury Bridge Coal & Wagon Co.*[74] as well as *Carruth v Imperial Chemical Industries Ltd* [75] it was held that a vote by show of hands is conclusive where a poll is not demanded and the chairman declares the result.[76]

405   Section 127 states that unless the by-laws otherwise provide, voting at a meeting of shareholders must be by a show of hands, except when a

---

[74]   (1879) 11 Ch D 109 (see p. 319)
[75]   (1937) Ac 707 (see p. 300)
[76]   Wainberg, *Company Meetings*, p. 71.

ballot is demanded by a shareholder or proxy holder entitled to vote at the meeting.

406   A vote by a show of hands pays no regard to the number of shares held by those participating in the vote. It is a vote based upon the number of persons present and voting. The Act by section 124 stipulates that unless the articles of the company otherwise provide, on a show of hands a shareholder or proxy holder has one vote. *Note that on a show of hands a proxy holder has only one vote irrespective of the number of shareholders he is representing by proxy.*

407   **Roll call voting** is used when the meeting wishes to set on record the vote of each member. Each member, delegate or representative indicates agreement, dissent, or abstention, when his name is called. This method of voting may be more appropriate for conventions.

408   **Voting by ballot** was traditionally considered as a secret vote in the sense that the name and vote of the person casting the ballot was not identifiable.

This had the merit of preventing undue influence on the exercise of one's vote but it made scrutiny difficult and anonymity is only applicable when each person voting has only a single vote in respect of the matter to be decided.

In the context of modern company practice, where on a poll the number of votes is related to the number of shares held and in respect of any proposal the number of votes cast for and against must be recorded, it does not appear practical in the vast majority of cases to have an anonymous ballot.

409   I make the foregoing observation because scrutineers must be able to ascertain if the ballot has been cast in accordance with the terms of any applicable proxy. How may this be done if it is 'anonymous'? Indeed if one looked at the polling paper used in *Butterworths Company Precedents* the name of the shareholder is required to be stated thereon.[77]

---

[77]   *Butterworths Company Precedents*, Vol. 2, p. 1028.

I am therefore of the view that in most cases there can be no provision for anonymous balloting in respect of any poll at company meetings.

POLLS

410   The right to demand a poll is a right conferred by the Act upon shareholders and proxy holders and this right cannot be abrogated by any provision to the contrary in the company's corporate instruments. The Act by section 127 provides that a shareholder or proxy holder may demand a ballot either before or after any vote by a show of hands.

I believe that the word poll was intended instead of ballot since a ballot is merely one of the methods of conducting a poll, but it maybe that the Act intended to confer upon shareholders not only the right to demand a poll, but also to determine the method how such poll should be conducted.

411   Section 124 provides that subject to the articles of the company (and the rights attached to the shares held) upon a poll a shareholder or proxy holder has one vote for every share held.

412   When a poll is demanded on the election of a chairman of any meeting or on a motion to adjourn the meeting, it must be taken forthwith. On any other question the poll may be held at such time as the chairman shall direct and the other business of the meeting should be dealt with pending the results of the poll, unless consideration of such other business was dependent upon the results of the poll.

413   A poll is perhaps the most representative method of voting in that it affords the opportunity for the maximum number of members to express their views on the proposal before the meeting according to their financial stake in the company.

414   For the avoidance of doubt, and particularly for the benefit of officers of companies that are governed by older enactments, note that members who were not present at the meeting at which a poll was demanded are

nevertheless entitled to vote on the poll. See *Regina* v *Wimbledon Local Board*[78] and *Regina* v *Lambeth*.[79]

415　The conduct of a poll requires detailed planning. Voting papers will be necessary. It is not usual to prepare these in advance since most polls are conducted at a date and time other than that of the meeting. However, while it is rare for a poll to be demanded on the election of a chairman or on the question of adjournment, the company secretary should always be prepared, since a poll on the question of adjournment or the election of a chairman must be held immediately. It is therefore always wise to have a supply of voting papers for this purpose.

416　Most polls are conducted by ballot. The general procedure is as follows:

- A ballot paper is handed to every person entitled to vote.

- The ballot should preferably be printed and have the proposal stated thereon.

- The ballot paper should also contain voting instructions.

- The name of the shareholder, or if the voter is a proxy holder then both the names of the shareholder and proxy holder (i.e. John Smith proxy for Bill Little), should be placed at the top or end of the ballot paper.

- The number of shares being voted for or against the proposal should be stated. See Appendix II Precedent O for specimen ballot paper.

- The ballot must be voted in accordance with any form of proxy which stipulates how the proxy holder must vote.

- A member need not vote all of his shares in a particular manner but may split his vote.

417　For the proper conduct of a poll the chairman must fix a date, time and place at which the poll will be conducted.

---

[78]　(1882) 8 Qbd 459 (see p. 348)
[79]　(1838) 8 A & E 356 (see p. 349)

It is the duty of the chairman to declare the poll opened and closed. He should not close the poll if there are persons at the polling station waiting to exercise their right to vote as every reasonable opportunity must be afforded members to cast their vote.

418   The chairman should appoint scrutineers to collect, examine and count the votes but it is the duty of the chairman to rule on the validity of any questionable ballots. It is also the duty of the chairman to declare the results of the poll and to declare the motion carried or lost. A sample scrutineers' report is shown as Appendix II Precedent Q.

419   For the avoidance of doubt, it is worth emphasising three provisions applicable to a poll.

    ♦   A demand for a poll properly made and seconded cannot be withdrawn by the proposer unless there are specific rules in the corporate instruments permitting such a withdrawal or the meeting unanimously agrees to the withdrawal. The principle is illustrated in *Regina* v *Mayor of Dover*.[80]

    ♦   The poll must be conducted in strict compliance with the Act and the company's corporate instruments. The chairman has no authority to enlarge the power or process of voting. This principle is clearly settled in *McMillan* v *Le Roi Mining Co*.[81]

    ♦   A poll is an enlargement of the meeting at which it was demanded. It is not an adjourned meeting. All persons who were entitled to attend the meeting may take part in the poll when held and the resolution passed pursuant to the poll is deemed to have been passed as of the date of the meeting and not as of the date when the poll was held. The matter is therefore more akin to a temporary suspension of the proceedings of the meeting so that a matter may be determined by a particular voting process.

---

[80]   (1903) 1 KB 668 (see p. 351)
[81]   (1906) 1 Ch 331 (see p. 353)

NEW VOTING PROVISIONS

420   The Act has introduced two innovative features designed to enhance minority shareholders' influence on the corporate affairs of their company. Those innovations are the concepts of cumulative voting and pooling arrangements.

421   **Cumulative voting:** This was introduced to enhance the influence of minority shareholders on the matter of the election of directors:

422   Stickler observes that "the main purpose of cumulative voting is to enable minority interest to obtain representation on the board by concentrating their total votes on one or more candidates".[82]

423   The provisions of the Act on cumulative voting are not mandatory but permissive, in that cumulative voting may only be exercised if the corporate instruments of the company make provision for its use. (See section 67.)

424   Cumulative voting may be exercised during the conduct of a poll and a specimen cumulative voting card is shown as Appendix II Precedent P.

425   This voting method enables each shareholder who is entitled to vote at an election of directors to cast a number of votes equal to the number of votes attached to the shares held by him, multiplied by the number of directors to be elected. He may then cast all such cumulative votes in favour of one candidate, or distribute them among the candidates in any manner.

426   **Pooling arrangements:** These provisions are wider in scope and are not dependent upon any enabling authorisation being given in the company's corporate instruments for their use.

427   Essentially a pooling arrangement is a special agreement between two or more shareholders to vote the shares held by them in a given manner. It is an alternative mechanism to enable a group of shareholders to

---

[82]   A. D. Stickler, *Canada Business Corporations Act — An Accountant's Review of the Highlights*, p. 28.

influence   corporate policy on matters brought before members for determination.

428   Section 132 of the Act provides that a written agreement between two or more shareholders of a company may provide that in exercising their voting rights the shares held by them will be voted as provided in the agreement and that such an agreement will be given legal recognition.

429   Unlike the provisions for cumulative voting to which the company is a party by virtue of the enabling provisions therefor contained in its corporate instruments, no notice should be taken by the company of any pooling arrangements as such arrangements are a private matter between certain shareholders whose rights, actions and remedies must be determined between themselves as provided for in the pooling agreement.

It is not intended that the company should become party to such pooling arrangements and any attempt to give notice thereof to the company should be resisted.

430   The pooling arrangement which is also known as a 'voting trust' agreement would normally provide for the deposit of the shares held by the parties to the agreement with a trustee who will be empowered by the agreement to vote the shares in such manner as provided for under the terms of the agreement.

LATE ATTENDANCE BY MEMBERS

431   The chairman is occasionally called upon to rule on the question of the entitlement to vote by members who arrive late for the meeting. A member who enters a meeting room while a vote is in progress is entitled to vote provided:

- ♦   The chair had not called for a voice vote or a show of hands to ascertain the mind of the meeting and in consequence thereof made a declaration.

- The chair had not finished calling the names in a roll call vote.

- The scrutineers had not collected the ballots for a written vote.[83]

- The by-laws of the company or any other applicable regulation or law did not otherwise prohibit.

CALLING FOR A RECOUNT

432   A candidate for election or a member may appeal to the chair for a recount of the votes if the result of the vote is close or if there is a significant number of spoiled ballots. The recommended procedure for dealing with such appeals is as follows:

Member or candidate
addressing the chair: *"Mr Chairman, I wish to appeal*
                                                 for a recount of the vote."

433   The chairman may then ask the appellant to provide reasons or support for the request, if not previously given.

434   The chair is then obliged to rule on the appeal, but it must be appreciated that rulings of the chair on the question of a recount may be open to challenge.

435   If the member or candidate considers that the ruling of the chair is not in order, he may appeal against the ruling as follows:

Member or candidate
addressing the chair: *"Mr Chairman, I wish to appeal*
                                                 against the ruling of the chair."

436   In this case the chairman should give a brief explanation of the ruling. The explanation   should   be   succinct   and   address   the   issue   under

---

[83]   Kerr and King, *Procedures for Meetings and Organisations,* p. 102.

consideration. It must be pointed out however that the ruling itself is not subject to debate.

The chairman should not use the occasion to demonstrate to the meeting the inherent power of the chair. The chairman should be guided by the overriding principle that the main function of the chair is to facilitate the efficient transaction of the business for which the meeting has been convened.

If the chairman demonstrates a sound knowledge of the rules and procedures applicable to corporate meetings to the point in his/her rulings, and is courteous towards members, he/she would find that in large measure the general body would be supportive of rulings from the chair.

437   Having given his/her explanation the chairman should ask the meeting to resolve the issue by deciding the question which may be put as follows:

"Is the ruling of the chair upheld?"

438   If the ruling is not upheld by an affirmative vote of the meeting, the chair is bound to take the necessary remedial action to correct the situation after which the meeting returns to its normal agenda.[84]

USE OF CASTING VOTE

439   In respect of any resolution which is required to be passed by a majority, if there is an equality of votes the motion is lost unless the chairman exercises the right, if any, of a casting vote.

440   The right to exercise such casting or second vote must be conferred by the company's corporate instruments. In the absence of such conferment the chairman has no second or casting vote.

---

[84]   Kerr and King, *Procedures for Meetings and Organisations*, p. 202.

CHAPTER 13

Postal voting

441   Postal voting is presently of little application to companies incorporated in the Caribbean, but as the number of their shareholders increase and become dispersed throughout the various islands of the area, it is a feature that will become of increasing importance.

442   There are, however, already special circumstances when postal voting or voting by post, as it is more familiarly called, is appropriate and even mandatory.

443   An example may be found by reference to the Insurance Legislation of Barbados.[85] Section 134 contains provisions for postal voting which are particularly applicable to certain insurance companies where there are no shareholders but only policy holders.[86]

---

[85]   The Insurance Act Cap 310 of the Laws of Barbados

[86]   Section 134 is as follows:

Notwithstanding anything contained in the instruments constituting, or in the articles of association or other rules of, any company not having shareholders, the company shall, within one year after it is registered under this Act, make arrangements for:

(a) the establishment of a postal voters' roll in relation to voting in contested elections of directors of the company or on questions as to the alterations of the instruments constituting the company or of the articles of association or other

---

444   Although the legislation overrides any negative provision or the absence of any provision in the company's corporate instruments on the question of voting, it is nevertheless strongly recommended that the company's own regulations should make specific provisions regulating the method and procedures which are to be applicable to the voting process.

445   The procedures to be put in place must seek to safeguard the integrity of the postal voting process.

446   Care must also be taken not to confuse postal voting with a poll. In *McMillan* v *Le Roi Mining Co. Ltd* [87] the Court decided that postal voting does not constitute a valid poll unless the rules of the company expressly provides for this.

447   In addition to the foregoing and for the avoidance of doubt certain formalities should be strictly observed.

448   Postal voting or voting by post implies that the postal ballot must reach the company by post.   It is questionable, unless the rules of the company provide otherwise, whether a postal ballot reaching the company by any other means is a valid ballot.

449   While ballot papers used in the postal voting process will vary from company to company, Appendix II Precedent R illustrates the documents used by a large Caribbean mutual company whose regulations, in conformity with the requirements of the Insurance Act, provide for postal voting.

---

rules of the company.

(b) the enrolment on the postal voters' roll of any member of the company entitled to vote in such elections or on such questions who applies to be so enrolled.

(c) the voting by post in any such election or on any such question by every member so enrolled; and

(d) the making of inspections of the postal voters' roll and the taking of copies of, or extracts from, the roll, on and after the close of nominations and before the close of the voting in any such election, by any person nominated for election as a director of the company and all regular votes of members given in pursuance of any such arrangements shall be valid and effectual for all purposes.

[87]   (1906) 1 Ch 331 (see p. 353)

450   Postal voting is merely a method of voting and as such does not displace the substantive rules of voting which speak to such issues as the persons entitled to vote etc.

451   To the extent that the regulations or the Act may require that persons desirous of voting by post should apply to have their names placed on a register of postal voters, the absence of such a person's name from the register of postal voters does not deprive him of his vote, but merely restricts the exercise of that right to vote by the postal method.

452   I wish to conclude this brief chapter by referring to the design and content of the postal ballot and to make some observations thereon.

453   It is becoming a practice in some areas for companies to send proxy forms to members that permit members to indicate on the proxy form how the holder of the proxy should vote in respect of the various agenda items. Such forms will sometimes indicate whether the holder should vote for, against, or abstain.

454   Unlike a proxy form, which is merely the registered member's instructions and authorisation to another person to vote on such member's behalf; a postal ballot is a mechanism which enables the member himself to vote.

455   Consequently the form of the postal ballot should be carefully designed. Preferably it should not be framed in a manner where there is a space or box to enable members to cast, what some may believe to be, a vote of abstention, for in such circumstances it may be argued that the company is offering the member three voting options namely; for, against, or a vote of neutrality otherwise called a vote of abstention as distinct from abstaining from voting.

456   It is a moot point, but I make the foregoing observation since in circumstances where a motion may require, say, a two-thirds majority of those voting, in order to pass, persons who abstained from voting on the question are not counted among the members voting.

457   The same may not hold true where the company's voting ballot purports to give its members three options or decision choices on the question. In

such circumstances, an obstreperous member may seek to challenge the chair, and thereby introduce an element of confusion in the meeting, if the presiding officer disallowed a ballot and claimed that a member had not voted merely by the fact that he had ticked the box or space marked 'abstain' on a ballot paper so prepared and sent to such member by the company.

In such a scenario a person may seek to allege that the company had offered the voter three choices and that the 'vote of abstention' was neither an affirmative nor a negative vote on the motion, but a vote of neutrality.

The question may be asked: "What happens then in the above scenario if in respect of a resolution requiring a two-thirds majority, 60 persons voted for, 30 against and 10 exercised the option granted to them by the company to cast a *vote* of abstention or of neutrality?" Did those 10 persons take part in the voting process? Or did they abstain from participating, i.e. voting?

458   In terms of its impact on the motion, the 'votes of abstention' may be imputed as   negative votes, and since the motion required a given percentage of votes cast to be in the affirmative in order to pass, it may be held to have failed although if the 'votes of abstention' were not counted the resolution would have passed.[88]

459   It may be argued, and it is the conventional wisdom, that there is no such thing as a vote of abstention, but the potential problems and the risk of confusion are however best avoided. A member may abstain from voting by merely not marking either of the boxes marked for or against on the ballot paper.

460   Unless it is clearly understood that the chair is not offering an alternative vote but merely seeking to ascertain the feel of the meeting so far as members, participation or views on the question before them, presiding officers should desist in a vote by show of hands from asking 'A*bstentions?* ' which some, as a matter of style, pose after calling *'Those for? Those against?*

---

[88]   For further reading on the matter see *Robert's Rules of Order.*

CHAPTER 14

Coping with disorder

461   The orderly conduct of any meeting is dependent upon those in attendance accepting the authority of the chair. Occasionally a meeting may be blessed with the presence of a member who believes passionately in Henry Adams' creed that "chaos often breeds life, while order breeds habit". Armed with such an article of faith the member will more often than not test the skill and patience of the presiding officer. In such circumstances a shrewd chairman should fortify himself with the wise counsel of St. Paul to "let all things be done decently and in order"[89] and hold fast to his responsibility to ensure that the meeting is orderly and conducted in a businesslike manner.

462   Sometimes there is a little heckling and the chairman will have to decide at what point he will intervene to restore order if the matter threatens to get out of hand. Occasionally, however, matters do get out of hand with debates deteriorating into insults, abuse and a great deal of cross talk between members. In those circumstances the chairman must act swiftly, tactfully and decisively in an effort to curtail discussion momentarily and restore order to the proceedings.

463   Sometimes there will be the occasional interjection from the floor in response to some point being made by a speaker during the course of his

---

[89]   King James Bible, 1 Cor. 14:40.

---

contribution to the debate. Brief occasional interjections may be ignored. Unfortunately some people may take this as a licence to become increasingly boisterous.

464   The chairman should seek to discourage members from making such unwelcome interjections. He should point out to the offending member that the preferred course of action would be for him to speak formally on the motion before the meeting so that the meeting may have the benefit of his keen insight.

465   If, after reasonable warnings, the offender persists he should be asked to leave the meeting. Should he refuse to do so he may be ejected.

EXPULSION

466   In rare circumstances it may be necessary to eject a member. The power to eject persons must be exercised with great care. It will invariably cause unpleasant exchanges of language and may even result in legal action. Before expelling a person the chairman should ask the offending member to take his seat or cease from interrupting the meeting as the case may be. If he refuses the chairman should ask him to leave the meeting.

467   If the member still persists in his interruption the chairman, accompanied by the stewards, should approach the member and enquire of him whether or not he intends to accept the chairman's ruling to cease his interruption of the meeting or to leave the meeting.

468   If the member does not yield to the ruling of the chair, the chairman should request the stewards to eject the member from the meeting. Care should be exercised however to ensure that every opportunity is given to the member to cease his interruption of the meeting or to leave the meeting voluntarily. If ejected, no more force than is necessary should be used. All expulsions should be carefully recorded.

469   The chairman's authority to order the ejection of the member, rests in the doctrine that, except when payment has been made to attend a meeting, in which case special provisions will apply, those attending meetings on

private property do so on licence of those who are entitled to possession of the property and such licence may be revoked at any time for reasonable cause.

470   Disturbance of the meeting constitutes reasonable cause. If the person is ordered by the chairman to leave the meeting and he refuses, he becomes a trespasser and may thus be ejected. However, if ejected without good cause or if unnecessary force is used, the person ejected may have a cause of action against those responsible for his ejection. Thus care and caution should be exercised in invoking this remedy but at the end of the day the chairman must endeavour to preserve order.

471   In certain circumstances the chairman has both the power and duty to adjourn the meeting for a brief period in an attempt to restore order. In *John* v *Rees* [90] the learned judge observed that the first duty of the chairman of a meeting is to preserve order.

472   If there is disorder his duty it to make an earnest attempt to restore order and to summon to his aid such assistance as is available. If all of this fails he should endeavour to adjourn the meeting as provided for in the regulations, such as obtaining a resolution to adjourn.

If this proves impossible he should exercise his inherent power to adjourn for a short while but the must be no longer than the necessities appear to dictate in order to restore order, say, fifteen minutes or so. It should be noted however that the chairman must exercise his powers bona fide for the purpose of forwarding and facilitating the meeting and not for the purpose of interruption or procrastination.

DEFAMATION, SLANDER AND LIBEL

473   Defamation may be defined as the publication of a statement which is detrimental to the reputation or business of a person. The defamation may be in the form of slander if it is merely a spoken statement. On the other hand if it is in written form the defamation will be libel.

---

[90]   (1969) 2 Wlr 1294 - 1317 (see p. 354)

474   The essence of a defamatory statement is that it damages the reputation of the person against whom it is made, in that it lowers his standing in society, or causes him to be shunned or avoided, or it makes imputations which are damaging to him in his profession, business or occupation.

475   Generally speaking company meetings enjoy a measure of privilege but there are still limits to members' freedom of speech and such privilege as may exist in company meetings will be lost if the untrue statement was made recklessly or with malice. Thus, a statement made at a meeting which questions the competence or honesty of a person may well be held to be defamatory.

476   The subject of defamation and the law relating thereto is complex and outside the scope of this book. Suffice it to say that company chairmen must at all times seek to ensure that shareholders are circumspect in their speeches and that these are kept within the bounds of probity.

477   While there are defences to an action against defamation such as justification, fair comment and privilege, it must be appreciated that such defences are normally risky and often quite expensive. Normally the plaintiff has only to prove that the statement was made, that it referred to him, and that it was defamatory. Shareholders, directors and others concerned with the conduct of meetings should avail themselves of the best of all defences: *avoidance*.

CHAPTER 15

Adjourning the meeting

478   The adjournment of the meeting is considered to be the ultimate
       suspensive device in the administration and conduct of meetings for it
       brings about a suspension of the entire proceedings. An adjournment may
       be:

       •   For a brief interval or period of time in order to restore order.

       •   For a statutory period for want of a quorum.

       •   To another place if, for example, the accommodation proves
            inadequate.

       •   For a given time and to a named place.

       •   For an indefinite time (an adjournment *sine die*).

479   A meeting which is a voluntary assembly, in the sense that there is no
       obligation to hold the meeting and those invited have no voting right on
       any issue being discussed or to be determined by the meeting, may be
       adjourned at any time at the discretion of the convenors or the presiding
       officer. In all other circumstances the right to adjourn is vested in the

meeting itself since the meeting is entitled to deal, uninterrupted, with the business for which it has been convened.

480   Adjournment is possible in four specific circumstances.

- By resolution of the meeting

- For want of a quorum

- Failure to maintain a quorum

- By interruption of the chairman

481   A motion to adjourn the meeting may be made by any member who has not yet spoken in the debate on the question then before the meeting. This is to ensure that those who have spoken do not then attempt to stifle discussion. The motion requires seconding, and if seconded, has priority over any matter then before the meeting and must be dealt with immediately.

482   Adjournment of the meeting may also be caused for want of a quorum or failure to maintain a quorum. If, during the course of a meeting, the number of persons in attendance falls below the number required to convene the meeting, then the meeting cannot continue unless the applicable statute or the company's corporate instruments provide otherwise. Any person present is entitled to raise a point of order — 'count quorum' — and the chairman should immediately require a count to be taken.

483   If it is confirmed that a quorum is not present then the meeting must be adjourned. There is a saving provision found in the Act which is mirrored in the corporate instruments of many companies. Section 123(2) provides that if a quorum is present at the opening of a meeting of shareholders, the shareholders present may, unless the by-laws otherwise provide, proceed with the business of the meeting, notwithstanding that a quorum is not present throughout the meeting. Company secretaries should note however that the by-laws should be consulted before advice is given to the presiding officer.

484   With respect to interruption by the chairman, the general rule is that in the absence of specific authority conferred by the company's corporate instruments the chairman cannot adjourn the meeting except in accordance with the corporate resolve of the meeting itself. These are however limited circumstances when the chairman has both the right and duty to adjourn the meeting.[91]

485   If the chairman improperly adjourns a meeting it does not affect the existence of the meeting; the meeting continues and may itself elect a new presiding officer and continue to deal with the business for which it was convened. See *Shaw* v *Thompson*[92] as well as *Catesby* v *Burnett*.[93]

486   Whether or not the chairman is vested with authority to adjourn the meeting of his own volition is a question of fact to be determined by careful scrunity of the corporate instruments. The precise wording and language used in the corporate instruments where such authority is given will be of significant importance in determining the scope of the chairman's authority. The following contrasting circumstances illustrate the point.

487   If the corporate instruments provide that the chairman may, with the consent of the meeting, and shall if so directed by the meeting, adjourn the meeting etc. then the power of the chairman to adjourn the meeting is subject to a vote of the meeting in the affirmative while on the other hand he is bound to adjourn the proceedings of the meeting if the meeting itself did adopt a motion of adjournment proposed by a member.

488   The situation is somewhat different if the words 'and if so directed by the meeting' as referrred to above were not included in the corporate instruments. In those circumstances the power of adjournment rests in the hands of the chairman subject to the concurrence of the meeting, but the chairman may not necessarily be bound to adjourn the meeting on the basis of a motion iniated from the floor of the meeting if he has valid and proper reasons for rejecting such a motion.

---

[91]   See chapter 14
[92]   (1876) 3 Ch D 233 p. 249 (see p. 358)
[93]   (1916) 2 Ch p. 325 (see p. 360)

This principle is supported by the decision emmanating from *Salisbury Gold Mining Co.* v *Hathorn*.[94]

489   The need to adequately plan for a meeting in order to avoid adjournment by reason of inadequate accommodation cannot be too strongly emphasised. It is a situation fraught with potential litigation. A recent Court of Appeal case ruled against a company and its chairman when the bungled events flowing from such a situation were brought before the Court.

490   The company had summoned a meeting to be convened at a location which proved too small to accommodate all members wishing to attend. The business before the meeting was one of urgency. However, shareholders attending the meeting could not be accommodated in a single room and communication between members and the chair proved difficult and unmanageable. The chairman, taking the advice of the company's legal advisors (who were present at the meeting), exercised a power to adjourn the meeting to another location in the afternoon of the same day. Certain members were unable to attend the reconvened meeting in the afternoon and as a consequence challenged the validity of the reconvened meeting.[95]

491   The Court was asked to decide (1) whether the chairman had power to adjourn the meeting without the consent of the meeting; (2) whether the power to adjourn was validly exercised. The judgement is instructive.

There was no suggestion that the chairman acted with malice. Indeed the Court empathised with the dilemma of the chairman especially having regard to the urgency of the business; but the rules were not followed and the decision went against the company.

492   At an adjourned meeting only the unfinished business of the meeting may be considered. No new business may be introduced since the adjourned meeting is a continuation of the meeting and not a new meeting. For this reason also, except the company's corporate instruments require, or unless the meeting was adjourned for more than 30 days or adjourned

---

[94]   (1897) AC 268 (see p. 362)
[95]   See *Byng* v *London Life Association Ltd and Another* CA 1988 - (1990) LRC p 500 (see p. 364)

sine die, it will not be necessary to give written notice of the adjourned meeting.

493   It should be noted however that if there is any irregularity in convening the meeting any adjournment thereof and the consideration of any unfinished business at the adjourned meeting will also be irregular. See *Re Portuguese Consolidated Copper Mines Ltd.*[96]

494   It is perhaps appropriate to conclude this chapter by highlighting an apparently *useful* mechanism, but which in reality is a pitfall which sometimes entraps corporate practitioners. It is the issue of postponement of meetings.

495   **A meeting once validly summoned cannot be postponed.** If the notice to convene the meeting has been issued the meeting must be held as arranged. If for valid reasons it was thought that the meeting should not be held on the date for which it was summoned, it is possible to start the meeting by proposing a resolution for its immediate adjournment.

496   One may send an informal letter to members stating that it is the intention of the directors to propose such a motion for the adjournment of the meeting and give a reasonable explanation why this will be done. This is an effort to inform members so that they do not waste time in attending, but there is always the risk that a minority of members may attend and refuse to pass the resolution for adjournment.

497   Directors should therefore, prior to sending such an informal letter to shareholders, make sure that they command sufficient votes to ensure the passing of the proposed motion for adjournment, for the meeting if properly summons by notice cannot be cancelled or postponed.

498   There is a fine line of distinction between adjournment and postponement.

Adjournment indicates that the business and proceedings of the meeting are suspended.

---

[96]   (1889) 42 Ch D 160 (see p. 366)

499   In *Smith* v *Paring Mines Ltd* [97] a notice was issued purporting to postpone the holding of a general meeting of shareholders which had previously been duly convened. One of the directors of the company who was in disagreement with the remainder of the board attended the meeting together with several shareholders and proceeded to conduct the business for which the meeting was called.

It was held that resolutions passed at the meeting were valid and effective, as the postponement of the meeting was inoperative without special power to postpone being given by the regulations governing the meeting.[98]

500   On the questions of resolutions passed at an adjourned meeting, it must be observed that although adjourned meetings are a continuation of the original meeting, the date on which any resolution passed at an adjourned meeting is deemed to take effect is, unlike a poll, the date of the adjourned meeting and not of the original meeting.[99]

501   Finally, adjournment must be distinguished from dissolution. When the business of the meeting is completed it is the duty of the chairman to dissolve the meeting.

---

[97]   (1906) 2 Ch 193 (see p. 368)
[98]   S. Shaw and D.Smith, *The Law of Meetings*, pp. 76-77.
[99]   This principle was made clear by the provisions of Section 144 of the United Kingdom 1948 Companies Act and has been folllowed by legal and corporate practitioners even in jurisdictions where the UK Companies Act do not apply.

CHAPTER 16

Minutes of the meeting

502 Among the records which a company is required by sections 170 and 172 of the Act to maintain at its registered office are minutes of meetings and resolutions of shareholders. Such records may be in a bound or loose-leaf form or in a photographic film form or may be entered or recorded by any system of mechanical or electronic data processing or by any other information storage device that is capable of reproducing any required information in an intelligible written form within a reasonable time.

503 The manner and style in which minutes are kept may vary from corporation to corporation and between meetings of the board and meetings of members but the basic principles involved in minutes-keeping apply to all kinds of meetings.

504 The Act imposes a duty of care on the company and its officers to take reasonable precautions to prevent loss or destruction of, or falsification of entries in the records. There are penalties for non-compliance.

505 Minutes are important because when the decisions of members are made on matters brought before them at a meeting, those decisions become resolutions of the meeting at which they were passed and the minutes constitute the only official evidence of members' corporate resolve.

506   We have previously observed that there is no statutory requirement for minutes to be approved, however they ought to be signed by the chairman of the meeting at which the proceedings were held or by the chairman of the next succeeding meeting of the board.

507   The preparation of minutes requires clarity and preciseness in writing. At the end of the meeting it is the duty of the company secretary to prepare the minutes in draft from notes made during the meeting.

508   The draft should be submitted to the chairman for his approval and, subject to any corrections, they should then be prepared for formal presentation to the board of directors at the next directors' meeting following the annual or special meeting of members as the case may be.

509   It is good corporate practice to have the minutes approved by resolution of the directors and for them to be signed both by the company secretary and the chairman of the board. Although not often done, ideally each page of the minutes should be initialled by the chairman and secretary.

510   Once the minutes have been signed, if an error is discovered or a decision needs to be altered, there must be no tampering with the minutes. The signed minutes must stand as the original record of the meeting. The correction or alteration must be dealt with as a separate matter at a later meeting and should be minuted accordingly.

511   The new minutes should make reference to the incorrectly recorded item or to the amended decision with reference to the matter previously dealt with at the prior meeting. The old minutes should also bear a reference in the margin to the new minutes so that a person consulting the minutes will be directed to the latter decision or the corrected item.

512   All minutes should record the following information:

   • The name of the company.

   • The type of meeting.

   • The date and venue of the meeting.

- Persons attending the meeting as of right.

- Persons attending the meeting by invitation.

- An accurate record of the business dealt with at the meeting.

- The precise wording of all motions, amendments and substantive motions put before the meeting, the result of any vote and the chairman's declaration of the mind or decision of the meeting on each such proposal.

513   In keeping proper minutes, probably the main difficulty arises when either the secretary or the chairman is unable to distinguish between minutes and a report.

514   A report is an account of what transpires at a meeting and narrates, in greater or less detail, the whole proceedings of the meeting, including the discussion upon the various matters considered, comments by the chairman, members' contributions and so on.

515   Minutes must not be ambiguous and must be an impartial record of the decisions and resolutions passed at the meeting. In the preparation of minutes it may be appropriate to include a little background data in connection with the business put before the meeting but minutes are not a report of proceedings.

516   Minutes are a record of the decisions made by the meeting and, it is therefore generally not appropriate to record individual members' contributions to the discussion of the meeting which precedes the resolution of the meeting. It should be noted however that in certain circumstances it may be appropriate to record the vote of dissenting shareholders depending upon the nature of business that is being considered. (See for example section 213 of the Act.)

517   As earlier indicated, the format of minutes is a matter of personal or corporate style and it is not the intention here to make any suggestions on the question of style. They should however be in such manner as would facilitate easy reference to the matters dealt with by members at the meeting.

518   Finally the company secretary should avoid any attempt to record reasons for decisions in the minutes. Members' reasons may be partially expressed or may be left unsaid. All of the reasons why members vote in a particular manner are unlikely to be known. Any attempt to record such is at best subjective, at worst speculative, and merely to report some of the reasons may be both misleading to the record and detrimental to the company. Minutes must be a record of fact: there is no room for conjecture. See Appendix II Precedent S.

519   On the question of minutes as evidence, minutes are prima facie evidence of the proceedings, even if signed, but that does not mean that other evidence of what actually occurred at a meeting would not be accepted by the Court. For example, properly grounded evidence may be accepted even if it were contrary to the resolutions as recorded in the minutes. Nevertheless, since minutes are a statutory requirement to be fulfilled, they will have statutory force as evidence as long as the statutory requirements and obligations are satisfied.

520   Where minutes of the proceedings are properly made and signed, they provide evidence not only of their contents but also of the regularity of the meeting itself; but direct evidence that, for example, the notice calling the meeting was not proper would rebut the minutes. See *Betts & Co. Ltd* v *MacNaghten.* [100]

521   The position however may be somewhat different if the corporate instruments contained a 'conclusive evidence' provision with reference to the minutes. Some authorities believe that it is good corporate practice for the corporate instruments to contain a provision that the minutes when signed shall be conclusive evidence. This they believe will prevent subsequent dispute on any matter which cannot be proved or disproved afterwards. The case cited is *Kerr* v *John Mottran Ltd.* [101]

---

[100]   (1910), 1 Ch 430 (see p. 330)
[101]   (1940) 1 Ch 657 (see p. 370)

CHAPTER 17

Shareholders' duties, rights and entitlement

522   There has been in recent times a growing tendency for security exchanges and commissions to demand that major issues affecting a public company's business or other extra-ordinary transactions be submitted to shareholders in general meeting for determination. This is an enlightened approach which also finds support in the Act.

523   Shareholders, if motivated by a common consideration focused on achieving that which is in the best interest of the company, can play a key role in the good governance of their company. By the same token it is to be observed that when the common interest of the company is supplanted by personal and often conflicting individual interest, the business of the company suffers great harm if for no other reason than that the energy of directors and management tends to be diverted from the pursuit of corporate goals.

524   Few matters impede the progress of companies so significantly as adversarial relationships between shareholders and directors.

525   Despite the inherent risk Henry Bosch A0, chairman of the working group of professional organisations which produced the Australian guide to corporate practices and conduct, had this to say: "Boards should

encourage, where appropriate, full participation of shareholders to ensure a high level of accountability and identification with company's goals".[102]

526   The Act confers a number of rights, upon shareholders. In some cases these rights or the manner of exercising them may be subject to modification by the company's corporate instruments. It is therefore important that before embarking on any particular course of action, shareholders should consult the applicable provisions of the Act as well as the corporate instruments of their company. If in doubt they may consult the company's secretary for guidance on procedural matters.

527   **Some of the rights conferred by statute on shareholders are as follows:**

- To confirm, repeal or amend by laws of the company.

- To elect and remove directors.

- To attend meetings of shareholders.

- To vote the shares registered in their names.

- To appoint proxies.

- To transfer their shares.

- To enter into voting agreements.

- To enter into unanimous shareholders' agreements.

- To submit proposals to the company.

---

[102]   H. Bosch, *Corporate Practice and Conduct* p. 30. The booklet was actually produced under the auspices of the Australian Institute of Company Directors, Australian Investment Managers Groups, Australian Society of Certified Practising Accountants, Australian Stock Exchange, Business Council of Australia, International Banks and Securities Association of Australia, Law Council of Australia (Business School Section), the Institute of Chartered Accountants in Australia and the Securities Institute of Australia under the chairmanship of Henry Bosch, AO.

- To requisition meetings.

- To approve or otherwise make a determination on proposals for extra-ordinary transactions submitted to them by the directors.

- To appoint auditors.

- To receive dividends if so declared payable by the directors.

- To receive the surplus assets of the company on its dissolution.

- For proper cause, to commence derivative actions, subject to the leave of the court.

528 **In addition to the foregoing rights shareholders are also entitled to:**

- Receive notice of meetings of members of their class.

- Receive financial statements of the company.

- Receive the auditor's report.

- Examine, at the registered office of the company, the financial statements of all subsidiary bodies corporate, the accounts of which are consolidated in the financial statements of the company.

- Examine the minutes of all meetings of shareholders.

- Examine the register of members.

- Receive of a copy of the basic shareholder list on request, subject to completion of certain formalities.

- Examine the register of mortgages and charges.

- Receive a definitive share certificate for the shares registered in their names.

- ♦   Petition the court, but only for cause shown, for an investigation order in respect of the company or any of its affiliated companies.

- ♦   Receive one copy of the company's corporate instruments and any unanimous shareholders' agreement.

529   One of the most interesting reforms in Caribbean corporate law is the concept of the unanimous shareholders' agreement.

The unanimous shareholders' agreement remedies a deficiency that has long existed in the region in that while shareholders could elect directors and dismiss them and appoint others in their place, they had little control over the actions of directors, who wielded virtually all decision making power once elected. This, in large measure, was because of the established principle that directors are agents of the company and not of the shareholders.

530   It was established in the *Quin & Axten* case previously referred to that the directors' power to manage the company's affairs could not be interfered with by any majority vote of the shareholders.

531   The unanimous shareholders' agreement was designed to modify this situation. It should be noted however that the agreement must be unanimous, and in the opinion of this writer is more appropriate to the small close company or family corporation.

532   On the question of shareholders' access to corporate information, it should be noted that notwithstanding that in recent times a substantial amount of information is now, by law, available to shareholders, there is still certain information to which shareholders have no right of access.

533   The corporate instruments of most companies will usually contain a provision, similar to the model general by-law found in the Companies Regulations made pursuant to the Act, which states that "no shareholder shall be entitled to any information respecting any details or conduct of the company's business which in the opinion of the directors it would be inexpedient in the interest of the company to communicate to the public".

534   The concept of confidentiality, when such is in the interest of the company, is supported by section 148 of the Act which provides that upon the application of a company for authorisation to omit from its financial statements any prescribed item, or to dispense with the publication of any particular prescribed financial statement, the Registrar may, if he reasonably believes that disclosure of the information therein contained would be detrimental to the company, permit its omission on such reasonable conditions as he thinks fit.

535   **Shareholders have no right of access to, neither are they entitled to:**

+   Examine the minutes of meetings of directors.

+   Receipt of any sensitive financial information of the company concerning its products, pricing, or remuneration of individual employees.

+   Details of any confidential management information, statistics or reports concerning the competitiveness of the company's products or otherwise, publication of which would not be in the best interest of the company.

536   Shareholders are however entitled to reasonable access to non-sensitive corporate data, to ask questions at annual meetings concerning the affairs of the company and to receive replies to general questions concerning any aspect of the company's business and corporate affairs.

537   Some years ago I circulated to my corporate clients a sample of questions which I believe shareholders may be entitled to ask and to which directors and officers should be prepared to respond.

The list was taken substantially from a booklet published by Coopers & Lybrand (USA) under the caption "Annual Meetings, Questions from Shareholders" and is partially reproduced in Appendix IV.

Over three hundred questions and follow-up questions are tabulated.

538   The appendix is included as a contribution to the educational process for both management as well as stockholders of Caribbean commercial enterprises.

To shareholders it is an aid as to the types of questions which may be properly asked at an annual meeting. At the same time it is hoped that the questions will assist the board, especially non executive directors, to better prepare themselves for the annual meeting.

Hitherto we have discussed the rights and entitlement of shareholders but what of their duties?

539   The duties of shareholders are not usually enshrined in any statute nor in the corporate instruments of the company but in the concept and philosophy of good corporate governance.

540   Good corporate governance requires meaningful interaction between stockholders and management. It must always be done with a view towards facilitating and enhancing the growth, development and corporate integrity of their company. Above all, the interaction must facilitate the purpose of the meeting.

541   Shareholders should not, as a general rule, attend meetings with a predetermined mental attitude against the company's management, so often encapsuled in the sentence: "*We are going up there to give them 'hell' this evening.*"

542   Neither should they arm themselves with the appendix of shareholder questions included in this book, and attend the meeting with the view of conducting a public oral examination of the board. Such behaviour will border on the abuse of privilege.

Some of the questions require research for a meaningful reply: there is no harm in informing the company secretary, at a reasonable time before the meeting, that you intend to ask a specific question. Indeed I recommend the procedure.

543   **Shareholders however have a duty to:**

- Elect those persons as members of the board who, in their opinion, will make the best contribution to directors' deliberations and management of the company's business. Considerations of personal friendships should be secondary.

- Patronise their company's product or service and do all in their power to enhance its reputation in the market.

- Attend meetings and make their contribution to the proceedings in an orderly and courteous manner.

- Exercise their right to vote by person or by proxy.

- Submit, via the company's public relations office or company secretary, useful proposals to the company's management, which may enhance the company's product, service or the efficiency of its operations.

- Encourage their board of directors and the management and employees of their company to strive constantly for corporate excellence and to excel in its service to customers.

- Remove from the board, through the proper corporate process, directors who are no longer able to make an adequate contribution to the management and corporate affairs of the company. (In making such determination the tests must neither be age, class, colour, creed, nor friendship, but a matter of competence and commitment and the physical and mental ability to perform the task of directing the company's affairs.)

CHAPTER 18

Meetings of the board

544   While this book is primarily concerned with the administration and conduct of shareholders' meetings, it would be incomplete if it did not address some of the basic issues concerning the conduct of meetings of the board.

545   The management powers of a corporation are sometimes divided between the directors and shareholders. In jurisdictions where incorporation is by Memorandum and Articles of Association, that is the contractual model, the Articles of Association sets out which corporate proceedings are to be conducted by the directors and which may be reserved as the responsibility of the shareholders.[103]

546   In jurisdictions where the statute is modelled after the Barbados Companies Act, the overriding provision is that subject to any restriction in the company's corporate instruments or any unanimous shareholders' agreement, the directors of a company must exercise the powers of the company directly or indirectly through the employees and agents of the company and direct the management of the business and affairs of the company (see section 58).

---

[103]   See *The Director's Manual*, para. 6-050 (CCH Canadian Ltd.)

---

547   Consequently, if directors therefore act within the powers given to them, they are not bound to follow the dictates of shareholders. The only manner in which shareholders can control directors, if they are acting within the powers given to them, would be to remove them as directors at a special meeting called for that purpose, or not to re-elect them as directors at the annual meeting at which they retire.

SOURCES OF AUTHORITY

548   Directors are by law empowered to manage and are charged with the responsibility for so doing. To enable them to carry out their function it is necessary for them to meet. Before dealing with the conduct and format of board meetings it may be appropriate to highlight the sources of authority for such meetings. These are found in:

- The Statute

- The company's corporate instruments

- The body of case law dealing with the management of companies.

549   Section 75 of the Act provides that subject to the company's corporate instruments, the directors of a company may meet at any place and upon such notice as the by-laws require. Harry Rajak, a senior lecturer at Kings College in the University of London, observed that "Management requires the taking of decisions, usually by organs and often in meetings. For this purpose, the Companies Act . . . and the Company's Articles of Association . . . provide a wide apparatus of administrative procedures and institutions. Sometimes the Act defers to the Articles and sometimes it overrides them".[104]

550   The model by-law found in the Companies Regulations[105] will probably be adopted by most companies either in its entirety or with minor modifications. See Appendix II Precedent T for draft model by-law. That model by-law contains a general provision dealing with the powers of

---

[104]   H. Rajak, *A Source Book of Company Law*, p. 463.
[105]   (S.I. 1984 No. 29) of the Laws of Barbados

directors, their number, election and tenure of office but it also provides for and regulates, in general terms, the holding of meetings of directors, the place of such meetings together with matters relating to the notice, quorum and voting at such meetings.

It is a fundamental principle that a quorum for a meeting of directors must be a disinterested quorum. It must be comprised of directors who are entitled to vote on the particular issues before the meeting. If a director is interested in a transaction which is a matter before the meeting and is not permitted by the company's corporate instruments to vote thereon, he cannot be counted for the purposes of the quorum with respect to that particular item of business and if the requisite quorum is not present the meeting is irregular and therefore cannot transact business.

551   While there will be differences in the corporate instruments of companies, there is likely to be a great deal of similarity on the question of directors and their meetings. Nevertheless, the company secretary must be fully aware of the specific provisions which apply to his respective company so as to be in a position to properly advise the board of directors.

552   Case law in the United Kingdom and Commonwealth territories has affirmed the principle that "the management of a company is vested in its directors who are, in effect, agents for the company in relation to the transactions into which they enter on behalf of the company, and trustees for the company so far as concerns the company's funds and property".[106] See *Great Eastern Railway Co.* v *Turner.*[107]

553   The power and constitution of the board meeting is put into proper perspective when one considers that every company is required by law to appoint directors. This is a statutory requirement that cannot be avoided. The company's corporate instruments will usually confer most of the powers of management of the company on the directors.

554   Directors in turn may delegate some of the powers vested in them to a managing director or a committee of directors, but there are certain powers which may not be delegated.

---

[106]   I. Shearman, *Shackleton on the Law and Practice of Meetings.* p. 229.
[107]   (1872) Lr 8 Ch 149 - 152 (see p. 371)

---

555   While the company's corporate instruments or any unanimous shareholders agreement may limit the powers which may be delegated in addition thereto, section 80(2) of the Act stipulates that no managing director and no committee of directors of a company may:

(a)   submit to the shareholders any question or matter requiring the approval of the shareholders;

(b)   fill a vacancy among the directors or in the office of the auditor;

(c)   issue shares except in the manner and on the terms authorised by the directors;

(d)   declare dividends;

(e)   purchase, redeem or otherwise acquire shares issued by the company;

(f)   pay a commission in respect of any issue of shares;

(g)   approve a management proxy circular to be sent to shareholders;

(h)   approve any financial statement; or

(i)   adopt, amend or repeal by-laws.

The foregoing matters are among those reserved for the corporate resolve of the collective board of directors.

556   It is a fundamental principle in corporate law that directors exercise their power and authority not as individuals, but collectively as a properly constituted board of directors.

557   "Individual directors, as such, have almost no usual authority beyond a power to execute documents, to clothe a transaction with formal validity which has already been authorised by the board . . . Where a director has a service agreement which requires him to perform a particular task (e.g. sales manager) then, like any other management executive, he will possess the usual authority that his function requires. This is a matter of ordinary agency law, but in terms of general power or management, directors must act collectively as a board, unless the articles give a power

to delegate to individual directors."[108] There are many cases which may be cited for authority. See *Rama Corporation Ltd* v *Proved Tin & General Investments Ltd* [109] *Houghton & Co.* v *Nothard, Lowe & Wills*[110] and *Kreditbank Cassel GMBH* v *Schenkers Ltd*.[111]

558   While the power to delegate in section 80 of the Act is not worded in terms which state that the provision is made subject to the by-laws of the company, the general wording is permissive in nature in so far as the authority to delegate. It is therefore my opinion that, for purposes of clarity, the company's corporate instruments should contain appropriate provisions authorising and regulating any delegation of directors' powers.

THE DECISION MAKING PROCESS

559   The board exercises its powers by means of resolutions. These resolutions may be made at meetings of the board, or by resolutions in writing under the authority of the Act or the company's corporate instruments.

560   A decision reached by casual phone conversation or correspondence is not valid, but may be ratified at a subsequent properly convened meeting.

561   In some cases board meetings are held under informal circumstances but the informality of the circumstances must not be confused with casual circumstances. The latter does not constitute a meeting. This was highlighted in the case of *Barron* v *Potter*.[112] Ian Shearman points out however that the principle that directors must actually meet as a board must not be pressed to legalistic excess and cites as authority *Bentley & Stevens* v *Jones* [113] a case in which an interlocutory injunction was sought on the grounds of irregularity on the question of a meeting, but the relief

---

108	*Gore Browne on Companies*, p. 68.
109	(1952) 2 QB 147 (see p. 374)
110	(1927) 1 KB 247 CA (see p. 377)
111	(1927) 1 KB 826 CA (see p. 380)
112	(1914) Ch 895 (see p. 382)
113	(1974) 1 Wlr 638 (see p. 384)

sought was refused on the ground that the regularities could all be cured by going through the proper process.[114]

562   I would caution however of giving too wide an interpretation to the judgement in the above case. The issues centred around a parent company removing a director from the board of its subsidiary. The decision of the parent company was arrived at by proper process but there was some irregularity at the level of the subsidiary board. It is therefore within that context that the judgement should be read, especially on the point that the irregularities could be cured by going through the proper process.

563   I venture to say that the judgement may not have been the same if the parties and their relationship to each other were different. Shearman did make the point however that "the importance of the act to the company will have some bearing on whether or not it will be vitiated by a technical irregularity. For example, matters such as winding up and the appointment of a liquidator would require a greater observance of strict formality than minor matters of administration".[115]

564   The Act affirms three avenues of decision making, namely:

    ◆   by decisions reached at meetings of the board;

    ◆   by resolutions in writing of the directors;

    ◆   by delegation of authority.

565   Unless there are special provisions in the company's corporate instruments, decisions at meetings of the board of directors are reached by a majority voting in favour of the proposition placed before the meeting.

566   It is important that board members understand and appreciate fully the principle of collective responsibility.

---

114   I. Shearman, *Shackleton on The Law and Practice of Meetings*, p. 255.
115   I. Shearman, *Shackleton on The Law and Practice of Meetings*, p. 256.

567   When a matter has been resolved by the board, all directors are bound by that resolution.

568   It is erroneous to believe that a director who merely abstained from voting on a resolution at a meeting of directors is not bound by the provisions of such resolution.

569   The Act clarifies this situation and section 96 is worth quoting in full.

(1)   *A director who is present at a meeting of the directors or of a committee of directors consents to any resolution passed or action taken at that meeting, unless*

(a)   *he requests that his dissent be or his dissent is entered in the minutes of the meeting*

(b)   *he sends his written dissent to the secretary of the meeting before the meeting is adjourned, or*

(c)   *he sends his dissent by registered post or delivers it to the registered office of the company immediately after the meeting is adjourned.*[116]

(2)   *A director who votes for or consents to a resolution may not dissent under subsection (1).*

(3)   *A director who was not present at a meeting at which a resolution was passed or action taken is presumed to have consented thereto unless, within 7 days after he becomes aware of the resolution, he*

(d)   *causes his dissent to be placed with the minutes of the meeting; or*

(e)   *sends his dissent by registered post or delivers it to the registered office of the company;*

---

[116]   The word adjourned mentioned in (b) and (c) should be interpreted to include ended and not merely an adjournment as mentioned in chapter 15

(4)   *A director is not liable under section 83, 84 or 95* [117] *if he relies in good faith upon.*

     (f)   *financial statements of the company represented to him by an officer of the company, or*

     (g)   *a report of an attorney-at-law, accountant, engineer, appraiser or other person whose profession lends credibility to a statement made by him.*

570   From the foregoing the reader will observe that mere abstention does not avoid liability. In fact, even voting against a resolution or absence from the meeting does not avoid liability if the resolution is carried by a majority vote of the board unless the director voting against requests that his dissent be entered in the minutes of the meeting.

571   Another fallacy sometimes encountered is the question of proxy voting by directors. There is no provision in the Act for a director to appoint a proxy. There are however two provisions which cater for the needs of directors who are unable to attend a meeting of the board.

572   One such provision is the appointment of an alternative director (see section 66(1).) It provides that a meeting of the shareholders of a company may, by ordinary resolution, elect a person to act as a director in the alternative to a director of the company, or may authorise the directors to appoint such alternate directors as are necessary for the proper discharge of the affairs of the company. Such alternate director shall have all the rights and powers of the director for whom he or she is elected or appointed in the alternative, except that the alternate director shall not be entitled to attend and vote at any meeting of the directors otherwise than in the absence of that other director.

573   The second provision may be found in section 79 of the Act which provides that, subject to the by-laws of a company, a director may, if all the directors of the company consent, participate in a meeting of the

---

[117]   Sections 83, 84 and 95 of the Act deal with the liability of directors arising out of: an issue of shares for a consideration other than money; consenting or voting for resolutions appertaining to redemption or acquisition of shares issued by the company, payment of commissions, dividends, and the giving by the company of financial assistance contrary to the solvency provisions of the Act; the exercise of a director's duty of care etc.

directors of the company or of a committee of the directors by means of such telephone or other communication facilities as permit all persons participating in the meeting to hear each other. Note that the prerequisite is the consent of all directors of the company and not only of those attending the meeting.

574   It is therefore recommended that either the company's corporate instruments should contain specific authorisation permitting directors attendance at meetings by electronic means or alternatively, as a matter of corporate governance, the directors should pass a unanimous resolution at the organisational meeting of the company or as soon thereafter as possible adopting a policy of directors participation in meetings by electronic means.

575   A director who participates in a meeting of directors by such electronic means is deemed to be present at the meeting. It is a moot point however if a director participating in a meeting by electronic means may be counted for the purpose of constituting a quorum or whether the director may only participate in a meeting that is otherwise validly convened.

576   In view of the absence of any known judicial ruling on the point and the fact that any business transacted at an irregular meeting is void, I am of the view that the preferred practice is to ensure that a quorum of directors is physically present at the venue of the meeting. Alternatively the corporate instruments of the company should contain a specific provision to the effect that a director participating in a meeting of the company by electronic means may also be counted for the purpose of forming a quorum.

577   In this era of global communication and the expansion of international business companies there is a rapid increase in the use of the electronic media for the holding of meetings.

Questions often arise as to where the meeting was held or deemed to be held. The venue of meetings may have significant legal or tax implications for the company. Where for example four directors, each located in a different country, are holding a meeting of an international business company by electronic means, it is important for the company secretary to ascertain and to properly minute a director's resolution as to the place where the meeting is being held.

By way of observation, the inference may be drawn that since the Act does not provide for the attendance of the company secretary at meetings by telephone or such other electronic means, the secretary is therefore deemed to be physically present at the place where the meeting is being held or deemed to be held.

PRACTICAL CONSIDERATIONS

578   Meetings of directors are as a rule less formal than shareholders' meetings. The fact that the former are held in private while the latter are usually larger in size and often held in public may contribute to the formal nature of such meetings. Nevertheless, the chairman of directors' meetings may at any time insist on observance of the formal rules of procedure.

579   **Notice:** Underlying the principle that directors have latitude in regulating their own proceedings, section 76 of the Act stipulates that a notice of a meeting of directors of a company must specify any matter referred to in subsection (2) of section 80[118] that is to be dealt with at the meeting; but unless the by-laws of the company otherwise provide, the notice need not specify the purpose of or the business to be transacted at the meeting.

580   No period of notice is specified in the Act and reference should therefore be made to the company's corporate instruments. The notice should however clearly state the place, date and time of the meeting. In the absence of any stipulation of the length of notice that is required, reasonable notice must be given. A week is considered reasonable. While, unless required, one need not state the business of the meeting, it is good corporate practice to circulate an agenda in general terms.

---

[118]   The matters referred to in section 80(2) relate mainly to: submission of proposals to shareholders, filing vacancies in the office of directors and auditors, issuing of shares, declaration of dividends, purchase or redemption of a company's shares, payment of commissions in respect of any share issue, approval of management proxy circulars, approval of financial statements, adoption amendment or repeal of by-laws.

581   Commenting on the absence of a strict requirement to give notice, one senior company secretary observed that, unlike shareholders who may choose whether or not to attend shareholders' meetings, directors have a duty to attend all meetings of the board irrespective of the business to be transacted.

582   **Board papers:** We have previously observed that a board is entitled to regulate its own affairs. The formality of board meetings and the content and format of board papers required to be supplied to the directors will depend upon the nature of the company i.e. whether private or public, whether the chairman is non-executive, the number of non-executive directors and the business to be dealt with at particular meetings.

583   In the more formal setting it is usual for the secretary to prepare or arrange for the preparation of one or more board papers to support the items listed on the agenda and to give members of the board pertinent information. This will enable them to reach an informed opinion on the several matters on which they are asked to make policy decisions or to pass resolutions.

584   Board papers should therefore be circulated with the agenda. It is unsatisfactory, except in extenuating circumstances, for board papers to be presented to members on their arrival at the meeting, because it is unlikely that members will be able to give the subject of the paper appropriate and meaningful consideration if they have not been given reasonable time to consider the issues.

585   Each board paper should state why it has been prepared, by whom and the date thereof. It should also set out the facts as clearly and impartially as possible and state precisely what the board is being asked to approve. In doing so the paper should document the arguments for, as well as against, the proposed course of action or the decision being sought, and conclude with a recommendation.

586   **The first board meeting:** The first board meeting of the company is likely to be concerned with a number of formal or procedural matters. Naturally the extent and complexity will vary from company to company, but the incorporator of the company may be requested to be present. The function of this person, if in attendance, may include calling this first

meeting to order and laying before members the Articles of Incorporation, evidencing the incorporation of the company. The incorporator should then ask the directors to appoint a presiding officer of the meeting to take the chair.

587   The draft agenda below gives some indication of the type of business which may require the attention of the directors at their first board meeting.

- To appoint a secretary for the meeting;

- To adopt a general by-law for the company;

- To adopt a common seal for the company;

- To appoint a chairman of the board;

- To appoint a managing director or chief executive officer;

- To appoint attorneys for the company;

- To appoint the first auditor;

- To appoint bankers of the company and open bank accounts;

- To receive and record directors' declaration of interest, if appropriate;

- To fix the accounting financial year end;

- To approve the form of share certificate and other corporate stationery;

- To allot shares and to authorise the issue of share certificates;

- To appoint a transfer agent, if required;

- To consider the company's business plan;

 • To appoint managers.

588 The above list of matters is not exhaustive and subsequent meetings will have at least two standard items on the agenda, in addition to the review of the company's business operations: namely, the reading and confirmation of the minutes of the previous meeting and matters arising therefrom.

589 **Board members at the AGM:** The seating arrangements at the head table at annual meetings is very much a matter of personal taste. A few observations, especially in the case of annual meetings of public companies, may however prove helpful:

 • All directors should be seated at the head table. This conveys a sense of unity, which is essential for good corporate management.

 • The company secretary should be seated near the chairman.

 • The company's chief finance officer, legal adviser and registrar or share transfer agent should all be in attendance, and should be seated within convenient access of the directors.

 • The company's auditor should not sit at the table but rather in the body of the meeting near the front of the room. There he or she will be within easy access of the directors but sitting in the body of the meeting emphasises his or her special relationship with members of the company, by whom he or she is appointed.

CHAPTER 19

Directors and officers

Their Duty of Care

590   While the theme of this book is the subject of meetings, the frequency with which directors and officers of companies are being challenged on questions of their duties renders it appropriate for some comment to be made on the matter since, in many cases, the challenges are made on issues which are rooted in decisions taken at meetings of the board.

591   Section 95 of the Act stipulates that every director and officer[119] of a company in exercising his powers and discharging his duties must act honestly and in good faith with a view to the best interest of the company and must exercise the care, diligence and skill that a reasonably prudent person would exercise in comparable circumstances.

    It further states that in determining what are the best interests of a company, a director must have regard to the interest of the company's employees in general as well as to the interest of its shareholders.

---

[119]   Section 2 (f) of the Act defines 'officer' in relation to a body corporate as, the chairman, deputy chairman, president or vice president, managing director, general manager comptroller, secretary or the treasure or any other person who performs for the body corporate functions similar to those normally performed by the aformentioned persons.

592   It must however be recognised that the interest of employees and shareholders may, at times, not be fully compatible. Cognisant of such potential incompatibility the Act clarifies the situation by stipulating that notwithstanding the foregoing considerations, the duty of care imposed upon directors is owed by them to the company alone.

593   Therefore while directors have an obligation to take the interest of employees and shareholders into account when seeking to ascertain that which is in the company's best interest, having done so, policy decisions must be made solely on the premise of that which is in the company's best interest for it is to the company and the company alone that directors owe their duty of care.

594   In the eyes of the law directors are agents of the company on whose behalf they act. In *Ferguson* v *Wilson*[120] the learned judge asked the question "What is the position of directors of a public company?"

He answered it thus: "They are merely agents of a company. The company itself cannot act in its own person, for it has no person, it can only act through directors, and the case is, as regard those directors, merely the ordinary case of principal and agent. Where an agent is liable those directors would be liable; where the liability would attach to the principal, and the principal only, the liability is the liability of the company".

595   Directors are however more than just agents. In some aspects their position may be akin to trustees. In *York and North Midland Railway* v *Hudson*[121], Mr Justice Romilly, Master of the Rolls, opined as follows: "the directors are persons selected to manage the affairs of the company . . . It is an office of trust which, if they undertake, it is their duty to perform fully and entirely. A resolution by shareholders therefore that shares or any other species of property shall be at the disposal of the directors, is a resolution that it shall be at the disposal of trustees".

596   The dual character of directors is perhaps best expressed in Lord Selbourne's words in *Great Eastern Railway Co.* v *Turner* [122] where he

---

[120] (1866) Lr 2 Ch 77 (see p. 386)
[121] (1853) 16 Beav 485 (see p. 388)
[122] (1872) Lr 8 Ch 149 - 152 (see p. 371)

157

said: "The directors are mere trustees or agents of the company . . . Trustees of the company's money and property, . . . agents in the transactions which they enter into on behalf of the company".[123]

597   A recent decision of the Supreme Court of Canada underscores another aspect of the trust relationship of directors in respect of their actions and dealings by their companies with third party funds, which by the terms of an agreement entered into by the company, such funds ought to have been held in trust but which in fact were mixed with the company's own funds to the detriment of the other party.

The Court held that the directors were personally liable from the breach arising out of the trust. See *Air Canada* v *M & L Travel Ltd, Martin and Valliant.*[124]

The same may apply in relation to employees' payroll deductions made by the company on behalf of the State where the enabling legislation constitute such deductions as trust funds.

598   This dual character of the status of directors may be summed up in the oft repeated statement that directors stand in a fiduciary relationship to the company. In this capacity they owe the company uncompromising honesty, loyalty and good faith in their dealings on behalf of the company. As agents a duty of care, diligence and skill is imposed upon them.

599   There continues to be much debate concerning the level of care, diligence and skill which is imposed by the Act, for the Act merely quantifies it at a level that a reasonable prudent person would exercise in comparable circumstances.

This issue was clearly settled in *Re City Equitable Fire Insurance Co. Ltd* [125] and observations from Mr Justice Romer's remarks in the judgement are worth noting.[126]

---

[123]   *Palmer's Company Law,* pp. 836 - 37
[124]   Supreme Court of Canada October 21, 1993. See CCH Corporation Law Reports, Volume 2 - 30-242 (see p. 390)
[125]   (1925) C 407 - 427 (see p. 393)
[126]   *Palmer's Company Law,* pp. 839 - 40

(a) "A director need not exhibit in the performance of his duties a greater degree of skill than may reasonably be expected from a person of his knowledge and experience. A director of a life insurance company, for instance, does not guarantee that he has the skill of an actuary."

(Law Reporters' comment: It is perhaps against this background that the Act provides by section 96(4) that a director who relies upon professional advice, reports and opinions may be shielded from certain liabilities).

(b) "A director is not bound to give continuous attention to the affairs of his company. His duties are of an intermittent nature to be performed at periodical board meetings and at meetings of any committee of the board".

(Law Reporter's comment: Here again the Act seems cognisant of the reality of the situation and provides by section 58 that directors may exercise their powers indirectly through the employees and agents of the company).

(c) "A director's duty . . . requires him to act with such care as is reasonably to be expected of him having regard to his knowledge and experience . . . He must give the company the advantage of his knowledge when transacting the company's business."

600   In North America, the issue of directors' and officers' duties is no less burning. Knepper puts it this way: "The duties that a corporate officer or director owes to his corporation are rooted not only in the elementary rules of equity, but also in business morality and public policy. They include undivided, unselfish and unqualified loyalty, unceasing effort never to profit personally at corporate expense, and unbending disavowal of any opportunity which would permit the director's private interests to clash with those of his corporation."[127]

601   The penalties imposed upon directors who fail to exercise the duty of care imposed upon them may be severe. Of equal, if not greater, concern is the liability to which they may be exposed while acting in good faith as agents of the company.

---

[127]   W. E. Knepper, *Liability of Corporate Officers and Directors*, p. 8.

602   Where directors have a discretion there are two principles by which they must be guided when exercising such discretion. First, directors must act bona fide — that is with honesty, good faith, sincerity and without deceit or fraud. Secondly; the discretion must be exercised for a proper purpose. It is, for example, an improper purpose for directors to use their fiduciary powers over the shares of a company by making an allotment purely for the purpose of destroying an existing majority or creating a new majority which did not previously exist.

The full treatment of this aspect of corporate governance is outside the specific scope of this book but there are a number of judicial decisions which underpin the principle that a discretion, if exercised, must not only be exercised in a bona fide manner but must also be for a proper purpose. For further research see *Hogg* v *Cramphorn*[128] *Howard Smith Ltd* v *Ampol Petroleum Ltd* [129] and *McCaine (London) Ltd* v *Cook & Watts Ltd.*.[130]

603   Note must also be taken of the fact that if the purpose for which the power was exercised was improper in nature a subsidiary purpose of a proper nature would not be a saving function. Legal proceedings against companies and directors by third parties are increasing at an alarming rate. The office of director for the incumbent is no longer an undisturbed status of peaceful repose in the corporate hierarchy, but rather one in which the holder may be exposed to considerable personal risk.

604   It is important that shareholders in the Caribbean recognise this changed corporate environment especially as it relates to directors' and officers' liabilities, the increased demands on their time and the additional responsibilities which are placed upon the shoulders of directors of sizable companies. It is therefore no longer reasonable to expect directors of such institutions to undertake the task without adequate protection and for a mere honorarium. If companies expect to attract people of calibre, commitment and reasonable ability, adequate remuneration must be paid for their services. In addition, some form of directors' and officers' liability insurance may be required in appropriate circumstances.

---

[128]   (1967) 1 Ch 254 (see p. 400)
[129]   (1974) AC 821 (see p. 403)
[130]   (1967) C.L.Y. 482 (see p. 405)

605　On the question of directors' and officers' liability insurance coverage, the advice of the Insurance Brokers Association of Ontario will become increasingly relevant to directors of companies in the Caribbean, especially those engaged in the offshore financial sector.

The association stated that "many privately held companies argue that directors' and officers' liability coverage is unnecessary. However there is evidence to suggest that more than half of all directors' and officers' claims made in Canada have come from parties other than shareholders."[131] Such claims may arise from a variety of causes, but the matters complained of are often rooted in improper decisions of the board, or decisions made and implemented through a process that was flawed.

606　Section 100 of the Act, in recognition of the changing corporate environment, provides that a company may purchase and maintain insurance for the benefit of any person such as an officer and for a director of the company against any liability incurred by him in specific circumstances in his capacity as a director or officer of the company.

607　In circumstances where there is in existence a unanimous shareholders' agreement the directors of such companies may consider it appropriate to request, in addition to the foregoing, a shareholders' indemnity if they are not satisfied that the corporate instruments of the company contains adequate indemnities as permitted by section 97 of the Act.

608　Notwithstanding all that has been penned on the subject of directors' and officers liabilities, directors must not be so preoccupied with the issue of personal liability that they became paralysed against taking bold initiatives on the company's behalf. In commerce, risk and progress are almost inseparable.

609　While directors who act negligently or recklessly impinge on their duty of care, directors are not liable for genuine mistakes or errors of judgement. See *Lagunas Nitrate Co.* v *Lagunas Nitrate Syndicate.*[132]

---

[131]　See *In Touch* 3 (Fall/Winter 1993/94) No. 2.
[132]　(1899) 2 Ch D 392 (see p. 406)

610   A thorny issue for creditors and directors alike is the matter of directors liability for corporate debts. In the United States there are some states which impose liabilities upon directors for corporate debts where they fail to make certain statutory reports or are guilty of certain specific delinquencies.

611   In the United Kingdom there are specific provisions which deal with offences, such as fraudulent trading or trading with intent to defraud creditors, where directors may be held personally liable.

612   The question of fraudulent trading is not easy to determine and the reported cases in England are replete with decisions swaying to and fro. The matter was perhaps best put in the unreported case of *Re White and Osmond (Parkstone) Ltd.*[133] In that case Mr Justice Buckley had this to say:

- "In my judgement, there is nothing wrong in the fact that directors incur a debt at a time when, to their knowledge, the company is not able to meet all its liabilities as they fall due.

- "What is manifestly wrong is if directors allow a company to incur credit at a time when the business is being carried on in such circumstances that it is clear that the company will never be able to satisfy its creditors.

- "However, there is nothing to say that directors who genuinely believe that the clouds will roll away and the sunshine of prosperity will shine upon them again and disperse the fog of their depression are not entitled to incur credit to help them to get over the bad time."[134]

613   The Act has no specific provision dealing with fraudulent trading. The matter would be decided on how the directors had exercised their duty of care and more particularly the directors' view of the company's position at the relevant time.

---

[133]   *This is an English Case* - 1960 (see p. 409)
[134]   *Palmer's Company Law*, Vol 1, p. 1192.

614   It is therefore important that when directors deal with the affairs of financially troubled companies their decisions, especially as to matters of borrowing or disposal of corporate property outside of the normal course of business, should be made by way of resolutions at properly convened meetings and carefully minuted. In the absence of these two indispensable requirements *(some may call them mere formalities)*, directors may find it difficult to refute an accusation or charge that they had acted negligently, recklessly or without due regard to the duty of care imposed upon them.

CHAPTER 20

That worthy servant called 'the Secretary'

615   It is almost impossible to consider the subject of corporate meetings without calling to mind the function and duties of the chairman and that obscure servant called the secretary.

616   The word 'secretary' is derived from the Latin word *secretarius* and denotes a notary or scribe. It is a title that was applied to various confidential officers and embraced as part of the root meaning of the word, the idea of secrecy or confidentiality.

617   The origin of the profession of secretary antedates recorded history and goes back to or beyond the era of the earliest Pharaoh.

618   Favourite administrators for French kings were sometimes given the title of 'secretary' as a special honour, a practice which has political usage even today in such titles as 'secretary of state', 'permanent secretary', 'secretary-general' etc.

619   Every association of persons however significant, whether the small social club or the State itself, has one or more persons to whom are allotted the important task of implementation of policy.

620   It has been said that the secretary's profession is one of the most ancient in the civilised world, for wherever there was the policy maker there too

was the man of letters and the pen to advise him, record his deeds and oversee the implementation of his policy.

621 The secretary is both a 'recorder' and a 'doer' and traditionally this person has stood in a unique position with the organisation he serves. Today's corporate secretary is often the confidante of the president or CEO and trusted advisor for a corporate-wide viewpoint.

622 The secretary's work is often hidden from view and his or her precise functions are seldom known.

623 The manual of the Corporation of Secretaries notes that the modern secretary occupies just as honourable a position as his ancient brothers, but the passage of time has added enormously to this person's importance. He or she is now indispensable to the conduct of industry, commerce and society and not the least so because their duties are often carried on behind the scenes and others receive the public credit.

624 This servant called the secretary is perhaps best described from the following digest of some remarks made by Sir Edwin Stockton at a secretaries conference held at Buxton in 1927. In the course of that presentation Sir Edwin remarked:

> "A good secretary endeavours to hide his employer's defects while allowing his virtues to appear in the full light of day. He shields him alike from the ubiquitous interviewer and the garrulous inventor who boasts a remedy for every ill.

> "He keeps from him the *[trivial]* things he need not know, and acquaints him with such things *[and all matters]* as he ought to know. In short, he is a man of discernment, discretion *[judgement]* and tact.[135]

> "He must have sound education, and correct and extensive information of the right kind. No busy man of affairs can find out for himself all that he requires to know,

---

[135] *Author's note:- The words in italics are my own*

he is bound to be dependent on his secretary to keep him posted in the things that matter.

"He should have specialised knowledge of the profession or business in which he is engaged, and, if that business be connected with a particular industry, be energetic enough and clever enough to master its technique, and to acquire from published statistics and other sources all that is to be known of similar businesses competing with his own.

"He would be quick to sense changing conditions, and to suggest appropriate means for meeting those changes, and keep himself abreast of all legislation that may affect or be likely to affect the industry.

"He must be a man of decision and energy, have self-discipline, self-control, sympathy for others, and a strong, true sense of justice, together with some personal charm, since these are the qualities required for the smooth control and management of a staff, and for securing its willing cooperation.

"In addition, he must possess the faculty of organisation and the habit of using it developed to a high degree, and a mind trained to deduce right conclusions from any given set of facts.

"The secretary may sometimes have little to do with the determination of policy. That, in general, is the prerogative of his superiors. But he will have much to do with the carrying out of policy once it has been decided. And here those special qualities already mentioned, which in the aggregate make up that elusive thing called personality, will play a most important part.

"The directors of a large corporation have not the opportunities for personal intercourse with customers or with the staff that the secretary has. The secretary is the liaison officer between the directors and the staff and outside persons dealing with the company, and will ensure by his advice that no policy shall be adopted that will antagonise the one or offend the others.

"Such a man as is here roughly sketched will perfect himself in all knowledge with which, as a business man, he ought to be acquainted. Particularly will he seek to master the intricacies of modern finance, and its bearing upon the financing of his own company. He will not be content to be a mere creature of routine, but will make his own openings for advancement. Slowly and discreetly he will win the esteem of his employers. His energy and initiative will diffuse itself throughout the whole organisation, bracing it up to full concert pitch, until by and by he will not only be the recipient of his superiors' orders, but their valued adviser as well, in whom an ever growing trust and confidence is reposed. This is the ideal position to which every secretary should aspire; this is the position which, in a very large number of instances, the secretary attains."[136]

625   The main duties of the secretary may be summarised as follows:

*   The secretary is the principal servant and chief administrative officer of his organisation. He or she acts as the main channel of communication between the enterprise and its governing body and between the enterprise and outside interest.

*   He or she advises the board of directors, records their decisions and makes sure that management policies and instructions reach the recipients concerned in a manner that is not distorted.

*   He or she provides information services for management, conducts the general correspondence of the enterprise and often directs its public relations activities.

---

[136]   Extract from Head, Fausset & Wilson, *Corporation of Secretaries' Manual of Secretarial Practice*, pp. 3 - 4.

- He or she maintains the statutory records of the body corporate.

- In respect of meetings, his or her duties are multifarious. They have the duty to advise not only the meeting but also the chairman on proper procedures.

- He or she advises the enterprise of its legal and statutory obligations.

- He or she is responsible for the administration of the register of members and the stock transfer function of their company.

- He or she is often in charge of personnel administration and the conduct of negotiations on conditions of service and the welfare of employees.

- He or she is responsible for all general undertakings which do not fall directly within the sphere of other functional departments.

626   The Act recognises the importance of the secretary and provides that directors must exercise all reasonable steps to ensure that the secretary is a person who appears to the directors to have the requisite knowledge and experience to discharge the functions of secretary of a public company (see Section 58(2)).

627   Not only does the Act require of directors of public companies to appoint a secretary, but it then goes on to list the qualifications of persons who may be assumed by the directors of a public company to have the requisite knowledge and experience to discharge the functions of secretary if the directors do not know otherwise.

628   Pennington observed that although the civil law tended to treat the secretary as a mere clerical assistant of the board, statutes creating new criminal offences usually make the secretary responsible for the company's crimes to the same extent as the directors. In this respect criminal law is more in accordance with reality.[137] Modern company law, such as the Act, has provided that 'officer' in relation to a body corporate includes the secretary (see section 2).

---

[137]   R. R. Pennington, *Company Law*, p. 508.

629   In the business management section of *The Administrator*,[138] Sir John Harvey-Jones, the chairman of Imperial Chemical Industries PLC, made some insightful observations on the role of the company secretary in an exclusive interview with Jon Preece for the journal.

Sir John stressed that the company secretary is an absolute key appointment, more important, said he, than that of any director. He opined that "the company secretary does as much as anybody to set the whole atmosphere of the board. He needs to understand not only the management's processes, aims and ambitions, but also the psychology of people on the board. He has to do all of this while not appearing to be manipulative but by being of irreproachable integrity."

The writer concluded by stating that Sir John has always spent a large amount of time with the company secretary planning meetings. "I did not do anything with the board without first sitting down and discussing it with the company secretary. As far as I was concerned the company secretary was my confidant."

In presiding over his board Sir John is said to have very open and positive views on board procedures which are meant to encourage discussion rather than prohibit it.

The aim has to be throughout to have a constructive discussion, to ensure doubts are aired. "I don't allow silence," says Sir John; "after discussing each subject I ask each member of the board what their opinion is and why and this includes the company secretary, as I have always believed that his view should be heard."

630   The conduct and administration of corporate meetings will be greatly enhanced if those who occupy the office of secretary are fully aware of their importance as officers of the company and of their responsibilities.

631   It is hoped that directors of companies in developing societies will see the need of filling the position of secretary with persons of competence, tact and sound judgement and that the persons so appointed will seek to equip themselves with such skills and knowledge as may be required for the proper discharge of their function.

---

[138]   See *The Administrator* p. 6 (April 1995)

Table of comparative references

This Table is included in order to improve the usefulness of the text for Canadian and Caribbean readers.

The sections of the legislation cited in the text are from the Companies Act CAP 308 of the laws of Barbados.

The companies legislation of Antigua and Barbuda, Belize, The Commonwealth of Dominica, Grenada, Guyana, St. Lucia, St. Vincent and Trinidad and Tobago are all based on the Caribbean Law Institute's model companies bill.

There is a great deal of similarity between such regional legislation and the Canada Business Corporations Act 1985. By referring to the table of comparative references, Canadian and Caribbean users may find comparative references to the relevant provisions of the respective enactments.

The legislation cited is as follows:

Antigua and Barbuda — *The Companies Act No. 18 of 1995.*

Bahamas — *The Companies Act No. 18 of 1992 .*

Belize — *The Laws of Belize 1980 Vol. 5 (The Companies Act).*

Canada — *Canada Business Corporations Act 1985*

Dominica — *The Companies Act 1994.*

Grenada — *The Companies Act No. 35 of 1994.*

Guyana — *The Companies Act No. 29 of 1991.*

Jamaica — *The Companies Act 1967.*

St. Lucia — *The Companies Act 1995*

St. Vincent — *The Companies Act No. 8 of 1994.*

Trinidad and Tobago — *The Companies Bill 1995.*

It should be pointed out that the provisions of the various Acts referred to in the Table of Comparative References may not be identical in wording. In particular there are substantial differences between the Companies Act of Jamaica and the comparative enactments of the other territories referred to in the text.

The comparative references shown in the table are intended as an aid to the userof the text and not a substitute for independent research or professional advice.

COUNTRY	SECTION	COMMENTS
Barbados	43	
Antigua	43	
Bahamas		not comparable but see Sec 45
Belize	44	
Canada	33	
Dominica	43	
Grenada	43	
Guyana	42	
Jamaica		
St. Lucia	43	
St. Vincent	43	
Trinidad & T	41&42	
Barbados	51	
Antigua	51	
Bahamas	61	
Belize	52	
Canada	42	
Dominica	51	
Grenada	51	
Guyana	50	
Jamaica		
St. Lucia	51	
St. Vincent	51	
Trinidad & T	55	
Barbados	52	
Antigua	52	Antigua - dividend payments out of unrealised
Bahamas	60	profits permitted for stock dividends. Bahamas
Belize	53	- dividends may be paid out of un-
Canada	43	realised appreciation of assets.
Dominica		see above note
Grenada		see above note
Guyana	50	see also section 51
Jamaica		
St. Lucia	52	
St. Vincent	52	see above note
Trinidad & T	56	see above note

COUNTRY	SECTION	COMMENTS
Barbados	53&54	loans to shareholders not permitted
Antigua	53&54	loans to shareholders permitted
Bahamas	30 & 31	not fully comparable.
Belize	54	
Canada	44	
Dominica	53&54	loans to shareholders permitted
Grenada	53&54	loans to shareholders permitted
Guyana	54	not fully comparable, see specific provisions
Jamaica	54, 179, & 186	different rules apply to private and public Cos
St. Lucia	53&54	
St. Vincent	53&54	loans to shareholders permitted
Trinidad & T	57&58	loans to shareholders not permitted
Barbados	58	
Antigua	58 to 61	
Bahamas	84	
Belize	59	
Canada	102(1)	
Dominica	58 to 61	
Grenada	58 to 61	
Guyana	59	
Jamaica		
St. Lucia	58 to 61	
St. Vincent	58 to 61	
Trinidad & T	62 to 65	
Barbados	59	
Antigua	62	only individuals may be directors of public
Bahamas	85	companies
Belize	60	
Canada	102(2)	
Dominica	62	
Grenada	62	see note above
Guyana	60	see note above
Jamaica	169	
St. Lucia	62	
St. Vincent	62	see note above
Trinidad & T	66	see note above

COUNTRY	SECTION	COMMENTS
Barbados	61	
Antigua	64	
Bahamas		
Belize	62	
Canada	103(1)	
Dominica	64	
Grenada	64	
Guyana	62	
Jamaica		
St. Lucia	64	
St. Vincent	64	
Trinidad & T	68	
Barbados	62	
Antigua	65	
Bahamas	70(2)	
Belize	63	
Canada	104	
Dominica	65	
Grenada	65	
Guyana	63	
Jamaica		not fully comparable but see sec 126
St. Lucia	65	
St. Vincent	65	
Trinidad & T	69	
Barbados	67	
Antigua	71	
Bahamas		
Belize	68	
Canada	107	
Dominica	71	
Grenada	71	
Guyana		provision is made for postal voting. See S133
Jamaica		
St. Lucia	71	
St. Vincent	71	
Trinidad & T	75	

COUNTRY	SECTION	COMMENTS
Barbados	79	
Antigua	81	
Bahamas	101	
Belize	80	
Canada	114(9)	
Dominica	81	
Grenada	81	
Guyana	80	
Jamaica		
St. Lucia	81	
St. Vincent	81	
Trinidad & T	85	
Barbados	80	
Antigua	82	
Bahamas	102 & 103	
Belize	81	
Canada	115	
Dominica	82	
Grenada	82	
Guyana	81	
Jamaica		not comparable but see Sec 190
St. Lucia	82	
St. Vincent	82	
Trinidad & T	86	
Barbados	83	
Antigua	85	
Bahamas	106	
Belize	84	
Canada	118(1)	
Dominica	85	
Grenada	85	
Guyana	84	
Jamaica	49(2)	
St. Lucia	85	
St. Vincent	85	
Trinidad & T	89	

COUNTRY	SECTION	COMMENTS
Barbados	84	
Antigua	86	
Bahamas	107	
Belize	85	
Canada	118(2)	see also section 119
Dominica	86	
Grenada	86	
Guyana	85	
Jamaica		
St. Lucia	86	
St. Vincent	86	
Trinidad & T	90	
Barbados	89	
Antigua	91	
Bahamas	112 to 114	
Belize	90	
Canada	120	
Dominica	91	
Grenada	91	
Guyana	90	
Jamaica	188	
St. Lucia	91	
St. Vincent	91	
Trinidad & T	95	
Barbados	95	
Antigua	97	
Bahamas	86	
Belize	96	
Canada	122	
Dominica	97	
Grenada	97	
Guyana	96	
Jamaica		
St. Lucia	97	
St. Vincent	97	
Trinidad & T	101	

COUNTRY	SECTION	COMMENTS
Barbados	96 & 97	
Antigua	98 & 99	
Bahamas	117 & 118	
Belize	97& 98	
Canada	123 & 124	
Dominica	98 & 99	
Grenada	99 & 99	
Guyana	97,98 & 99	
Jamaica		
St. Lucia	98 & 99	
St. Vincent	98 & 99	
Trinidad & T	102 & 103	
Barbados	109	notice not less than 21 nor more than 50 days
Antigua	111	notice not less than 7 nor more than 30 days
Bahamas	127	21 days presumed
Belize	110	
Canada	135	notice not less than 21 nor more than 50 days
Dominica	111	notice not less than 7 nor more than 30 days
Grenada	111	notice not less than 7 nor more than 30 days
Guyana	111	21 days presumed. See sec 155
Jamaica	128 & 129	varying lengths of time
St. Lucia	111	notice not less than 7 nor more than 30 days
St. Vincent	111	notice not less than 7 nor more than 30 days
Trinidad & T	115	notice not less than 10 nor more than 30 days
Barbados	110	dividend payments not an AGM item
Antigua	112	sanction of dividends is an AGM agenda item
Bahamas		
Belize	111	
Canada	135(5)	dividend payments not an AGM item
Dominica	112	sanction of dividends is an AGM agenda item
Grenada	112	sanction of dividends is an AGM agenda item
Guyana	112	dividend payments not an AGM item
Jamaica		dividend payments may be an AGM item
St. Lucia	112	sanction of dividends is an AGM agenda item
St. Vincent	112	sanction of dividends is an AGM agenda item
Trinidad & T	116	sanction of dividends is an AGM agenda item

COUNTRY	SECTION	COMMENTS
Barbados	111	
Antigua	113	and shareholders' participation by telephone
Bahamas	98	
Belize	112	
Canada	136	
Dominica	113	and shareholders' participation by telephone
Grenada	113	and shareholders' participation by telephone
Guyana	113	
Jamaica		
St. Lucia	113	and shareholders' participation by telephone
St. Vincent	113	and shareholders' participation by telephone
Trinidad & T	117	and shareholders' participation by telephone
Barbados	121	
Antigua	123	
Bahamas		not comparable but see sections 56 and 58
Belize	122	
Canada	138	
Dominica	123	
Grenada	123	
Guyana	123	
Jamaica		not comparable but see sections 109 and 110
St. Lucia	123	
St. Vincent	123	
Trinidad & T	127	
Barbados	123	
Antigua	125	
Bahamas	75	
Belize	124	
Canada	139	
Dominica	125	
Grenada	125	
Guyana	128	
Jamaica		
St. Lucia	125	
St. Vincent	125	
Trinidad & T	129	

COUNTRY	SECTION	COMMENTS
Barbados	124	
Antigua	126	
Bahamas	76	
Belize	125	
Canada	140	
Dominica	126	
Grenada	126	
Guyana	129	
Jamaica	130	proxy holder may only vote on a poll
St. Lucia	126	
St. Vincent	126	
Trinidad & T	130	
Barbados	127	
Antigua	129	
Bahamas	76	
Belize	128	
Canada	141	
Dominica	129	
Grenada	129	
Guyana	132	
Jamaica		not fully comparable but see section 131
St. Lucia	129	
St. Vincent	129	
Trinidad & T	133	
Barbados	128	
Antigua	130	
Bahamas		
Belize	129	
Canada	142	
Dominica	130	
Grenada	130	
Guyana	134	
Jamaica		
St. Lucia	130	
St. Vincent	130	
Trinidad & T	134	

COUNTRY	SECTION	COMMENTS
Barbados	129	
Antigua	131	
Bahamas	71	
Belize	131	
Canada	143	
Dominica	131	
Grenada	131	
Guyana	135	
Jamaica	129	not fully comparable
St. Lucia	131	
St. Vincent	131	
Trinidad & T	135	
Barbados	132	
Antigua	134	
Bahamas		
Belize	134	
Canada	146	
Dominica	134	
Grenada	134	
Guyana		
Jamaica		
St. Lucia	134	
St. Vincent	134	
Trinidad & T	138	
Barbados	134	
Antigua	136	
Bahamas		
Belize	136	
Canada	189	
Dominica	136	
Grenada	136	
Guyana	140	
Jamaica		
St. Lucia	136	
St. Vincent	136	
Trinidad & T	140	

COUNTRY	SECTION	COMMENTS
Barbados	135	
Antigua	137	
Bahamas		
Belize	137	
Canada	147	
Dominica	137	
Grenada	137	
Guyana	141	
Jamaica		
St. Lucia	137	
St. Vincent	137	
Trinidad & T	141	
Barbados	136	
Antigua	138	
Bahamas	79	
Belize	138	
Canada	148	
Dominica	138	
Grenada	138	
Guyana	142	
Jamaica	130	
St. Lucia	138	
St. Vincent	138	
Trinidad & T	142	
Barbados	137	
Antigua	139	
Bahamas	82	
Belize	139	
Canada	148(4)	
Dominica	139	
Grenada	139	
Guyana	143	
Jamaica		
St. Lucia	139	
St. Vincent	139	
Trinidad & T	143	

COUNTRY	SECTION	COMMENTS
Barbados	138	
Antigua	140	
Bahamas		
Belize	141	
Canada	148(5)	
Dominica	140	
Grenada	140	
Guyana	144	
Jamaica		
St. Lucia	140	
St. Vincent	140	
Trinidad & T	144	
Barbados	139	
Antigua	141	
Bahamas		
Belize	142	
Canada	149	
Dominica	141	
Grenada	141	
Guyana	145	
Jamaica		
St. Lucia	141	
St. Vincent	141	
Trinidad & T	145	
Barbados	140	
Antigua	142	
Bahamas		
Belize	143	
Canada	150	
Dominica	142	
Grenada	142	
Guyana	146	
Jamaica		
St. Lucia	142	
St. Vincent	142	
Trinidad & T	146	

COUNTRY	SECTION	COMMENTS
Barbados	144	
Antigua	146	
Bahamas		
Belize	147	
Canada	153	
Dominica	146	
Grenada	146	
Guyana	150	
Jamaica		
St. Lucia	146	
St. Vincent	146	
Trinidad & T	150	
Barbados	147	
Antigua	149	
Bahamas		not fully comparable but see sections 58 & 59
Belize	150	
Canada	155	
Dominica	149	
Grenada	149	
Guyana	153-155,168	
Jamaica		not fully comparable but see sec 121 to 123
St. Lucia	149	
St. Vincent	149	
Trinidad & T	153	
Barbados	148	
Antigua	150	
Bahamas		
Belize	151	
Canada	156	
Dominica	150	
Grenada	150	
Guyana	159-161	
Jamaica		
St. Lucia	150	
St. Vincent	150	
Trinidad & T	154	

COUNTRY	SECTION	COMMENTS
Barbados	150	
Antigua	152	
Bahamas	125	
Belize	153	
Canada	158	
Dominica	152	
Grenada	152	
Guyana	158	
Jamaica		
St. Lucia	152	
St. Vincent	152	
Trinidad & T	156	
Barbados	152	threshold $1m gross revenue $1m assets
Antigua	154	threshold $4m gross revenue $2m assets
Bahamas		
Belize	155	
Canada	160	
Dominica	154	threshold $4m gross revenue $2m assets
Grenada	154	threshold $2m gross revenue $1m assets
Guyana	156	threshold to be prescribed by minister
Jamaica		not comparable but see sections 30 & 32
St. Lucia	154 & 155	no threshold but cert of solvency required
St. Vincent	154	threshold $4m gross revenue $2m assets
Trinidad & T	158	threshold $4m gross revenue $2m assets
Barbados	170	
Antigua	177	
Bahamas		
Belize	173	
Canada	157	
Dominica	177	
Grenada	177	
Guyana	189	
Jamaica		not fully comparable but see section 142
St. Lucia	177	
St. Vincent	177	
Trinidad & T	181	

COUNTRY	SECTION	COMMENTS
Barbados	172	
Antigua	187	
Bahamas		
Belize	175	
Canada		
Dominica	187	
Grenada	187	
Guyana	191	
Jamaica		
St. Lucia	187	
St. Vincent	187	
Trinidad & T	191	
Barbados	179	
Antigua	195	
Bahamas	35 & 36	
Belize	182	
Canada	76	not fully comparable
Dominica	195	
Grenada	195	
Guyana	199	
Jamaica	73 to 75	
St. Lucia	195	
St. Vincent	195	
Trinidad & T	199	
Barbados	184	
Antigua	200	
Bahamas		
Belize	187	
Canada		not fully comparable but see section 60
Dominica	200	
Grenada	200	
Guyana	204	
Jamaica	80	
St. Lucia	200	
St. Vincent	200	
Trinidad & T	204	

COUNTRY	SECTION	COMMENTS
Barbados	201	
Antigua	214	
Bahamas		
Belize	205	
Canada	137	see also section 173
Dominica	214	
Grenada	214	
Guyana		see section 114
Jamaica		
St. Lucia	214	
St. Vincent	214	
Trinidad & T	219	
Barbados	202	
Antigua	215	
Bahamas		
Belize	206	
Canada		see section 173
Dominica	215	
Grenada	215	
Guyana		
Jamaica		not comparable but see section 72
St. Lucia	215	
St. Vincent	215	
Trinidad & T	220	
Barbados	208	
Antigua	221	
Bahamas	167	
Belize	213	
Canada	183	
Dominica	221	
Grenada	221	
Guyana	219 & 493	
Jamaica		not comparable but see section 194
St. Lucia	221	
St. Vincent	221	
Trinidad & T	226	

COUNTRY	SECTION	COMMENTS
Barbados	213	
Antigua	226	
Bahamas	168	
Belize	219	
Canada	190	
Dominica	226	
Grenada	226	
Guyana	220	
Jamaica	195	
St. Lucia	226	
St. Vincent	226	
Trinidad & T	231	
Barbados	488(U)	
Antigua	543(1)	
Bahamas	2	
Belize		
Canada	2	
Dominica	543(1)	
Grenada	543(1)	
Guyana	535(v)	
Jamaica		
St. Lucia	543(1)	
St. Vincent	543(1)	
Trinidad & T	4	

APPENDIX II

Precedents

The Precedents which follow are not a substitute for professional advice and should be amended as the circumstances may require

PRECEDENT A

(Text Reference Chapter 5)

MINUTES OF AN ORGANISATIONAL MEETING

MINUTES OF THE ORGANISATIONAL MEETING OF THE DIRECTORS
OF   , HELD AT   ON   , THE   DAY OF
, 199   AT   A.M./P.M.

PRESENT:

1.	CHAIRMAN FOR THE MEETING:	On a motion duly made and seconded it was resolved that be appointed chairman of the meeting.
2.	CERTIFICATE OF INCORPORATION:	The chairman reported that the company had been incorporated on the day of , 19 under the Companies Act Cap 308 and the Certificate and Articles of Incorporation bearing such date were then tabled.

The Instruments of Incorporation were examined and thereafter on motions duly moved and seconded, IT WAS RESOLVED as follows:

3.   ADOPTION OF
BY-LAW NO. 1:

THAT By-Law No. 1, a copy of which was produced to the meeting, be adopted as the general by-law of the company relating generally to the conduct of its affairs and that the said by-law should, in accordance with the provisions of the Companies Act CAP 308, be submitted to the shareholders of the company at a meeting of such Shareholders for confirmation, amend- ment or repeal.

4.   APPOINTMENT
OF SECRETARY:

THAT   be appointed secretary of the company to hold such office at the discretion of the directors.

5.   APPOINTMENT OF
ATTORNEY-AT-LAW:

THAT   be appointed attorney-at-law of the company to hold such office at the discretion of the directors.

6.   APPOINTMENT
OF AUDITORS:

THAT   of   be appointed auditors of the company to hold office until the close of the first Annual Meeting of the shareholders.

7.   REGISTERED OFFICE:

THAT the registered office of the company be situated at

8.   APPOINTMENT
OF BANKERS:

THAT   be appointed bankers of the company and that the directors be authorised to open and operate bank accounts in the name of the company and that the resolutions contained in the appropriate banking mandates, copies of which are hereto attached, be and are hereby adopted as resolutions of this meeting and that the secretary be authorised to forward the completed documents to the appropriate branch office of the bank.

9.   ADOPTION OF FORM OF
     SHARE CERTIFICATE:

THAT the form of share certificate, a copy whereof was produced to the meeting and is attached to these minutes, be and is hereby adopted as the form of share certificate to be issued by the company.

10. STATUTORY
     RECORDS:

THAT the secretary be authorised to obtain the following corporate records for use by the company

     (a) Minute book

     (b) Share register

     (c) Seal register

11. ADOPTION OF
     COMMON SEAL:

THAT the seal, an impression of which appears in the margin hereto, be adopted as the common seal of the company.

12. FINANCIAL YEAR:

THAT the financial year of the company shall end on

13. ISSUE OF SHARES:

THAT   common shares be issued as fully paid shares to the undermentioned persons for a consideration of $ per share, the company having already received the full consideration in respect of each such share:

Name   No. of Shares

14.   APPOINTMENT
       OF OFFICERS: (a)   THAT   be appointed
                                                  chairman of the board of directors.

                                   (b)   THAT   be appointed
president (or managing director) of
the company.

                                   (c)   THAT   be appointed
chief financial officer of the company.

Approved on the   day of   19 .

....

       CHAIRMAN   SECRETARY

PRECEDENT B

(Text Reference Chapter 7)

CHECK LIST FOR PLANNING THE ANNUAL MEETING OF MEMBERS

1. Check and agree: (a) Venue for the meeting (See chapter 8)

(b) Target date for annual meeting

2. Check and agree date: (a) Completion of audit

(b) Receipt of draft financial statements

(c) Board meeting to consider and approve accounts

(d) Auditor's report

(e) Signing accounts

(f) Annual meeting

3. Check and agree date (a) Accounts to be sent to printers

(b) Draft accounts to be received and reviewed

(c) Date draft to be returned to printers

		(d) Final statements to be received from printers
4.	Check and agree:	(a) Minimum notice required
		(b) Date for despatch to shareholders
		(c) Date for return of proxy forms
		(d) Date for filing with the Registrar of Companies
		(e) Date for notification to stock exchange
5.	Settle arrangements for:	(a) Stewards
		(b) Scrutineers
		(c) Layout and seating arrangements of head table
		(d) Proposers and seconders of motions
		(e) Voting cards or ballot papers
		(f) Attendance registers
6.	Note and arrange for:	(a) Filing company returns, if required
		(b) Payment of dividends
		(c) Notification to stock exchange, where appropriate
7.	Make diary notes relative to next annual meeting	

PRECEDENT C

(Text Reference Chapter 7)

AGENDA FOR PRE-AGM DIRECTORS' MEETING

ABC LIMITED

Agenda for Meeting of the Board of Directors to be held at
on   the   day of
19   at   o'clock

1.   To approve the minutes of the board meeting held on the   day of
       , 19 .

2.   Matters arising out of the minutes.

3.   To receive the share transfer report and to ratify the transfers processed.

4.   To receive a report on the use of the company's seal and to confirm the
      affixing of the seal to the documents stated therein.

5.   To receive and consider a proof print of the directors' report and of the
      accounts for the year ended the   day of   , 19 , together with the
      draft of the chairman's statement to be circulated therewith.

6.   To recommend (or declare) a dividend.

7.   To fix a date for the annual meeting.

8.   To consider the management accounts for the month ending:

9.   To consider   being the subject of Board Paper No:

10.   Any other business.

PRECEDENT D

(Text Reference Chapter7)

DRAFT MINUTES OF PRE-AGM DIRECTORS' MEETING

ABC LIMITED

Minutes of a Meeting of the Board of Directors held

at   on   the   day of   , 19 .

Present were:

50.   Minutes:

The minutes for the meeting of the board of directors held on the   day of   , 19 , copies having been circulated to the directors were approved by members and signed by the chairman.

51.   Matters arising out of the minutes:

(a)

(b)

(c)

52.   Share Transfer Report:

A share transfer report from the company's registrar and transfer agent dated   was produced to the meeting.

Resolved:

That the share transfers listed therein be confirmed.

53.   Use of Corporate Seal:

The secretary produced the seal book to the meeting.

Resolved:

That the affixing of the company seal to the documents set out against items numbers   to   inclusive in the said seal book be confirmed.

54.   Draft Reports and Accounts:

There were produced to the meeting for consideration a proof print of the report of the directors and the accounts for the year ended   , 19
and a draft of the chairman's statement to be circulated with the report and accounts.

Resolved:

(a)   That in accordance with the minutes of the previous annual meeting the remuneration of the auditors be fixed at $.

(b)   That the report of the directors, the chairman's statement and the accounts for the year ended   19   including the final dividend of   per share recommended therein (making a total dividend of   per share for the year) be approved and that (subject to the approval of the company in general meeting) such dividend be paid on the   day of   , 19   to shareholders registered at the close of business on the   day of
19 .

(c)   That the company's bankers be requested to open dividend account no.:   in the name of the company and be authorised to honour warrants dated   19   , drawn on the said account bearing the (facsimile or autographic) signatures(s) of and

(d)   That the signing of the balance sheet by two directors on behalf of the board be authorised.

(e)   That the draft management proxy circular submitted to the meeting by the secretary be approved.

55.   Date of Annual Meeting:

Resolved:

(a)   That the   annual meeting of the company be convened and held at   on   the   day of   19 at   a.m./p.m. to transact the ordinary business of the company and that the secretary be authorised to issue notices accordingly, together with a form of proxy in accordance with the proof print submitted to and approved by this meeting.

(b)   That the secretary be authorised to circulate with the notice convening the meeting the management proxy circular in accordance with the draft submitted to and approved by this meeting.

56.   Notification to Stock Exchange:

Resolved:

That the secretary be authorised to release forthwith to the stock exchange and to the company's press agents a preliminary announcement of the results for the year ended,   19 .

57.   Management Accounts:

There were produced to the meeting:

(a)   A list of bank balances at   19   and revised cash flow
        statement for the three months to   19   .

(b)   Management statements as at   19   .

(c)   The managing directors' report.

The directors noted the reports and accounts.

58.   Office Hours:

Board Paper No: *(This is by way of example only)*

The question of office hours was discussed and it was decided that with
effect from   19   , the office should close each day at   p.m. instead
of   p.m. Mr   dissented from this decision and asked that
his dissent be recorded in the minutes.

59.   Any other business.

The meeting terminated at   p.m.

PRECEDENT E

(Text Reference Chapter 8)

NOTICE AND AGENDA FOR ANNUAL GENERAL MEETING

ABC LIMITED

NOTICE AND AGENDA FOR ANNUAL MEETING

Notice is hereby given that the Twentieth Annual Meeting of the Shareholders of the Company will be held at 7 Gallows Heights, Illaby, St Jerome on Monday the   day of   , 19   at   a .m.

AGENDA

1.   Reading the minutes of the previous annual meeting of the company.

2.   To receive the reports of the auditors and the directors and to consider the audited financial statements for the year ended   19 .

3.   To elect directors of the company.

4.   To reappoint the retiring auditors for a further year and to authorise the directors to fix their remuneration.

5.   Question and answer period to discuss any other business of the company which may properly be considered at an annual meeting.

Dated this   day of   19 .

BY ORDER OF THE BOARD
D. E. Featherspoon
Secretary

7 Gallows Heights
Illaby
St Jerome

Note: A member entitled to attend and vote at the meeting is entitled to appoint a proxy to attend and vote instead of him. A proxy need not also be a member.

PRECEDENT F

(Text Reference Chapter 8)

CHAIRMAN'S EXTENDED AGENDA FOR ANNUAL GENERAL MEETING

ABC LIMITED

Chairman's Agenda for Twentieth Annual Meeting of the Shareholders of the Company to be held at 7 Gallows Heights, Illaby, St Jerome on Monday the day of   , 199   .

1.	Chairman:	Ladies and gentlemen, a quorum being present, I call the meeting to order and welcome you to the twentieth annual meeting of shareholders.
		Mr Secretary, please read the notice convening the meeting and thereafter the minutes of the previous annual meeting.

(Secretary will read the notice)

(Secretary will read the minutes of the previous annual general meeting)

2.	Chairman:	I now ask Mr of the firm of , the company's auditors, to read the report of the auditors to the members.

(Mr   will read the report.)

3.	Chairman:	The directors' report and audited accounts of the company have been in your hands for the

statutory period and I invite Mr   to propose their adoption.

Mr   : I move that the report of the directors and the audited financial statements for the year ended   now before the meeting be received and adopted.

Chairman: I invite Mr   to second the motion.

Mr   : I second the motion.

Chairman: The adoption of the directors' report and the accounts have been proposed and seconded and I now invite any member who desires to comment on the report and accounts to so indicate.

(After dealing with any questions)

Chairman: I now put the motion to the meeting. Those in favour please indicate by a show of hands. Any against?

I declare the resolution carried.

4.   Chairman: I move that the dividend of   per share as propose by the directors be declared payable on the   day of   19   to the holders of common shares registered at the close of business on   the day of   19

I invite Mr   to second the motion.

Mr   : I second the motion.

Chairman: Are there any comments from members? If not, those in favour please indicate by a show of hands. Those against?

I declare the resolution carried.

5.   Chairman: I invite Mr   to move the next resolution.

Mr   : I move that Mr X, a director retiring by rotation be re-elected a director of the Company and I ask Mr   to second the motion.

Mr   : I do second the motion.

Chairman: I do put the motion to the meeting. Are there any comments? If not, those in favour? Those against?

I declare the resolution carried.

6.   Chairman: Your board of directors has recommended that Mr Y be elected a director of the company to fill the vacancy arising from the retirement of Mr W and I do so move.

Mr   : I second the motion.

Chairman: Are there any questions or comments from members?

(After dealing with such, if any)

Chairman: I now put the motion to the meeting. Those in favour? Those against?

I declare the resolution carried.

7.   Chairman: The next resolution is: That   the retiring auditors be re-appointed auditors of the company for a further year and that the directors be authorised to fix their remuneration. I do invite a shareholder to formally propose this resolution.

Shareholder: I propose the resolution as read.

Chairman: Thank you. Will another shareholder please second the resolution?

Shareholder: I second the resolution.

Chairman: Thank you. I now put the resolution to the meeting. Those in favour? Those against?

I declare the resolution carried.

8. Chairman: That completes the prescribed business of the meeting. As is our customary practice there will be a question and answer period for the next minutes to discuss any other matter which may properly be considered at an annual meeting.

(After a suitable period the chairman to close the meeting and invite members to join the directors for light refreshments.)

PRECEDENT G (i)

(Text Reference Chapter 8)

FORM OF PROXY

A B C LIMITED

FORM OF PROXY

I   , the undersigned, being a shareholder of the company hereby appoint   of   or failing him   of   as my proxy to attend and act for me and on my behalf at the annual meeting of the shareholders of the company to be held on the   day of   , 19   and at any adjournment or adjournments thereof in the same manner, to the same extent and with the same powers as if the undersigned were present at the same meeting or such adjournment or adjournments thereof.

Dated this   day of   , 19   .

....
Signature of shareholder

Note: Proxies must be received at the office of the secretary not less than 48 hours
         before the time of the meeting.

PRECEDENT G (ii)

(Text Reference Chapter 8)

FORM OF PROXY (ALTERNATE FORM OF PROXY)

ABC LIMITED

I/We *(block capitals, please)*   of   a member/members of the above-named company, hereby appoint the chairman of the meeting or failing him the secretary of the company as my/our proxy to vote for me/us on my/our behalf at the annual general meeting to be held at 12 noon on   day, the   day of   , 19   , and at any adjournment thereof.

Please indicate with an X in the spaces below how you wish your votes to be cast.

RESOLUTION 1	To receive the reports and accounts	For: ____	Against: ____
RESOLUTION 2	To declare or approve payment of dividend recommended by the directors	For: ____	Against: ____
RESOLUTION 3	To elect a director	For: ____	Against: ____
RESOLUTION 4	To elect a director	For: ____	Against: ____
RESOLUTION 5		For: ____	Against: ____

Dated the   day of   , 19   .

....
Signature of shareholder

Note: Proxies must be received by the company at least 48 hours before the time of the meeting

PRECEDENT H

(Text Reference Chapter 8)

SPECIMEN PROXY INFORMATION CIRCULARS

The following management information circular and dissidents information circular mirror closely the Canadian precedents. The management information circular is required to be sent pursuant to section 140 of the Companies Act CAP 308 of the Laws of Barbados.

The dissidents information circular is also governed by the said provisions and is enclosed as a precedent for the guidance of shareholders where, in appropriate circumstances, it is desirable to use a dissidents proxy solicitation.

The precedents are given by way of example and should be amended as the circumstances may require.

Acknowledgement

The information circulars are adapted from *Canadian Corporation Precedents*, 3rd ed. (Toronto, Ontario: Carswell, 1987).

ANNUAL MEETING OF SHAREHOLDERS

MANAGEMENT INFORMATION CIRCULAR

ABC LIMITED

MANAGEMENT SOLICITATION

This management information circular is furnished in connection with the solicitation of proxies by the management of ABC Limited (the "Corporation") for use at the annual meeting of the shareholders of the Corporation to be held at the offices of the Corporation, 7 Gallows Heights, Illaby, St Jerome, on   the   day of   , 19   at the hour of   o'clock in the   noon for the purposes set out in the notice of the meeting. This solicitation is made by the management of the Corporation. It is expected that the solicitation will primarily be by mail. Proxies may also be solicited personally or by telephone by officers and directors of the Corporation. The cost of solicitation will be borne by the Corporation. Except as otherwise stated, the information contained herein is given as of   , 19   .

The form of proxy forwarded to shareholders with the notice of the meeting confers discretionary authority upon the proxy nominees with respect to amendments or variations of matters identified in the notice of the meeting or other matters which may properly come before the meeting.

The form of proxy affords the shareholder an opportunity to specify that the shares registered in his name shall be voted or withheld from voting in respect of the election of directors, the appointment of auditors and the authorisation of the directors to fix the remuneration of the auditors.

On any ballot that may be called for, the shares represented by proxies in favour of management nominees will be voted or withheld from voting in respect of the election of directors, the appointment of auditors and the authorisation of the directors to fix the remuneration of the auditors, in each case in accordance with the specifications made by shareholders in the manner referred to above.

In respect of proxies in which the shareholders have not specified that the proxy nominees are required to vote or withhold from voting in respect of the election of directors, the appointment of auditors and the authorisation of the directors to fix the remuneration of the auditors, the shares represented by proxies in favour of management nominees will be voted in favour of the election as directors of the persons listed herein, the appointment of auditors and the authorisation of the directors to fix the remuneration of the auditors.

Management knows of no matters to come before the meeting other than the matters referred to in the notice of meeting. However, if any other matters which are not now known to management should properly come before the meeting, the shares represented by proxies in favour of management nominees will be voted on such matters in accordance with the best judgement of the proxy nominee.

A proxy given by a shareholder for use at the meeting may be revoked at any time prior to its use. In addition to revocation in any other manner permitted by law, a proxy may be revoked by an instrument in writing executed by the shareholder or by his attorney authorised in writing or, if the shareholder is a corporation, under its corporate seal or by an officer or attorney thereof duly authorised, and deposited either at the registered office of the Corporation at any time up to and including the last business day preceding the day of the meeting, or any adjournment thereof, at which the proxy is to be used, or with the chairman of such meeting on the day of the meeting, or any adjournment thereof, and upon either of such deposit the proxy is revoked. The registered office of the Corporation is located at *(address)*.

Authorised Capital, Voting Shares and
Principal Holders Thereof

The authorised capital of the Corporation consists of an unlimited number of preference shares, issuable in series, and an unlimited number of common shares (the "Common Shares"), of which no preference shares and Common Shares are issued and outstanding as at   , 19   . Each Common Share carries one vote in respect of each matter to be voted upon at the meeting. Only holders of outstanding Common Shares whose names appear on the list of shareholders as provided for under section 121 of the Act are entitled to vote at the meeting, except to the extent that a person has transferred any of his Common Shares after that date and the transferee of such shares establishes proper ownership and demands not later than 10 days before the meeting that his name be included in the list of shareholders for the meeting, in which case the transferee is entitled to vote his shares at the meeting.

The following table sets forth the only persons who, to the knowledge of the directors and officers of the Corporation, beneficially own or exercise control or direction over more than 5 percent of the Common Shares, the approximate number of Common Shares controlled or directed by each such person and the percentage of the Common Shares of the Corporation represented by the number of Common Shares so owned, controlled or directed is indicated below:

Name of Shareholder	No. of Common Shares	Percentage of Class

Election of Directors

The present term of office of each director will expire immediately prior to the closure of the annual meeting of shareholders. It is proposed that each of the persons whose name appears hereunder be elected as a director of the Corporation to serve until the close of the next annual meeting of shareholders or until his successor is elected or appointed. It is intended that on any ballot that may be called for relating to the election of directors, the shares represented by proxies in favour of management nominees will be voted in favour of the election of such persons as directors of the Corporation, unless a shareholder has specified in his proxy that his shares are to be withheld from voting in the election of directors. In the event that any vacancies occur in the slate of such nominees, it is intended that discretionary authority shall be exercised to vote the shares represented by such proxies for the election of such other person or persons as directors nominated in accordance with the best judgement of management.

Name and address	Present principal occupation and position with the Corporation	Period of service as director	Common Shares of the Corporation beneficially owned, directly or indirectly or controlled or directed as at , 19 .

Each of the above nominees, with the exception of Mr X was elected to his present term of office by a vote of shareholders of the Corporation at a meeting the notice of which was accompanied by a management information circular.

The principal occupation of Mr X within the five preceding years has been as follows:

(insert details)

Directors and Executive Compensation

The Corporation has two executive directors and three executive officers. These persons received aggregate cash compensation of $ for services rendered during the financial year beginning   , 19 , and ending   ,19 .

Each of the directors who are not officers of the Corporation received an annual fee of $ for all services rendered to the Corporation as a director during the last full fiscal year.

Indebtedness of Directors and Officers

No present or proposed director or officer and none of their respective associates or affiliates is or has been indebted to the Corporation (or its subsidiaries) at any time since   ,19   with the exception of   Inc., a company controlled by   , the president and chief executive officer of the Corporation (see Interest of Insiders in Material Transactions).

Interest of Insiders in Material Transactions

During the financial year ended   , 19 , the Corporation advanced funds to   Inc., a company controlled by   , the president and chief executive officer and a director of the Corporation. The largest amount outstanding on the funds advanced to date was $. The amount currently outstanding on the advance of funds is $. The funds were advanced in the form of a promissory note payable on demand. Prior to   , 19 , the funds were advanced at the prime rate of interest; after   , 19 , the interest on the funds advanced is payable at the prime rate less 3/8 of 1 percent.

On   , 19   , the Corporation and   Ltd entered into a joint venture agreement. Pursuant to the terms of the joint venture agreement, Ltd committed itself to make investments to a total of $ in business selected by the Corporation. In addition,   Ltd has the right, once it has invested the initial $, to increase the amount of its commitment to $, a director of the Corporation, is chairman and chief executive officer of Ltd.

Directors' and Officers' Insurance

Directors' and officers' liability insurance has been obtained for the directors and officers of the Corporation (and its subsidiaries). The insurance is in effect for a (five) year period which began   , 19   , and an annual premium of $ is paid by the Corporation. No portion of the premium is directly paid by any of the directors or officers of the Corporation (or its subsidiaries). The aggregate insurance coverage obtained under the policy is limited to $ per policy year. Under the policy, the director or officer must absorb   percent of each loss.

Appointment of Auditors

Management proposes to nominate   , Chartered Accountants, of (address), the present auditors, as the auditors of the Corporation to hold office until the close of the next annual meeting of shareholders.   was first appointed auditor of the Corporation on   ,19   , shortly after its incorporation. It is intended that on any ballot that may be called relating to the appointment of auditors, the shares represented by proxies in favour of management nominees will be voted in favour of the appointment of   as auditors of the Corporation, unless a shareholder has specified in his proxy that his shares are to be withheld from voting in the appointment of auditors.

Remuneration of Auditors

In the past, the directors have negotiated with the auditors of the Corporation on an arm's length basis in determining the fees to be paid to the auditors. Such fees have been based upon the complexity of the matters in question and the time incurred by the auditors. Management believes that the fees negotiated in the past with the auditors of the Corporation were reasonable in the circumstances and would be comparable to fees charged by auditors providing similar services. Accordingly, on any ballot that may be called for relating to the authorisation of the directors to fix the remuneration of the auditors, the shares represented by proxies in favour of management nominees will be voted in favour of the resolution authorising the directors to fix the remuneration of the auditors, unless a shareholder has specified in his proxy that his shares are to be withheld from voting in the authorisation of the directors to fix the remuneration of the auditors.

Management Agreement

Pursuant to an agreement (the "management agreement") made as of   , 19 , between the Corporation and (name and address of the manager) (the "Manager"), the Manager has agreed to render advice and management services to the Corporation in connection with the day-to-day operations of the Corporation in a manner consistent with the policies determined from time to time by the board of directors of the Corporation. Pursuant to the management agreement, the Manager will provide the following:

(a)   clerical, corporate and accounting services;

(b)   secretarial services;

(c)   office space;

(d)   office equipment; and

(e)   general office supplies.

In consideration for the services provided by the Manager under the management agreement, the Corporation has agreed to pay to the Manager a monthly fee of $, together with those expenses actually and properly incurred by the Manager on behalf of the Corporation. In addition, if the Manager is required to provide technical services or project management to the Corporation, the Manager is entitled to receive per diem charges for (engineering and supervisory) personnel. The management agreement may be terminated by either party at the end of a month by written notice of termination given to the other at least 60 days prior to the end of such month.

The names and addresses of the insiders of the Manager are as follows:

(Shareholder Proposals for Next Meeting)

Proposals of shareholders to be presented at the 19   annual meeting of shareholders of the Corporation must be received by the secretary of the Corporation before   ,19   , to be considered for inclusion in the management information circular and form of proxy relating thereto.

Certificate

The contents and the distribution of this information circular have been approved by the board of directors of the Corporation.

Dated this   day of   , 19 .

....
(To be signed by chairman or secretary)

ANNUAL MEETING OF SHAREHOLDERS

DISSIDENTS' INFORMATION CIRCULAR

ABC LIMITED

Solicitation By

This information circular is furnished in connection with a solicitation of proxies by and on behalf of (describe solicitation group) (the "Investors") for use at the annual and/or special meeting of the shareholders of ABC Limited (address) (the "Corporation") to be held at 7 Gallows Heights, Illaby, St Jerome, on   ,
the   day of   19   , at o'clock in the   noon. The purpose of the meeting is set forth in the notice of the meeting which the Corporation has forwarded to shareholders and which was attached to the Management Information Circular referred to under "Management's Solicitation" below.

It is expected that the solicitation will be by mail, telephone and personal contact. (The Investors have retained the firm of   Inc., investment dealers, as soliciting agents to assist in the solicitation of proxies on their behalf for use at the meeting. For such services, the Investors will pay   Inc. a fee not to exceed $ and will reimburse such soliciting agents for its reasonable out-of-pocket expenses.) The costs of solicitation by or on behalf of the Investors will be borne by the Investors.

This solicitation is not made by or on behalf of management of the Corporation.

Management's Solicitation

An information circular dated   , 19   (the "Management Information Circular") has been previously forwarded to the shareholders in connection with the solicitation of proxies by the management of the Corporation. Reference is hereby made to the information contained in the Management Information Circular, which information is incorporated herein by reference.

Information Respecting Proxies

The form of proxy accompanying this information circular confers discretionary authority upon the proxy nominees with respect to any amendments or variations to the matters identified in the notice of meeting or other matters which may properly come before the meeting. The form of proxy affords a shareholder the opportunity to specify that the shares registered in his name will be voted or withheld from voting in respect of the election of directors, the appointment of auditors and the authorisation of the directors to fix the remuneration of the auditors. The form of proxy also affords a shareholder the opportunity to specify that the shares registered in his name will be voted in favour of or against (the resolution to agree to and adopt the Scheme of Arrangement represented by the arrangement dated   , 19   (a copy of which was annexed as an Appendix to the Management Information Circular). Reference is made to the Management Information Circular for details respecting the Scheme of Arrangement proposed for consideration at the meeting.

The shares represented by proxies solicited by the Investors will be voted or withheld from voting in respect of the election of directors, the appointment of auditors and the authorisation of the directors to fix the remuneration of the auditors and voted in favour of or against the adoption of the Scheme of Arrangement, in each case in accordance with the specifications made by shareholders in the manner referred to above.

In respect of proxies solicited by the Investors in which the shareholders have not specified that the proxy nominees are required to vote or withhold from voting, or vote for or against, the matters specified above, the shares represented by proxies solicited by the Investors will vote for the election as directors of the persons named herein, for the appointment of auditors and the authorisation of the directors to fix the remuneration of the auditors and against the adoption of the Scheme of Arrangement.

The Investors know of no other matters to come before this meeting other than the matters referred to above. However, if any other matters which are not known to the Investors should properly come before the meeting, the shares represented by the proxies solicited by the Investors will be voted on such matters in accordance with the best judgement of the proxy nominee.

Proxies given by shareholders for use at the meeting may be revoked at any time prior to their use. (In addition to revocation in any other manner permitted by law, a proxy may be revoked by an instrument in writing executed by the shareholder or by his attorney authorised in writing or, if the shareholder is a corporation, under its corporate seal or by an officer or attorney thereof duly authorised, and deposited either at the head office of the Corporation at any time up to and including the last business day preceding the day of the meeting, or any adjournment thereof, at which the proxy is to be used or with the chairman of such meeting on the day of the meeting, or adjournment thereof, and upon either of such deposits the proxy is revoked.)

Interest of Investors in Scheme of Arrangement

The Investors have no material interest, direct or indirect, in the Scheme of Arrangement other than as stated below:

(Insert particulars of interest of Investors)

Scheme of Arrangement and Recommendations of Investors

The details of the Scheme of Arrangement proposed for consideration at the special meeting of the shareholders of the Corporation are contained in the Management Information Circular referred to above.

The Investors are soliciting the support of the holders of (common) shares of the Corporation in order to oppose the resolution to be placed before the special meeting of shareholders to agree to and adopt the Scheme of Arrangement and thereby effectively prevent the completion of the transaction described in the Management Information Circular on the basis therein proposed.

In the opinion of the Investors, the Scheme of Arrangement is neither fair nor equitable to the shareholders of the Corporation for the following reasons:

(Insert details of reasons for opposition)

(The Investors have received indications of support from substantial shareholders holding in the aggregate a significant percentage of the outstanding shares of the Corporation.)

Reasons for Investors' Solicitation

(Insert appropriate description, including the circumstances under which each dissident became involved in the solicitation and the nature and extent of his activities as a dissident)

In view of the foregoing, the Investors no longer have confidence in the ability of the present directors of the Corporation to manage the business and affairs of the Corporation in a manner which is consistent with the best interests of the Corporation and its shareholders.

Election of Directors

Each person whose name appears below is proposed by the Investors to be elected as a director of the Corporation to serve until the next annual meeting of the shareholders of the Corporation or until his successor is appointed. In the event that any vacancy occurs in the slate of such nominees, the Investors will nominate another person as director. If a vote by ballot is demanded, the shares represented by proxies in favour of the Investors' nominees will be voted in favour of the election of such persons as directors of the Corporation, unless a shareholder has specified in his proxy that his shares are to be withheld from voting in the election of directors.

Name and address	Present principal occupation and position with the Corporation	Period of service as director	Common Shares of the Corporation beneficially owned, directly or indirectly or controlled or directed as at , 19 .

The Investors have been advised that each of the foregoing nominees is prepared to act as a director of the Corporation if elected.

(Include interest of nominees for director in material transactions and details of any contract, arrangement or understanding between any nominee and any other person, pursuant to which the nominee is to be elected)

Appointment of Auditors

Management proposes to nominate   , Chartered Accountants, the present auditors of the Corporation, to hold office until the next annual meeting of shareholders. If a vote by ballot is demanded, it is intended that the shares represented by proxies in favour of the investors' nominees will be voted (in favour) of the appointment of   , Chartered Accountants, as auditors of the Corporation, unless a shareholder has specified in his proxy that his shares are to be withheld from voting in the appointment of auditors.

Voting Shares and Interest of Investors Therein

The following table sets forth the only persons who, to the knowledge of the Investors, beneficially own or exercise control or direction over more than 5 percent of the (common) shares, the approximate number of (common) shares controlled or directed by each such person and the percentage of (common) shares of the Corporation represented by the number of (common) shares so owned, controlled or directed:

Name of Shareholder	No. of Common Shares	Percentage of Class

To the knowledge of the Investors, a change in effective control of the Corporation has not occurred since the beginning of the last financial year of the Corporation.

The Investors and their associates beneficially own, directly or indirectly, or exercise control or direction over, the following (common) shares of the Corporation:

(Insert details, including shareholdings in affiliates of the Corporation)

The Investors have made the following trades in securities of the Corporation during the preceding two years:

Investor	Date	No. of shares Purchased	No. of shares Sold	Price

(Insert details, including details of any indebtedness outstanding which was incurred for the purpose of acquiring or holding the above securities)

None of the Investors has been, during the preceding year, a party to a contract, arrangement or understanding with any person in respect of securities of the Corporation, including joint ventures, loan or option arrangements, puts or calls, guarantees against loss or guarantees of profit, division of losses or profits or the giving or withholding of proxies.

Information Regarding the Investors

Name and address	Principal occupation or employment	Principal employment during past five years

(Insert appropriate information)

None of the persons whose names appear in the above table has been a dissident within the preceding five years except for *(insert name, body corporate involved, relationship of dissident to principals and subject matter and outcome of the solicitation)*.

Information Regarding Partners, Directors, Officers
and Certain Shareholders of .... Corporation

(Insert details)

Interest in Material Transactions

(Insert details, including interest of all nominees for director, and interest of each dissident and his associates. Also include details of any contract between a dissident or his associates and any person with respect to future employment by the corporation or any of its affiliates, or future transactions to which the corporation or any of its affiliates will or may be a party.)

Certificate

The contents and sending of this information circular have been approved by the Investors.

Dated this   day of   , 19   .

(Signature of dissident or dissidents)

PRECEDENT I (i)

(Text Reference Chapter 8)

CONSENT AS TO SHORT NOTICE

ABC LIMITED

(The Companies Act CAP 308 Sec. 111)

We, being all of the shareholders of ABC Limited entitled to receive notice and vote at the annual meeting of the company hereby consent to the calling of the annual meeting of the company and voting upon any resolutions required to be considered thereat notwithstanding the short notice given for convening the meeting.

Dated this   day of   19 .

Signature of shareholders: ....

                                    ....

                                    ....

(See also Precedent I (ii))

PRECEDENT I (ii)

(Text Reference Chapter 8)

ALTERNATIVE FORM OF CONSENT AS TO SHORT NOTICE

ABC LIMITED
(The Companies Act CAP 308 Sec. 111)

We the undersigned being all of the shareholders of ABC Limited entitled to receive notice and to vote at the annual meeting of shareholders hereby consent:

(a)   To the company sending us copies of the accounts, proxies and management proxy circular less than 21 days before the date of the meeting

and

(b)   To the calling of the annual general meeting of the company and voting upon any resolutions required to be considered thereat notwithstanding that less than 21 days notice has been given for convening the meeting.

Dated this   day of   19 .

Signature of shareholders: ....

....

....

PRECEDENT J

(Text Reference Chapter 11)

BY-LAW (OR ARTICLES) TO LIMIT NOMINATIONS FROM THE FLOOR AT ANNUAL MEETINGS

DIRECTORS' ELIGIBILITY FOR ELECTION

Except otherwise provided by the by-laws no person shall be eligible for election as a director at any general meeting unless either:

(a)   he is recommended for election by the board of directors; or

(b)   not less than 10 clear days nor more than 50 clear days before the date appointed for the annual general meeting, written notice, executed by not less than the number of persons holding at least 5 percent of the issued and outstanding voting shares in the capital of the company, has been given to the company of the intention to propose such person for election together with a letter of consent signed by that person confirming his willingness to be nominated and to serve as a director if elected.

PRECEDENT K

(Text Reference Chapter 11)

MOTION FOR ELECTION OF DIRECTORS

Resolved:

That Mr   , a director retiring by rotation and being eligible for re-election be, subject to the articles and by-laws of the company, re-elected a director of the company to hold office until the close of the second annual meeting next following his election.

OR

Resolved:

That Mr   , having indicated his willingness to serve as a director, be, subject to the articles and by-laws of the company, elected a director of the company to hold office until the close of the third annual meeting next following his election.

PRECEDENT L

(Text Reference Chapter 11)

PROCEDURAL MOTION TO ELECT MULTIPLE PERSONS BY SINGLE RESOLUTION

Resolved:

That the motion for the election of three persons to fill the three vacancies on the board of directors be put before the meeting in a single resolution and be voted upon accordingly.

PRECEDENT M

(Text Reference Chapter 11)

WRITTEN CONSENT OF NOMINEE TO SERVE AS DIRECTOR IF ELECTED

I,   *(full name)* residing at   not being a person disqualified from holding the office of a director, hereby consent to act as a director of ABC Limited if elected.

Dated this   day of   19 .

....
(Signature)

PRECEDENT N (i)

(Text Reference Chapter 12)

NOTICE INCORPORATING RESOLUTION APPOINTING CORPORATE REPRESENTATIVE

To: The Secretary
                  ABC Limited

   Resolved:

   "That Mr   or failing him Mr   be and is
   hereby appointed pursuant to section 125 of the Companies Act
   CAP 308 of the laws of Barbados to act as the company's
   representative at any meeting of the members or creditors of
   ABC Limited."

   Dated this   day of   19 .

                  ....
                            Chairman
                                                        Seal

                  ....
                            Secretary

PRECEDENT N (ii)

(Text Reference Chapter 12)

ALTERNATE NOTICE INCORPORATING RESOLUTION APPOINTING CORPORATE REPRESENTATIVE

TO WHOM IT MAY CONCERN

Resolved:

"That Mr   or failing him Mr   be and is hereby appointed pursuant to section 125 of the Companies Act CAP 308 of the laws of Barbados to act as the company's representative at any meeting of the members or creditors of other companies in which the company is or may hereafter become interested as a member or creditor."

Dated this   day of   19 .

....
Chairman

Seal

....
Secretary

PRECEDENT O (i)

(Text Reference Chapter 12)

BALLOT PAPER

ABC LIMITED
ANNUAL MEETING
, 19 .

Ballot paper for voting on the adoption of the directors' report and audited accounts for the year ended , 19 .

Agenda item no:

FOR/AGAINST
(delete as appropriate)

PRECEDENT O (ii)

(Text Reference Chapter 12)

FORM OF BALLOT PAPER FOR USE AT POLL
(sometimes called a poll card)

ABC LIMITED
Special Meeting of Shareholders..........., 19 .

NAME OF SHAREHOLDER	SHARES HELD*	RESOLUTION NO.:	VOTES	
			FOR	AGAINST
		1		
		2		
		3		
Signature of member, proxy or corporate representative	If ballot is being cast by proxy name of proxy holder .... (Block Letters)	If "X" only is marked all shares held will be voted according to marked preferences * If number of shares held not known, leave blank and scrutineer will complete.		

PRECEDENT O (iii)

(Text Reference Chapter 12)

ALTERNATE FORM OF BALLOT PAPER
FOR USE AT POLL
(sometimes called a poll card)

ABC LIMITED

Special Meeting of the Shareholders held on   , 19 .

POLL

On the special resolution as set out in the notice convening the meeting

BALLOT PAPER FOR VOTING ORDINARY SHARES

NAME OF SHAREHOLDER (Block letters please)	SHARES HELD (If number of shares not known see note 2)	Votes FOR	Votes AGAINST
*If ballot is being cast by proxy or corporate representative Name of such person _____ (Block letters please)		*(Leave blank please)*	

NOTES & INSTRUCTIONS

1. Please print your name and state the number of shares held. Thereafter indicate the number of shares voted for and/or against the resolution.

2. If you do not indicate the number of shares voted for or against the resolution but merely mark an "X" for or against, all of the shares registered in your name will be allocated according to your marked preference.

3. Members may split their votes and vote some shares for and some against the resolution. If the shares voted or the aggregate shares cast for and against the resolution exceed the number of shares held, the votes cast for and/or against the resolution will be adjusted rateably.

4. If the name of the shareholder and/or proxy holder is not stated, the ballot will be treated as a spoilt ballot.

PRECEDENT P

(Text Reference Chapter 12)

CUMULATIVE VOTING CARD

ABC LIMITED

ANNUAL MEETING   19 .

Cumulative Voting Card for the Election of Three Directors

Name of member (Block letters)	Shares held If no. of shares held not known, see note	Name of candidates (Please vote for not more than 3 persons)	Number of votes FOR	Leave blank (for official use)
		Bedford, A. J.		
		Collins, D. R.		
Name of proxy (if applicable)	Cumulative votes = Shares held x 3	Smith, O. L.		
		Wiseman, A. Z.		
* Signature of member, proxy or corporate representative:				

Notes: 1. Cumulative voting enables you to vote all of your cumulative votes for one candidate or to allocate your cumulative votes according to your preference among up to 3 persons or your choice.

2. If you do not allocate your votes but merely make 'X' against the candidate of your choice, your votes will be allocated equally among the candidates of your choice.

* The signature of the ballot paper is an optional feature, but is recommended by some authorities on ballot papers for cumulative voting.

PRECEDENT Q

(Text Reference Chapter 12)

SCRUTINEERS' REPORT ON BALLOTING

Report of the Scrutineers

The Chairman of the Meeting

The undersigned scrutineers hereby report that at the annual (or special) meeting of the shareholders of ABC Limited (the Company) held on   the   day of   19 , the result of the balloting by the holders of common shares ("shares") of the Company on the resolution indicated below, which was submitted to the meeting, was as follows:

1.   Resolution to approve the employees' stock option plan and to approve the grant of the options specified therein.

    <u>Shareholders present in person</u>   <u>No of shares</u>

    Voted for the resolution:

    Voted against the resolution:

    <u>Shareholders represented by proxy</u>

    Voted for the resolution:

Voted against the resolution:

Abstained on instructions from voting on the resolution:

Of the total number of shares represented in person and/or by proxy at the said meeting;

The total number of shares voted for the resolution was:

The total number of shares voted against the resolution was:

The percentage of the votes cast which were affirmative votes was   percent.

Dated this   day of   199 .

_____

Scrutineer

_____

Scrutineer

PRECEDENT R

(Text Reference Chapter 13)

POSTAL BALLOT AND DECLARATION, ETC.

ABC LIMITED

INSTRUCTIONS FOR POSTAL VOTING

BEFORE VOTING

(a) You must complete the attached Declaration of Identity before a witness. A person who is qualified to witness your signature is either:

(i) a manager of the company;

(ii) a notary public;

(iii) a justice of the peace;

(iv) a commissioner of oaths;

(v) a medical practitioner;

(vi) an attorney-at-law;

(vii) an accountant of a recognised national or international accounting body;

(viii) a bank manager;

(ix) a head teacher of a recognised primary or secondary school;

(x) a head of a government department;

(xi) a chief registering officer or returning officer of a constituency;

(xii) a permanent secretary;

(xiii) a manager or chairman of a statutory corporation;

(xiv)   a priest or minister of religion;

(xv)   a police officer of gazetted rank.

(b)   The witness must either know you personally or you must carry some form of identification with you.

(c)   In the presence of the witness print and sign your name in the spaces provided and then request the witness to sign and complete the Declaration.

(d)   If the shareholder is a corporation the Declaration of Identity must be signed by a duly authorised officer who should state next to his or her signature the capacity in which he or she signs.

(e)   In the case of shareholders jointly owning a policy (*or shares*) any one of such shareholders may sign the Declaration of Identity.

PRECEDENT R

(Text Reference Chapter 13 continued)

POSTAL BALLOT AND DECLARATION, ETC

YOU MAY NOW VOTE

(a)   [   ] candidates are contesting the election of directors for [   ] vacancies.

(b)   You may vote for [   ] candidates or less. Do not vote for more than [   ] candidates.

(c)   Mark ONE "X" ONLY next to each of the names of the candidates of your choice. Do not make any alterations or other marks on the ballot paper.

(d)   AFTER VOTING, PEEL THE TAPE OFF THE BALLOT PAPER, FOLD AND SEAL IT AND PLACE IT IN THE OFFICIAL BALLOT ENVELOPE TOGETHER WITH YOUR COMPLETED DECLARATION OF IDENTITY.

(e)   SEAL the official ballot envelope carefully and stick the appropriate stamp on the envelope before posting.

(f)   POST to reach the Addressee not later than [*time*] ON [
                    , 19]. DO NOT DELIVER THE ENVELOPE TO ANY OTHER PERSON OR PLACE.

FOLLOW ALL OF THE ABOVE INSTRUCTIONS FOR COMPLETING THE DECLARATION OF IDENTITY AND THE BALLOT PAPER AND FOR POSTING OR YOUR VOTE MAY BE INVALID.

PRECEDENT R

(Text Reference Chapter 13 continued)

POSTAL BALLOT AND DECLARATION, ETC.

ABC LIMITED

ANNUAL GENERAL MEETING

to be held on the   day of   , 19

ELECTION OF DIRECTORS - DECLARATION OF IDENTITY

I,   (*please print*) hereby declare that I am a shareholder to whom a postal ballot paper was sent.

Dated this   day of   19   .

....
Signature of shareholder

The abovenamed shareholder, who is known to me */identified himself/herself to me *, signed this Declaration in my presence.

Signature of witness: ....

Name of witness: ....
Please print

Address: ....
Please print

Profession or description: ....
Please print

* Delete where not applicable

PRECEDENT R

(Text Reference Chapter 13 continued)

POSTAL BALLOT AND DECLARATION, ETC.

ABC LIMITED

ANNUAL GENERAL MEETING

to be held on the   day of   , 19

ELECTION OF DIRECTORS - POSTAL BALLOT PAPER

CANDIDATE	
Mr A	
Mr B	
Ms C	
Mr D	
Ms E	
Mr F	

PRECEDENT R

(Text Reference Chapter 13 continued)

Postal Ballot and Declaration, etc.

ABC LIMITED

Instructions for

Authentication and Counting of Ballot Papers

Authentication:

The first step is to authenticate the declaration of identity and the ballot paper. This involves:

(1) Opening each official ballot envelope

(2) Checking each declaration of identity for:

    (a) Policy holder's name (check against voters' list that he or she is a policy holder);

    (b) Policy holders' signature;

    (c) Witness' signature and particulars.

(3) Stapling together the declaration and ballot paper where either one does not satisfy any of the above and placing them in the box for rejected declarations.

(4) If the declaration and ballot paper are authenticated, doing the following:

    (a) Validating both the declaration and the ballot paper with a rubber stamp.

    (b) Placing the declaration in the approved box.

(c)   Placing the ballot paper in a sealed ballot box.

All authentication must be completed before ballot papers are opened and counting starts or a completely different team must be earmarked for counting.

COUNTING

(1)   The sealed ballot box can now be opened and ballots counted.

(2)   Tally sheets should be supplied and tallying should take place as usual.

(3)   If there are any questionable or spoilt votes they are to be passed to the presiding officer whose ruling will be final.

(4)   After counting has been completed summary sheets and the scrutineers' report will be prepared.

PRECEDENT S

(Text Reference Chapter 16)

DRAFT MINUTES OF AN ANNUAL MEETING OF SHAREHOLDERS

ABC LIMITED

Minutes of the   Annual General Meeting held at

     on the   day of   19   at   p.m.

Present were: Mr   Chairman of the Board.

     Directors

In attendance: Auditors

     Secretary

     members as recorded in the attendance sheets
Nos.   to   inclusive.

1.   Notice: The secretary read the notice convening the meeting.

2.   Minutes: The minutes of the   annual meeting were read by the secretary.

3.   Auditors' report: Mr   the representative of the auditors read the auditors' report to the members of the company.

4.   Directors' report and accounts: The Chairman proposed that the report of the directors and the audited accounts for the year ended 19   now laid before the meeting be received and adopted and that the final dividend of   cents per share recommended therein be (approved or declared) payable on the   day of   19   to the holders of common shares registered at the close of business on the   day of 19 .

    Mr   seconded the motion.

    After replying to questions and receiving the comments of members the Chairman put the resolution to the meeting and after voting thereon declared it carried.

5.   Election of director retiring by rotation: Mr   proposed that Mr   the director retiring by rotation, and being eligible for re-election, be re-elected a director of the company to serve until the close of the second annual meeting next following his election. Mr   seconded the motion which was then put to the meeting and thereafter declared carried by the Chairman.

6.   Election of director to fill vacancy: The Chairman, upon the recommendation of the board, proposed that Y be elected a director of the company to fill the vacancy arising from the retirement of W. Mr seconded the motion which was then put to the meeting and after deliberation and voting thereon, was declared carried by the Chairman.

    Before consideration of the next item the chairman paid tribute to W for his considerable contribution to the management of the company. Mr then formally proposed a vote of appreciation which was carried by acclamation.

7.   Re-appointment of retiring auditors: Mr   proposed that Messrs   the retiring auditors be re-elected auditors of the company for a further year and that the directors be authorised to fix their remuneration.

Mr   seconded the resolution which was put to the meeting and declared carried.

8.   Question & Answer Period: The prescribed business of the meeting being concluded, the Chairman opened the meeting for a period of questions and answers on any matter pertaining to the company which may properly be discussed at an annual meeting. There then ensued a period of discussion and after responding to the questions as summarised in the company's 19   newsletter to shareholders, declared the meeting closed and invited shareholders to join the directors for refreshments. The proceedings terminated with a vote of thanks to the board, proposed by Mr   and carried by acclamation.

....
Chairman

....
Secretary

PRECEDENT T

(Text Reference Chapter 18)

MODEL GENERAL BY-LAW

General By-Law No. 1 for companies incorporated

under the Companies Act CAP 308 of the Laws of

Barbados or similar legislation

Note: This model by-law is drafted in accordance with the provisions of the Companies Act of Barbados. Where applicable, see table of comparative references.

THE COMPANIES ACT CAP 308

BY-LAW NO. 1

of

ABC LIMITED

TABLE OF CONTENTS

THE COMPANIES ACT CAP 308

BY-LAW NO. 1

A BY-LAW RELATING GENERALLY TO THE

CONDUCT OF THE AFFAIRS

OF

ABC LIMITED

This By-Law is hereby adopted as the general By-Law of: ABC Limited (hereinafter called the "Company").

1. INTERPRETATION

1. In this By-Law and all other by-laws of the Company, unless the context otherwise requires:

(a) "Act" means the Companies Act Cap 308 as from time to time amended and every statute substituted therefor and, in the case of such substitutions, any references in the By-Law of the Company to provisions of the Act shall be read as references to the substituted provisions therefor in the new statute or statutes;

(b) "Regulations" means any Regulations made under the Act, and every regulation substituted therefor and, in the case of such substitution, any references in the by-laws of the Company to provisions of the Regulations shall be read as references to the substituted provisions therefor in the new regulation;

(c) 'By-laws' means any By-Law of the Company from time to time in force;

(d)   All terms contained in the by-laws and defined in the Act or the Regulations shall have the meanings given to such terms in the Act or the Regulations; and

(e)   The singular includes the plural and the plural includes the singular; the masculine gender includes the feminine and neuter genders; the word "person" includes bodies corporate, companies, partnerships, syndicates, trusts and any association of persons; and the word "individual" means a natural person;

(f)   The headings used in the by-laws are inserted for reference purposes only and are not to be considered or taken into account in construing the terms or provisions thereof or to be deemed in any way to clarify, modify or explain the effect of any such terms or provisions.

2. REGISTERED OFFICE

2.1   The registered office of the Company shall be in Barbados at such address as the directors may fix from time to time by resolution.

2.2   The Company may also maintain other offices at such other places both within and outside Barbados as the directors may from time to time determine.

3. SEAL

3.1   The common seal of the Company shall be such as the directors may by resolution from time to time adopt.

3.2   The seal, an impression whereof is made on these by-laws is, at the date hereof declared to be the common seal of the Company

4. DIRECTORS

4.1   **Numbers and powers:** The number of directors, or the minimum and maximum number of directors, of the Company is set out in the articles of the Company. Subject to any unanimous shareholder agreement, the directors shall manage the business and affairs of the Company and may exercise all such powers and do all such acts and things as may be exercised or done by the Company and are not by the Act, the articles, the by-laws, any special resolution of the Company, a unanimous shareholder agreement or by statute expressly directed or required to be done in some other manner.

4.2 Eligibility for election: Except otherwise provided by the by-laws no person shall be eligible for election as a director at any general meeting unless either:

(a) he is recommended for election by the board of directors or

(b) not less than 10 clear days nor more than 50 clear days before the date appointed for the annual general meeting, written notice, executed by not less than the number of persons holding at least five percent of the issued and outstanding shares in the capital of the Company, has been given to the Company of the intention to propose such a person for election together with a letter of consent signed by that person confirming his willingness to be nominated and to serve as a director if elected.

4.3 Election: Subject to the articles or any unanimous shareholders' agreement and to by-laws, directors shall be elected by the shareholders on a show of hands unless a poll is demanded in which case such election shall be by ballot.

4.4 Tenure: Unless otherwise determined by the Articles or the by-laws or any resolution of the shareholders and unless his tenure is sooner determined, a director shall hold office from the close of the meeting from the date on which he is elected or appointed until the close of the third annual meeting of the shareholders next following or until his successor is elected or appointed, which ever shall first occur, but, if qualified, he shall be eligible for re-election.

4.4.1 A director who is also an officer shall cease to be a director when he ceases to be an officer, but shall be eligible for re-election if qualified.

4.4.2 A director shall cease to be a director:

(a) if he becomes bankrupt or compounds with his creditors or is declared insolvent;

(b) if he is found to be of unsound mind; or

(c) if by notice in writing to the Company he resigns his office. Any such resignation shall be effective at the time it is sent to the Company or at the time specified in the notice, whichever is later;

(d) if he absents himself from more than four consecutive meetings of the directors without leave;

(e) if he is otherwise prohibited under any legislation in Barbados from being a director of any company in Barbados.

4.4.3 The shareholders of the Company may, by ordinary resolution passed at a special meeting of the shareholders, remove any director from office and a vacancy created by the removal of a director may be filled at the meeting of the shareholders at which the director is removed.

4.5   Rotation of directors: At the annual general meeting held each year one-third or the number nearest thereto of the directors shall retire but shall be eligible for re-election if qualified. The retiring directors shall be those who have been longest in office, and, as between two or more who have been equal length of time the directors or director to retire shall, in default of agreement between them, be determined by lot. The length of time a director has been in office shall be computed from the date of commencement of his last unbroken service as a director. Directors retiring by rotation shall, if willing, continue in office until their places are filled.

4.6   Casual vacancy among the directors: Where there is any vacancy or vacancies among the directors, the directors then in office may exercise all of the powers of the directors so long as a quorum of the directors remains in office. Any vacancy occurring among the directors may be filled, for the remainder of the term, by such directors.

4.7 Leave of absence: The directors may, at their discretion, grant leave of absence to not more than one-third the number of directors in office at the same time. Such leave for any one director shall not normally exceed six months in any one calendar year.

4.8 Committee of directors: The directors may appoint from among their number a managing director or a committee of directors and subject to section 80(2) of the Act may delegate to the managing director or such committee any of the powers of the directors.

4.8.1 Audit committee: If any of the issued securities of the Company are part of a distribution to the public, or the number of shareholders for the time being exceeds twenty in number, the board of directors shall elect annually from among their number an audit committee to be composed of not fewer than three directors, a majority of whom are not officers or employees of the Company or any of its affiliates.

4.8.2 Each member of the audit committee shall serve during the pleasure of the board of directors and, in any event, only so long as he shall be a director. The directors may fill vacancies in the audit committee by election from among their number.

4.8.3 The audit committee shall have power to fix its quorum at not less than a majority of its members and to determine its own rules of procedure subject to any regulations imposed by the board of directors from time to time and to the following paragraph.

4.8.4 The auditor of the company is entitled to receive notice of every meeting of the audit committee and, at the expense of the Company, to attend and be heard thereat; and, if so requested by a member of the audit committee, shall attend every meeting of the committee held during the term of office of the auditor. The auditor of the Company or any member of the audit committee may call a meeting of the committee.

5. BORROWING POWERS OF DIRECTORS

5.1 The directors may from time to time:

(a) borrow money for the benefit of the Company upon the credit of the Company;

(b) issue, reissue, sell or pledge debentures of the Company

(c) subject to section 53 of the Act, give a guarantee on behalf of the Company to secure performance of an obligation of any person; and

(d) mortgage, charge, pledge or otherwise create a security interest in all or any property of the Company, owned or subsequently acquired, to secure any obligation of the Company.

5.2 Subject to the articles or any unanimous shareholders agreement the directors may from time to time by resolution delegate to any officer of the company all or any of the powers conferred on the directors by paragraph 5.1 hereof to the full extent thereof or such lesser extent as the directors may in any such resolution provide.

5.3 The powers conferred by paragraph 5.1 hereof shall be in supplement of and not in substitution for any powers to borrow money for the purposes of the Company possessed by its directors or officers independently of a borrowing by-law.

6. MEETINGS OF DIRECTORS

6.1 Place of meeting: Meetings of the directors and of any committee of the directors may be held within or outside Barbados.

6.2 Notice: Meetings of the directors may be convened from time to time at such place, on such day and at such time as the chairman of the board, or the deputy chairman of the board, or the president or vice president or managing director or any two directors may determine, and the secretary shall call meetings when directed or authorised by any of the said officers or by any two directors. Subject to subsection 76(1) of the Act the notice of any such meeting need not specify the purpose of or the business to be transacted at the meeting. Notice of any such meeting shall be served in the manner specified in paragraph 18.1 hereof not less than five days (exclusive of the day on which the notice is delivered or sent but inclusive of the day for which notice is given) before the meeting is to take place. A director may in any manner waive notice of the meeting of the directors and attendance of a director at a meeting of the directors shall constitute a waiver of notice of the meeting except where a director attends a meeting for the express purpose of objecting to the transaction of any business on the grounds that the meeting is not lawfully called.

6.2.1 It shall not be necessary to give notice of a meeting of the directors to a newly elected or appointed director for a meeting held immediately following the election of directors by the shareholders or the appointment to fill a vacancy among the directors.

6.2.2 Adjournment: Any meeting of directors or of any committee of directors may be adjourned from time to time by the chairman of the meeting with the consent of the meeting, to a fixed time and place and no notice of the time and place for the holding of the adjourned meeting need be given to any director if the time and place of the adjourned meeting is announced at the original meeting. Any adjourned meeting shall be duly constituted if held in accordance with the terms of the adjournment and a quorum is present thereat. The directors who formed a quorum at the original meeting are not required to form the quorum at the adjourned meeting. If there is no quorum present at the adjourned meeting, the original meeting shall be deemed to have terminated forthwith after its adjournment.

6.3 Quorum: A majority of the directors shall constitute a quorum for the transaction of any business at any meeting thereof and notwithstanding any vacancy among the directors, a quorum may exercise all the powers of the directors. No business shall be transacted at a meeting of directors unless a quorum is present.

6.3.1 Provided that all the directors agree, a director may participate in a meeting of directors or of any committee of the directors by means of such telephone or other communication facilities as permit all persons participating in the meeting to hear each other and a director participating in such meeting by such means is deemed to be present at that meeting.

6.4 Voting: Questions arising at any meeting of the directors shall be decided by a majority of votes. In case of an equality of votes the chairman of the meeting in addition to his original vote shall have a second or casting vote.

6.5 Resolution in lieu of meeting: Notwithstanding any of the foregoing provisions of this By-Law a resolution in writing signed by all the directors entitled to vote on that resolution at a meeting of the directors or any committee of the directors is as valid as if it had been passed as a meeting of the directors or any committee of the directors.

7. REMUNERATION OF DIRECTORS

7.1 The directors shall be paid such remuneration as the board may by resolution from time to time determine. Any remuneration so payable to a director who is also an officer or employee of the Company or who is counsel or attorney-at-law to the Company or otherwise serves it in a professional capacity shall, unless the board shall otherwise determine, be in addition to his salary as such officer or employee or to his professional fees as the case may be.

7.1.1 In addition, the board may by resolution from time to time award special remuneration out of the funds of the Company to any director who performs any special work or services for, or undertakes any special mission on behalf of the Company outside the work or services ordinarily required of a director of the Company, and the confirmation of any such resolution or resolutions by the shareholders shall not be required. The directors shall also be paid such sums in respect of their out-of-pocket expenses properly incurred in attending board, committee of shareholders' meetings or otherwise in respect of the performance by them of their duties as the board may determine.

8. SUBMISSION OF CONTRACTS OR TRANSACTIONS TO SHAREHOLDERS FOR APPROVAL

8.1 The directors in their discretion may submit any contract, act or transaction for approval or ratification at any annual meeting of the shareholders called for the purpose of considering the same and, subject to the provisions of section 89 of the Act, any such contract, act or transaction that is approved or ratified or confirmed by a resolution passed by a majority of the votes cast at any such meeting (unless any different or additional requirement is imposed by the Act or by the Company's articles or any other By-Law) shall be valid as though it had been approved, ratified or confirmed by every shareholder of the Company.

9. FOR THE PROTECTION OF DIRECTORS AND OFFICERS

9.1 No director or officer of the Company shall be liable to the Company for:

(a) the act, receipts, neglects or defaults of any other director or officer or employee or for joining in any receipt or act for conformity;

(b) any loss, damage or expense incurred by the Company through the insufficiency or deficiency of title to any property acquired by the Company or for or on behalf of the Company;

(c) the insufficiency or deficiency of any security in or upon which any of the moneys of or belonging to the Company shall be placed out or invested;

(d) any loss or damage arising from the bankruptcy, insolvency or tortuous act of any person, including any person with whom any moneys, securities or effects shall be lodged or deposited;

(e) any loss, conversion, misapplication or misappropriation of or any damage resulting from any dealings with any moneys, securities or other assets belonging to the Company;

(f) any other loss, damage or misfortune whatever which may happen in the execution of the duties of his respective office or trust or in relation thereto;

unless the same happens by or through his failure to exercise the powers and to discharge the duties of his office honestly and in good faith with a view to the best interests of the Company and in connection therewith to exercise the care, diligence and skill that a reasonably prudent person would exercise in comparable circumstances.

9.2 Nothing herein contained shall relieve a director or officer from the duty to act in accordance with the Act or regulations made thereunder or relieve him from liability for a breach thereof.

9.2.1 The directors for the time being of the Company shall not be under any duty or responsibility in respect of any contract, act or transaction whether or nor made, done or entered into in the name or on behalf of the Company, except such as are submitted to and authorised or approved by directors at a meeting of the directors or by a resolution in lieu of meeting pursuant to paragraph 6.5 of these systems.

9.2.2 If any director or officer of the Company is employed by or performs services for the Company otherwise than as a director or officer or is a member of a firm or a shareholder, director or officer of a body corporate which is employed by or performs services for the Company, the fact of his being a shareholder, director or officer of the Company shall not disentitle such director or officer or such firm or body corporate, as the case may be, from receiving proper remuneration for such services.

10. INDEMNITIES TO DIRECTORS AND OFFICERS

10.1 Subject to section 97 of the Act, except in respect of a action by or on behalf of the Company to obtain a judgement in its favour, the Company shall indemnify a director or officer of the Company, a former director or officer of the Company or a person who acts or acted at the Company's request as a director or officer of a body corporate in which the Company is or was a shareholder or creditor, and his personal representatives, against all costs, charges and expenses, including an amount paid to settle an action or satisfy a judgement, reasonably incurred by him in respect of any civil, criminal or administrative action or proceeding to which he is made a party by reason of being or having been a director or officer of such company, if

(a) he acted honestly and in good faith with a view to the best interests of the Company; and

(b) in the case of a criminal or administrative action or proceeding that is enforced by a monetary penalty, he had reasonable grounds for believing that his conduct was lawful.

11. OFFICERS

11.1 **Appointment:** The directors shall as often as may be required appoint a secretary and, if deemed advisable, may as often as may be required appoint any or all of the following officers: a chairman, a deputy chairman, a managing director, a president, one or more vice presidents, a treasurer, one or more assistant secretaries or one or more assistant treasurers. A director may be appointed to any office of the Company but none of the officers except the chairman, the deputy chairman, the managing director, the president and vice-president need be a director. Two or more of the aforesaid offices may be held by the same person. In case and whenever the same person holds the offices of secretary and treasurer he may but need not be known as the secretary-treasurer. The directors may from time to time appoint such other officers and agents as they deem necessary who shall have such authority and shall perform such duties as may from time to time be prescribed.

11.2 **Remuneration:** The remuneration of all officers appointed by the directors shall be determined from time to time by resolution of the directors. The fact that any officer or employee is a director or shareholder of the Company shall not disqualify him from receiving such remuneration as may be determined.

11.3 **Powers and duties:** All officers shall sign such contracts, documents or instruments in writing as require their respective signatures and shall respectively have and perform all powers and duties respectively as may from to time be assigned to them by the directors.

11.4 Delegation: In case of the absence or inability to act of any officer of the Company except a managing director or for any other reason that the directors may deem sufficient the directors may delegate all or any of the powers of such officer to any other officer or to any director.

11.5 Chairman: A chairman shall, when present, preside at all meetings of the directors, and any committee of the directors or the shareholders.

11.6 Deputy chairman: If the chairman is absent or is unable or refuses to act, the deputy chairman (if any) shall, when present, preside at all meetings of the directors, and any committee of the directors, or the shareholders.

11.7 Managing director: A managing director shall exercise such powers and have such authority as may be delegated to him by the directors in accordance with the provisions of section 80 of the Act.

11.8 President: A president shall be the chief executive officer of the Company. He shall be vested with and may exercise all the powers and shall perform all the duties of a chairman and deputy chairman if none be appointed or if the chairman and the deputy chairman are absent or are unable or refuse to act.

11.9 Vice President: A vice president or, if more than one, the vice presidents, in order of seniority, shall be vested with all the powers and shall perform all the duties of the president in the absence or inability or refusal to act of the president.

11.10 Secretary: The secretary shall give or cause to be given notices for all meetings of the directors, any committee of the directors and the shareholders when directed to do so and shall have charge of the minute books of the Company and, subject to the provisions of paragraphs 14.1 and 14.3 hereof, of the records (other than accounting records) referred to in section 170 of the Act. The secretary shall keep or cause to be kept a record of all the proceedings of all meetings held by the directors and by the shareholders of the Company and shall have charge of the seal of the Company, all of which he shall deliver as and when instructed or authorised by resolution of the board of directors and not otherwise. He shall perform such duties as are incident to his office or as may be required of him from time to time by the board of directors.

11.11 Treasurer: Subject to the provisions of any resolution of the directors, a treasurer shall have the care and custody of all funds and securities of the Company and shall deposit the same in the name of the Company in such bank or banks or with such other depository or depositories as the directors may direct. He shall keep or cause to be kept the accounting records referred to in section 172 of the Act. He may be required to give such bond for the faithful performance of his duties as the directors in their uncontrolled discretion may require but no director shall be liable for failure to require any such bond or for the insufficiency of any bond or for any loss by reason of the failure of the Company to receive any indemnity thereby provided.

11.12 Assistant secretary and assistant treasurer: The assistant secretary or, if more than one, the assistant secretaries in order of seniority, and the assistant treasurer or, if more than one, the assistant treasurers in order of seniority, shall respectively perform all the duties of the secretary and the treasurer, respectively, in the absence or inability or refusal to act of the secretary or the treasurer, as the case may be.

11.13 General manager or manager: The directors may from time to time appoint one or more general managers or managers and may delegate to him or them full power to manage and direct the business and affairs of the Company (except such matters and duties as by law or the articles must be transacted or performed by the directors or by the shareholders) and to employ and discharge agents and employees of the Company or may delegate to him or them any lesser authority. A general manager or manager shall conform to all lawful orders given to him by the directors of the Company and shall at all reasonable times give to the directors or the secretary or any of them all information they may require regarding the affairs of the Company. Any agent or employee appointed by the general manager or manager may be discharged by the directors.

11.14 Vacancies: If the office of any officer of the Company becomes vacant by reason of death, resignation, disqualification or otherwise, the directors by resolution shall, in the case of the secretary, and may, in the case of any other office, appoint a person to fill such vacancy.

12. SHAREHOLDERS' MEETINGS

12.1 Annual meeting: Subject to the provisions of section 105 of the Act, the annual meeting of the shareholders shall be held on such day in each year and at such time as the directors may by resolution determine at any place within Barbados or, if all the shareholders entitled to vote at such meeting so agree, outside Barbados.

12.2 Special Meeting: Special meetings of the shareholders may be convened by order of the chairman, the deputy chairman, the managing director, the president, a vice president or by the directors at any date and time and at any place within Barbados or, if all the shareholders entitled to vote as such meeting so agree, outside Barbados. Whenever and as soon as there is not a quorum of directors in office, it shall be the duty of the secretary to call a special meeting of shareholders to elect directors to fill the vacancies, provided that if such lack of quorum shall occur within a month before the regular time for the annual meeting, the secretary may call the annual meeting instead of a special meeting.

12.2.1 The directors shall, on the requisition of the holders of not less than five percent of the issued shares of the Company that carry a right to vote at the meeting requisitioned, forthwith convene a meeting of shareholders, and in the case of such requisition the following provisions shall have effect:

(1) The requisition must state the purpose of the meeting and must be signed by the requisitionists and deposited at the registered office, and may consist of several documents in like form each signed by one or more of the requisitionists.

(2) If the directors do not, within 21 days from the date of the requisition being so deposited, proceed to convene a meeting, the requisitionists or any of them may themselves convene the meeting, but any meeting so convened shall not be held after three months from the date of such deposit.

(3)   Unless subsection (3) of section 129 of the Act applies, the directors shall be deemed not to have duly convened the meeting if they do not give such notice as is required by the Act within 14 days from the deposit of the requisition.

(4)   Any meeting convened under this paragraph by the requisitionists shall be called as nearly as possible in the manner in which meetings are to be called pursuant to the by-laws and divisions E and F of part 1 of the Act.

(5)   A requisition by joint holders of shares must be signed by all such holders.

12.3 Notice: A printed, written or typewritten notice stating the day, hour and place of meeting shall be given by serving such notice on each shareholder entitled to vote at such meeting, on each director and on the auditor of the Company in the manner specified in paragraph 18.1 hereof, not less than 21 days or more than 50 days (in each case exclusive of the day for which the notice is delivered or sent and of the day for which notice is given) before the date of the meeting. Notice of a meeting at which special business is to be transacted shall state (a) the nature of that business in sufficient detail to permit the shareholder to form a reasoned judgement thereon, and (b) the text of any special resolution to be submitted to the meeting.

12.4 Waiver of notice: A shareholder and any other person entitled to attend a meeting of shareholders may in any manner waive notice of a meeting of shareholders and attendance of any such person at a meeting of shareholders shall constitute a waiver of notice of the meeting except where such person attends a meeting for the express purpose of objecting to the transaction of any business on the grounds that the meeting is not lawfully called.

12.5 Omission of notice: The accidental omission to give notice of any meeting or any irregularity in the notice of any meeting or the non receipt of any notice by any shareholder, director or the auditor of the Company shall not invalidate any resolution passed or any proceedings taken at any meeting of the shareholders.

12.6 Record dates: For the purpose of Section 106 (1) of the Act and for the purpose of determining shareholders who are entitled to receive notice of a meeting of shareholders of the Company, the directors of the Company may fix in advance a date as the record date for the determination of shareholders; but the record date must not precede by more than 50 days or by less than 21 days the date on which the meeting is to be held.

12.7 Votes: Every question submitted to any meeting of shareholders shall be decided in the first instance by a show of hands unless a person entitled to vote at the meeting has demanded a ballot and, if the articles so provide, in the case of an equality of votes the chairman of the meeting shall on a ballot have a casting vote in addition to any votes to which he may be otherwise entitled.

12.7.1 At every meeting at which he is entitled to vote, every shareholder, proxy holder or individual authorised to represent a shareholder who is present in person shall have one vote on a show of hands. Upon a ballot at which he is entitled to vote, every shareholder, proxy holder or individual authorised to represent a shareholder shall, subject to the articles, have one vote for every share held by the shareholder.

12.7.2 At any meeting, unless a ballot is demanded, a declaration by the chairman of the meeting that a resolution has been carried or carried unanimously or by a particular majority or lost or not carried by a particular majority shall be conclusive of the fact.

12.7.3 When the chairman, the deputy chairman, the president and the vice president are absent, the persons who are present and entitled to vote shall choose another director as chairman of the meeting; but if no director is present or all the directors present decline to take the chair, the persons who are present and entitled to vote shall choose one of their number to be chairman.

12.7.4 A poll may, either before or after any vote, by a show of hands, be demanded by any person entitled to vote at the meeting. If at any meeting a poll is demanded on the election of a chairman or on the question of adjournment it shall be taken forthwith without adjournment by ballot in such manner and either at once, later in the meeting or after adjournment as the chairman of the meeting directs. The result of a poll shall be deemed to be the resolution of the meeting at which the ballot was demanded. A demand for a poll may be withdrawn.

12.7.5 If two or more persons hold shares jointly, one of those holders present at a meeting of shareholders may, in the absence of the other, vote the shares; but if two or more of those persons are present, in person or by proxy vote, they must vote as one on the shares jointly held by them.

12.7.6 At each meeting of shareholders two or more scrutineers may be appointed by the chairman to serve at the meeting. Such scrutineers need not be shareholders of the Company.

12.8 Proxies: Votes at meetings of shareholders may be given either personally or by proxy or, in the case of a shareholder who is a body corporate or association, by an individual authorised by a resolution of the directors or governing body of that body corporate or association to represent it at meetings of shareholders of the Company.

12.8.1 A proxy shall be executed by the shareholder or his attorney authorised in writing and is valid only at the meeting in respect of which it is given or any adjournment thereof.

12.8.2 A person appointed by proxy need not be a shareholder.

12.8.3 Subject to the provisions of part v of the Regulations, a proxy may be in the following form:

I,   the undersigned being a shareholder of
hereby appoint   of   or failing
him,   of   , as my proxy to
attend and act for me and on my behalf at the
meeting of the shareholders of the said Company to be held on
the   day of   19 , and at any adjournment or
adjournments thereof in the same manner, to the same extent and
with the same powers as if the undersigned were present at the
said meeting or such adjournment or adjournments thereof.

Dated this   day of   19   .

....
Signature of shareholder

12.9 Adjournment: The chairman of any meeting may, with the consent of the meeting, adjourn the same from time to time to a fixed time and place and no notice of such adjournment need be given to the shareholders unless the meeting is adjourned by one or more adjournments for an aggregate of 30 days or more in which case notice of the adjourned meeting shall be given as for an original meeting. Any business that might have been brought before or dealt with at the original meeting in accordance with the notice calling the same may be brought before or dealt with at any adjourned meeting for which no notice is required.

12.10 Quorum: Subject to the Act, the articles and any unanimous shareholders' agreement and except in the case of a company having only one shareholder a quorum for the transaction of business at any meeting of the shareholders shall consist of two persons present in person, each being either a shareholder entitled to vote thereat, or a duly appointed proxy holder or representative of a shareholder so entitled and representing in aggregate at least 10 percent of the shares entitled to vote at the meeting. If a quorum is present at the opening of any meeting of the shareholders, the shareholders present or represented may proceed with the business of the meeting notwithstanding a quorum is not present throughout the meeting.

12.10.1 If a quorum is not present within 30 minutes of the time appointed for a meeting of shareholders, the meeting stands adjourned to the same day two weeks thereafter at the same time and place, and, if at the adjourned meeting a quorum is not present within 30 minutes of the appointed time, the shareholders present constitute a quorum.

12.10.2 When a company has only one shareholder, or has only one shareholder of any class or series of shares, that shareholder present in person or by proxy constitutes a meeting.

12.11 Resolution in lieu of meeting: Notwithstanding any of the foregoing provisions of this By-Law a resolution in writing signed by all the shareholders entitled to vote on that resolution at a meeting of the shareholders is, subject to section 128 of the Act, as valid as if it had been passed at a meeting of the shareholders.

13. SHARES

13.1 Allotment and issuance: Subject to the Act, the articles and any unanimous shareholders' agreement, shares in the capital of the Company may be allotted and issued by resolution of the directors at such times and on such terms and conditions and to such persons or class of persons as the directors determine.

13.2 Certificate: Share certificates and the form of share transfer shall (subject to section 181 of the Act) be in such form as the directors may by resolution approve and such certificates shall be signed by a chairman or a deputy chairman or a managing director or a president or a vice president and the secretary or an assistant secretary holding office at the time of signing.

13.2.1 The directors or any agent designated by the directors may in their or his discretion direct the issuance of a new share or other such certificate in lieu of and upon cancellation of a certificate that has been mutilated or in substitution for a certificate claimed to have been lost, destroyed or wrongfully taken, on payment of such reasonable fee and on such terms as to indemnity, reimbursement of expenses and evidence of loss and of title as the directors may from time to time prescribe, whether generally or in any particular case.

14. TRANSFERS OF SHARES AND DEBENTURES

14.1 Transfer agent: The directors may from time to time by resolution appoint, or remove, a transfer agent and/or registrar, who may but need not be the same person or Company, to keep the register of holders of shares or debentures of any class and the register of transfers of such shares and/or debentures.

14.2 Transfer: The shares or debentures of the Company may be transferred by a written instrument of transfer signed by the transferor or where the transferor is a body corporate by a duly authorised officer and naming the transferee.

14.3 Registers: Registers of shares and debentures issued by the Company shall be kept at the registered office of the Company or at such other place in Barbados as may from time to time designated by resolution of the directors.

14.4 Surrender of certificates: Subject to section 179 of the Act, no transfer of shares or debentures shall be registered unless or until the certificate representing the shares or debentures to be transferred has been surrendered for cancellation.

14.5 Shareholder indebted to the Company: If so provided in the articles, the Company has a lien on a share registered in the name of a shareholder or his personal representative for a debt of that shareholder to the Company. By way of enforcement of such lien the directors may refuse to permit the registration of a transfer of such share.

15. DIVIDENDS

15.1 Record date: The directors may by not less than 7 days notice given fix in advance a date preceding by not more than 30 days the date for the payment of any dividend or the date for the issue of the warrant or other evidence of right to subscribe for securities of the Company as a record date for the determination of the persons entitled to receive payment of such dividend or to receive the right to subscribe for such securities, as the case may be, and in every such case only such persons as shall be holders of record at the close of business on the date so fixed shall be entitled to receive payment of such dividend or to receive the right to subscribe for securities and to be issued the warrant or other evidence in respect of such, notwithstanding the transfer of any securities after any such record date is fixed.

15.2 The directors may from time to time by resolution declare and the Company may pay dividends on the issued and outstanding shares in the capital of the Company subject to the provisions (if any) of the articles and sections 51 and 52 of the Act.

15.2.1 In case several persons are registered as the joint holders of any shares, any one of such persons may give effectual receipts for all dividends and payments on account of dividends.

16. VOTING IN OTHER COMPANIES

16.1 All shares or debentures carrying voting rights in any other body corporate that are held from time to time by the Company may be voted at any and all meetings of shareholders, debenture holders (as the case may be) of such other body corporate and in such manner and by such person or persons as the directors of the Company shall from time to time determine. The officers of the Company may for and on behalf of the Company from time to time:

   (a)   execute and deliver proxies; and

   (b)   arrange for the issuance of voting certificates or other evidence of
            the right to vote;

in such names as they may determine without the necessity of a resolution or other action by the directors.

17. INFORMATION AVAILABLE TO SHAREHOLDERS

17.1 Except as provided by the Act, no shareholder shall be entitled to any information respecting any details or conduct of the Company's business which in the opinion of the directors it would be inexpedient in the interests of the Company to communicate to the public.

17.2 The directors may from time to time, subject to rights conferred by the Act, determine whether and to what extent and at what time and place and under what conditions or regulations the documents, books and registers and accounting records of the Company or any of them may be open to the inspection of shareholders and no shareholder shall have any right to inspect any document or book or register or accounting record of the Company except as conferred by statute or authorised by the directors or by a resolution of the shareholders.

18. NOTICES

18.1 **Method of giving notice:** Any notice or other document required by the Act, the Regulations, the articles or the by-laws to be sent to any shareholder, debenture holder, director or auditor may be delivered personally or sent by prepaid mail or cable or telex or facsimile transmission to any such person at his latest address as shown in the records of the Company or its transfer agent and to any such director at his latest address as shown in the records of the Company or in the latest notice filed under section 66 or 74 of the Act, and to the auditor at his business address.

18.2 **Waiver of notice:** Notice may be waived or the time for the notice may be waived or abridged at any time with the consent in writing of the person entitled thereto.

18.3 **Undelivered notices:** If a notice or document is sent to a shareholder or debenture holder by prepaid mail in accordance with this paragraph and the notice or document is returned on three consecutive occasions because the shareholder or debenture holder cannot be found, it shall not be necessary to send any further notices or documents to the shareholder or debenture holder until he informs the Company in writing of his new address.

18.4 **Shares and debentures registered in more than one name:** All notices or other documents with respect to any shares or debentures registered in more that one name shall be given to whichever of such persons is named first in the records of the Company and any notice or other document so given shall be sufficient notice or delivery to all the holders of such shares or debentures.

18.5 Persons becoming entitled by operation of law: Subject to section 184 of the Act, every person who by operation of law, transfer or by any other means whatsoever becomes entitled to any share is bound by every notice or other document in respect of such share that, previous to his name and address being entered in the records of the Company is duly given to the person from whom he derives his title to such share.

18.6 Deceased shareholders: Subject to section 184 of the Act, any notice or other document delivered or sent by prepaid mail, cable or telex or left at the address of any shareholder as the same appears in the records of the Company shall, notwithstanding that such shareholder is deceased, and whether or not the Company has notice of this death, be deemed to have been duly served in respect of the shares held by him (whether held solely or with any other person) until some other person entered in his stead in the records of the Company as the holder or one of the holders thereof and such service shall for all purposes be deemed a sufficient service of such notice or document on his personal representatives or on all persons, if any, interested with him in such shares.

18.7 Signature to notice: The signature of any director or officer of the Company to any notice or document to be given by the Company may be written, stamped, typewritten or printed or partly written, stamped, typewritten or printed.

18.8 Computation of time: Where a notice extending over a number of days or other period is required under any provisions of the articles or the by-laws the day of sending the notice shall, unless provided, not be counted in such number of days or other period.

18.9 Proof of service: Where a notice required under paragraph 18.1 hereof is delivered personally to the person to whom it is addressed or delivered to his address as mentioned in paragraph 18.1 hereof, service shall be deemed to be at the time of delivery of such notice.

18.9.1 Where such notice is sent by post, service of the notice shall be deemed to be effected 48 hours after posting if the notice was properly addressed and posted by prepaid mail.

18.9.2 Where the notice is sent by cable or telex or facsimile transmission, service is deemed to be effected on the date on which the notice is so sent.

18.9.3 A certificate of an officer of the Company in office at the time of the making of the certificate or of any transfer agent of shares of any class of the Company as to facts in relation to the delivery or sending of any notice shall be conclusive of those facts.

19. CHEQUES, DRAFTS AND NOTES

19.1 All cheques, drafts or orders for the payment of money and all notes and acceptances and bills of exchange shall be signed by such officers or persons and in such manner as the directors may from time to time designate by resolution.

20. EXECUTION OF INSTRUMENTS

20.1 Contracts, documents or instruments in writing requiring the signature of the Company may be signed by:

(a) The chairman, a deputy chairman, a managing director, a president or a vice president together with the secretary or the treasurer; or

(b) any two directors together with the secretary;

and all contracts, documents and instruments in writing so signed shall be binding upon the Company without any further authorization or formality. The directors shall have power from time to time by resolution to appoint any officer or person on behalf of the Company either to sign certificates for shares in the Company or contracts, documents and instruments in writing generally or to sign specific contracts, documents or instruments in writing.

20.1.1 The common seal of the Company may be affixed to contracts, documents and instruments in writing signed as aforesaid or by any officer or person specified in paragraph 20.1 hereof.

20.1.2 Subject to section 134 of the Act:

(a) a chairman, a deputy chairman, a managing director, a president or a vice president together with the secretary or the treasurer, or

(b) any two directors together with the secretary.

shall have authority to sign and execute (under the seal of the Company or otherwise) all instruments that may be necessary for the purpose of selling, assigning, transferring, exchanging, converting or conveying any such shares, stocks, bonds, debentures, rights, warrants or other securities.

21. SIGNATURES

21.1 The signature of a chairman, a deputy chairman, a managing director, a president, a vice president, the secretary, the treasurer, an assistant secretary or an assistant treasurer or any officer or person, appointed pursuant to paragraph 20 hereof by resolution of the directors, may be printed, engraved, lithographed or otherwise mechanically reproduced upon any certificate for shares in the Company or contract, document or instrument in writing, bond, debenture or other security of the Company executed or issued by or on behalf of the Company. Any document or instrument in writing on which the signature of any such officer or person is so reproduced shall be deemed to have been manually signed by such officer or person whose signature is so reproduced and shall be as valid to all intents an purposes as if such document or instrument in writing is delivered or issued.

22. FINANCIAL YEAR

22.1 The directors may from time to time by resolution establish the financial year of the Company.

23. GENERAL OVERRIDING PROVISION

23.1 Where in any matter the provisions of these by-laws are in conflict with the Articles of Incorporation, then the provisions as contained in the articles shall prevail.

ADOPTED by resolution of the directors on the   day of   19   and
approved by resolution of the shareholders on the   day of   19 .

(Seal)

Chairman - Board of Directors

Secretary

APPENDIX III

Compendium
of
legal cases

TABLE OF CASES

TEXT REFERENCE - FOOTNOTE 1

SALOMON v *SALOMON & CO.*

(1897) AC 22

Company - Private Company - One Man Company - Limited Liability

Facts

A trader sold a solvent business to a limited company with a nominal capital of 40,000 shares of £1 (sterling) each, the company's shareholders consisting only of the vendor, his wife, a daughter and four sons, who subscribed for one share each, all the terms of the sale being known to and approved by the shareholders.

In part payment of the purchase-money debentures forming a floating security were issued to the vendor. Twenty thousand shares were also issued to him and were paid out of the purchase money. These shares gave the vendor the power of outvoting the six other shareholders. No shares other than these 20,007 were ever issued. All the requirements of the Companies Act 1862 were complied with. The vendor was appointed managing director. However bad times came, the company was wound up, and after satisfying the debentures there was not enough to pay the ordinary creditors. The creditors claimed that there was no real difference between Mr Salomon and Salomon & Co. and that he ought not to enjoy the preference which the debentures conferred.

Held,

It is not contrary to the true intent and meaning of the Companies Act 1862, for a trader, in order to limit his liability and obtain the preference of a debenture-holder over other creditors, to sell his business to a limited company consisting only of himself and six members of his own family, the business being then solvent, all the terms of sale being known to and approved by the shareholders, and all the requirements of the Act being complied with.

TEXT REFERENCE - FOOTNOTE 6

AUSTRALIAN AUXILIARY STEAM CLIPPER CO.

V

MOUNSEY

(1958) 4 K & J 733

Directors Having Power By The Company's Articles Of Association To Do All Acts That The Company Might Do, Not Being Acts Which The Companies Acts Or The Company's Articles Of Association Required To Be Done By The Company In General Meeting

Facts

On the 4th of August 1857, at an extraordinary general meeting of the company duly held for that purpose, the following special resolution was duly passed: "That the company be empowered, by the issue of debentures, to raise such sum of money as it may require, not exceeding in whole 50,000 pounds sterling, and be authorised to assign the company's vessels to trustees to secure the due payment of the principal and interest to be secured thereby." This resolution was subsequently confirmed at another general meeting of the plaintiff company.

The act complained of is simply that the company having already mortgaged all their ships but one, and being in want of a further sum of money for the purposes of their business, the directors applied to the bankers, who were already creditors of the company to advance the requisite sum; and finding that the bankers required security as well for their past as for future advances, they make a mortgage to the trustee for the bank of one of the company's ships.

The contention of the plaintiffs was that the directors had no power to raise money by mortgaging the company's ships for such an act was not within the powers of a general meeting of the company. The company was established for the purpose of making profit, not by buying and selling ships, but by sailing them. The ships were the instruments by which the trade was to be carried on. The company owned them solely to enable them to carry on that trade; and it is impossible that any one partner or majority of partners can do an act which would bring the entire business of the company to an end.

The plaintiffs further contended that assuming a majority of the company had such a power and that such a power was ever delegated to the directors, it was, in fact, revoked by the resolution of August 1857. They averred that it is impossible to contend that the powers given by the resolution were cumulative; the object of the resolution was to limit the amount to be raised by the directors under the previous powers, whatever they might be; and after the resolution was passed, it was impossible for the directors to exercise their previous powers, except in the modified form prescribed by that resolution.

The questions are:

(1) What are the powers of the directors of the plaintiffs' company under their Memorandum and Articles of Association?

(2) Did the directors have power to borrow money upon the mortgage of one of the company's ships?

The learned trial judge held that he found no clause in the Articles of Association directing how money is to be raised for carrying on the business of the company. His Lordship further noted that nevertheless every concern of this description requires money from time to time, for the purpose of carrying it on; and nothing being specified as to borrowing, the measures to be adopted for that purpose are precisely those which it would fall within the province of the directors to take, until checked by some regulation of the company in general meeting, as prescribed by the 55th clause of the Articles of Association.

In resolving the issue the learned trial judge stated that the question comes to this: whether, because directors require a special power for such an extraordinary transaction as that of borrowing money on behalf of the company by means of debentures, they should therefore require a special power for such an ordinary transaction as that of borrowing money by the means which these directors have adopted.

Held,

The directors were at liberty to raise the money in question in the manner they had done until arrested by some regulation prescribed by the company in general meeting. There was no such arresting regulation in the instant case. There is no allegation of fraud, nor any allegation that the money which has been secured was not wanted for the purposes of the company.

TEXT REFERENCE - FOOTNOTE 9

MacDOUGALL v GARDINER

(1875) 1 Ch D 13

Authority Of Chairman Of Meeting - Motion For Adjournment - Mode Of Taking Votes

Facts

The Articles of Association of a company gave power to the chairman at any general meeting of the company, with the consent of the meeting, to adjourn the meeting and also provided for a poll if demanded by five shareholders.

At a general meeting of the company the adjournment of the meeting was moved, and on being put was declared by the chairman who was one of the directors to be carried. A poll was duly demanded, but the chairman ruled that there could not be a poll on the question of adjournment and left the room.

One of the shareholders filed a bill on behalf of himself and all other shareholders except the directors, against the directors and the company stating these facts and alleging that the course taken at the meeting was taken in collusion with the directors, with a view of stifling discussion, and that the directors were intending to carry out certain measures injurious to the company without submitting the terms to a general meeting; and praying for a declaration that the conduct of the chairman was illegal and improper, and for an injunction to restrain the directors from carrying out the proposed arrangement without submitting them to the shareholders for approval.

Held,

The action brought could not be sustained as it violated the rule laid down in *Mozley* v *Alston 1 Ph 790* and *Foss* v *Harbottle 2 Hare, 461* and asked the interference of the Court in the internal management of the company. Whether, on a motion for the adjournment of the meeting of shareholders, the votes ought to be taken according to the number of shareholders or of the shares they represent, quaere.

TEXT REFERENCE - FOOTNOTE 12

ROYAL BRITISH BANK v TURQUAND

(1856) 6 E & B 327

A Person Dealing With A Company Is Entitled To Assume, In The Absence Of Facts Putting Him On Inquiry, That There Has Been Due Compliance With All Matters Of Internal Management And Procedure Required By The Articles

Facts

Turquand was sued, as the official manager of a coal mining and railway company incorporated under the Act of 1844, on a bond for £2,000 (sterling) which had been given by the company to the plaintiff bank to secure its drawings on current account. The bond was given under the seal of the company and signed by two directors and the secretary, but the company alleged that under the terms of its registered deed of settlement (its corporate documents) the directors had power to borrow only such sums as had been authorised by a general resolution of the company, and in this case no sufficiently specific resolution had been passed.

The Court of Exchequer Chamber, affirming the judgement of the Court of Queen's Bench, held that even so the company was bound by the bond.

Held,

Jervis C.J.: . . . We may now take for granted that the dealings with these companies are not like dealings with other partnerships, and that the parties dealing with them are bound to read the statute and the deed of settlement. But they are not bound to do more. And the party here, on reading the deed of settlement, would find not a prohibition from borrowing, but a permission to do so on certain conditions. Finding that the authority might be made complete by a resolution, he would have a right to infer the fact of a resolution authorising that which on the face of the document appeared to be legitimately done.

TEXT REFERENCE - FOOTNOTE 13

The rule in FOSS v HARBOTTLE

FOSS v HARBOTTLE

(1843) 2 Hare 461

Facts

The bill in this case was brought by two shareholders in the Victoria Park Co. (incorporated by statute) against the company's five directors and others, alleging that the property of the company had been misapplied and wasted and certain mortgages improperly given over the company's property. It asked that the defendants should be accountable to the company and also sought the appointment of a receiver. The vice chancellor ruled, however, that it was incompetent for the plaintiffs to bring such proceedings, the sole right to do so being that of the company in its corporate character.

Held,

The Court will not ordinarily intervene in a matter which it is competent for the company to settle itself or, in the case of an irregularity, to ratify or condone by its own internal procedures. Where it is alleged that a wrong had been done to a company, prima facie the only proper plaintiff is the company itself.

TEXT REFERENCE - FOOTNOTE 21

BAMFORD AND ANOTHER v *BAMFORD AND OTHERS*

(1970) 1 Ch 212

Company - Director - Improper Exercise Of Power - Ratification By General Meeting

Facts

A public company had an authorised capital of 1,000,000 pounds sterling in five million shares of 4s. each, of which 4,500,000 shares were issued. By its articles the power to allot the unissued shares was vested in the directors of the company. A bid having been made by another company to take over its shares, the directors allotted the uninsured 500,000 shares at par to a principal distributor of the company's products.

The plaintiffs, two shareholders in the company, issued a writ against the defendants, the directors and the company, claiming, *inter alia* a declaration that the allotment was invalid on the ground that the directors in making the allotment had not acted bona fide, but from an improper motive in that their primary purpose was to block the take-over bid.

As a counter to that writ the directors gave notice convening a general meeting of the shareholders of the company to consider a resolution ratifying and approving the allotment. The plaintiffs issued a second writ claiming, *inter alia*, a declaration that any resolution passed at the proposed meeting was and would be a nullity. At the meeting the resolution was passed on a poll by the substantial majority of the votes of the shareholders, the allotted shares not being voted.

The two actions were then consolidated and by consent an order was made for the trial of the preliminary point of law whether, even if the directors had acted in bad faith as alleged by the plaintiffs, the allotment was not capable of being ratified and approved by a general meeting of the shareholders of the company.

Plowman J. held, that the allotment was capable of being thus ratified and being approved by a general meeting of the company's shareholders, and he therefore, held that since the allotment had been approved by the shareholders, it was thereby validated, even if the directors had acted from an improper motive in making the allotment. He accordingly dismissed the plaintiffs' action.

ON APPEAL BY THE PLAINTIFFS:

Held,

Dismissing the appeal, that even if the directors had acted in bad faith, and from an improper motive in making the allotment of the 500,000 unissued shares, any impropriety on their part could be and had been waived by a majority of the votes of the shareholders at the general meeting of the company; and, therefore, even if the allotment was initially voidable, it has been subsequently validated by the shareholders, and was thus a valid allotment.

TEXT REFERENCE - FOOTNOTE 22

BALL v *METAL INDUSTRIES LTD*

(1957) SLT 124

Facts

Shareholders had requisitioned an extraordinary general meeting for the appointment of three new directors. Subsequently, the chairman of the company gave notice of intention to move at the meeting a resolution for the removal from office of one of the existing directors

The court granted an injunction restraining the company from proceeding with this resolution.

Held,

Lord Hill Watson: The removal of a director from the board is a matter of very considerable importance. I think it would be quite wrong that a matter of this nature should be brought by a shareholder before an extraordinary general meeting of the company, convened pursuant to section 132, when the matter is not covered by the terms of the requisition, and when the directors have not convened the meeting . . . for that particular purpose.

TEXT REFERENCE - FOOTNOTES 24 & 75

CARRUTH v *IMPERIAL CHEMICAL INDUSTRIES LTD*

(1937) Ac 707

Company - Reduction Of Capital - Variation And Extingushment Of Rights - Separate Class Meeting

Facts

A company was incorporated under the Companies Acts 1908 to 1917 for the purpose of acquiring shares and other interests in various other companies. At the material date the capital of the Company consisted of £95,000,000 (sterling) divided into 22,727,000 preference shares of £1 (sterling) each, 43,767,355 ordinary shares of £1 (sterling) each 745,290 deferred shares of 10s. each, 15,133,000 unclassified shares of £1 (sterling) each and 5,000,000 unclassified shares of 10s. each.

By one of the Articles of Association the profits of the company were to be applied towards payment to the holders of cumulative preference shares of a dividend of 7 percent; secondly, towards payment to the ordinary shareholders of a non-cumulative dividend of 7 percent, and the balance towards payment of a further dividend on the ordinary shares and a dividend on the deferred shares, the dividends paid on the ordinary shares to be nearly as possible twice that paid on the deferred shares.

By clause 6 of its Memorandum of Association the company was empowered to increase its share capital and to issue shares of the original or new capital with any preference or priority over any other shares and to vary the regulations of the company as far as necessary to give effect to any such preference or priority "but so that unless provided by the terms of issue of any shares any preferential or other special rights for the time being annexed to any special class of shares shall not be affected or abrogated without the sanction of a separate meeting of the holders of shares of that class held pursuant to the articles registered herewith".

By Art. 36 the board of directors was authorised, with the sanction of the Court previously given, in a general meeting, to convert any paid up shares into stock.

By Art. 44 the company might by special resolution reduce its capital by paying off capital cancelling capital which had been lost or was unrepresented by available assets, reducing the liability on the shares "or otherwise as 'might' seem expedient, 'or it might' by ordinary resolution cancel shares not taken or agreed to be taken by any person".

By Art. 71 the holders of any class of shares might by an extraordinary resolution passed at a meeting consent on behalf of all the holders of shares of that class to the issue of shares ranking equally therewith, or having priority thereto, or to the abandonment of any preference or priority, or to the amalgamation into any one class of the shares or any two or more classes, or to any scheme for the reduction of the company's capital and generally consent to any alteration, transaction or arrangement which persons holding all the shares of that class could consent to.

By Art. 72 any meeting for the purpose of Art. 71 was to be convened and concluded in the same way as nearly as possible as an extraordinary meeting of the company. At any such meeting, immediately upon a declaration of a result of a show of hands, a poll might be demanded in writing by the chairman.

At the date of the meetings mentioned below there were 63,000 persons holding both ordinary and deferred shares, 65,000 holding ordinary shares only, and 17,000 holding deferred shares only.

In the year 1935 the board of directors came to the conclusion that in the best interests of the company the capital, namely £95,000,000 (sterling) divided as above stated, should be reduced and varied by amalgamating the said ordinary and deferred shares into one class of ordinary shares; and thereafter that the capital of the company should be increased to its former amount of £95,000,000 (sterling) by the creation of 5,434,141 additional unclassified shares of £1 (sterling) each.

A circular notice containing this proposal was sent to the shareholders together with: (1) a notice of an ordinary general meeting of the company to be held at a certain place on 1 May 1935, at 10.30 a.m., and three other notices of other meetings to be held at the same place on the same day, namely (2) a notice of an extraordinary general meeting of the company for the purpose of passing, among other resolutions, a resolution for the reduction of capital, (3) a notice of a separate meeting of the ordinary shareholders, and (4) a notice of a separate meeting of deferred shareholders; the last mentioned meetings to be held respectively at 10:45 a.m., 11:00 a.m. and 11:15 a.m. or as soon thereafter as the meeting immediately proceeding should be concluded, with the object of passing as an extraordinary resolution under no. 71 of the Articles of Association a resolution consenting to the reduction and reorganisation of the company's capital as above stated.

At the ordinary general meeting on 1 May 1935, 1,600 shareholders were present of whom 565 were holders of deferred shares.

Notice convening the extraordinary general meeting was taken as read. The chairman stated that the meeting would be followed by a meeting of the ordinary shareholders, and then by a meeting of deferred shareholders; that he proposed to make one speech and to take the vote at the two meetings to follow without any further speeches. He then explained to the general meeting the proposals of the board and the reasons for submitting those proposals and then moved the special resolutions which had been set out in the notice convening the meeting. These were put to the vote and defeated on a show of hands, whereupon the chairman demanded a poll, after which he adjourned the meeting to a later hour when the result of the poll would be declared.

The class meeting of the ordinary shareholders followed. The chairman moved as an extraordinary resolution the proposals set out in the notice convening the meeting. This was carried by the requisite majority, but the chairman gave notice demanding a poll to be taken forthwith, and adjourned the meeting to a later hour when the result of the poll would be declared.

The class meeting of the deferred shareholders followed, and the same course was pursued. On a show of hands the resolution was declared to have been negatived.

The chairman then demanded a poll to be taken forthwith, and adjourned the meeting to a later hour when the result of the poll would be declared.

The extraordinary general meeting and the class meetings of the ordinary and deferred shareholders were resumed at the hour named. The chairman then announced the results of the polls and declared that the resolutions had been duly carried as special resolutions and as extraordinary resolutions respectively.

The reduction of capital effected by the special resolution passed at the extraordinary general meeting having been confirmed by an order of the Court of Appeal affirming an order of the chancery division made upon by the petition of the company:

Held,

(1) that the meetings were duly summoned.

(2) that the reduction in capital was not *ultra vires.*

(3) that, although, if the question had been open, the meeting of the deferred shareholders was not a separate meeting, the resolution must for the purpose of the petition be taken to have been duly passed, as it had not been challenged by the appropriate procedure.

(Per Lord Russell of Killowen and Lord Maugham) that although prima facie a separate meeting of a class should be a meeting attended only by members of the class, the meeting of deferred shareholders having been properly convened, the presence of shareholders of another class was a matter relating to the conduct of the meeting, which lay in the hands of the chairman with the assent of those who were properly present and constituted the meeting, and, as no objection was taken at the meeting, those present must be taken to have assented to the meeting being so conducted, and the resolution was accordingly valid.

(4) that the scheme was fair to both classes of shareholders.

TEXT REFERENCE - FOOTNOTE 27

In Re RAILWAY SLEEPERS SUPPLY CO.

(1885) 29 CH D 204

Time - Computation Of - Interval - Company - Special Resolution - Companies Act 1862

Facts

At an extraordinary general meeting duly convened and held on the 25th of February 1885 a special resolution was passed for the reduction of the capital of the company, and at another extraordinary general meeting convened and held on the 11th of March, that resolution was confirmed.

On 17 March the company presented a petition asking for the sanction of the Court to the proposed reduction of capital, but doubts having been entertained whether the provisions of section 51 of the Act with regard to the interval of time to elapse between the meetings passing and confirming a special resolution had been complied with, this was a motion on behalf of certain respondents to the petition, who were also shareholders, that all further proceedings under the petition might be stayed on the ground that the resolution was not passed and confirmed as a special resolution at such interval as is required by the Act.

Held

The interval of not less than 14 days which under section 51 of the Companies Act 1862, is to elapse between the meetings passing and confirming a special resolution of a company is an interval of 14 clear days, exclusive of the respective days of the meeting, and therefore a special resolution for reduction of capital passed at a meeting held on the 25th of February 1885, and confirmed at a meeting held on the 11th of March 1885, was held to be bad.

Chitty, J.: The general rule of law in the computation of time is that fractions of a day are not reckoned . . . In the case before me only 13 clear days elapsed between the two meetings.

TEXT REFERENCE - FOOTNOTE 30

YOUNG v *LADIES' IMPERIAL CLUB LTD*

(1920) 2 KB 523

Expulsion Of Member - Resolution Of Committee - Validity - Construction Of Committee

Facts

One of the rules of a ladies' proprietary club provided that if the conduct of any member should, in the opinion of the executive committee, be injurious to the character and interests of the club, the committee should have power to suspend the member from the use of the club and to recommend her to resign, and if she did not do so within a certain time, the committee could erase her name from the list of members, provided that no member could be so suspended or recommended to resign unless a resolution to that effect should have been passed by a certain majority of the members of the committee actually present at a meeting specially convened for the purpose.

Acting under the rule the committee of the defendant club recommended the plaintiff, who was a member, to resign, and as she did not do so, the committee erased her name from the list of members.

The notice convening the meeting of the committee stated that the object of the meeting was "to report on and discuss the meeting concerning the plaintiff and Mrs L." and it was sent to each member of the committee except one, who had previously intimated to the chairman that she would be unable to attend meeting of the committee.

In an action for a declaration that the plaintiff was still a member of the club:

Held on appeal,

(1) That the omission to summon the absent member of the committee invalidated the proceedings of that body.

(2) That the notice did not state the object of the meeting with sufficient particularity.

On both these grounds the plaintiff was entitled to succeed.

TEXT REFERENCE - FOOTNOTE 31

In Re WEST CANADIAN COLLIERIES LTD

(1962) Ch 370

Company Meeting - Service Of Notice - Accidental Omission To Serve All Members - Table A Provision - Whether Meeting Duly Convened - Whether Resolution Duly Passed

Facts

By section 141 (5) of the Companies Act, 1948: "For the purposes of this section, notice of a meeting shall be deemed to be duly given and the meeting to be duly held when notice is given and the meeting held in manner provided by this Act or the articles."

The registrar of a company, in sending out to members of the company notices of a special resolution for the reduction of capital to be proposed at the annual general meeting, inadvertently omitted to send notices to nine of the members. Article 75 of the company's Articles of Association, which was identical in terms with Article 51 of Table A provided that the accidental omission to give notice of a meeting to, or the non-receipt of notice of a meeting by, any person entitled to receive notice should not invalidate the proceedings at that meeting. The special resolution was passed at the meeting.

On a petition for confirmation of the reduction of capital:

Held,

That the omission to give notice to the nine members was "accidental" within the meaning of Article 75 and that therefore, it did not invalidate the proceedings at that meeting. It must be implicit in Article 75 that a meeting, the proceedings of which were to be taken to be valid notwithstanding the omission to give notice to the members, was to have been deemed to be duly convened for the purposes of the articles, including in those purposes the manner of convening the meeting, since in the absence of such an implication there could be no meeting the proceedings of which could be validated by Article 75. Accordingly, the notice of the meeting had been duly given and the resolution duly passed for the purposes of section 141 of the Companies Act 1948, and the deduction would therefore be confirmed.

TEXT REFERENCE - FOOTNOTE 32

KAYE v *CROYDON TRAMWAYS CO.*

(1898) 1 Ch 358

Company - Ultra Vires - Sale Of Undertaking - Compensation To Directors - Notice Of Extraordinary Meeting - Sufficiency Of Notice

Facts

By a provisional agreement made between two companies for the sale of the undertaking of the one to the other, the purchasing company agreed to pay, in addition to the sum payable to the selling company, a substantial sum to the directors of the selling company as compensation for the loss of office, and the agreement was made conditional upon its adoption by the shareholders of the selling company. The notice convening the meeting of shareholders to consider the agreement described it simply as an agreement for the sale of an undertaking. The selling company was governed by the Companies Clauses Act, 1845:

Held on appeal,

(1) That the provision in favour of the directors did not render the agreement *ultra vires*, but

(2) That the notice, by reason of its omission to refer to this provision, did not fairly disclose the purpose for which the meeting was convened, and did not comply with section 71 of the Companies Clauses Act.

TEXT REFERENCE - FOOTNOTE 33

REX v *WAKE*

(1728) 1 Barn KB 80

What Persons Have Authority To Administer The Oath Of Office To The Members Of A Corporation - Points Of Consequence - Rule On Notice

Facts

On rule to show cause, why informations in the nature of quo warranto should not be filed against several defendants for exercising several offices in the borough of Southwold in Suffolk, several points of consequence fell into debate. Some difficulties fell into the debate about notice.

Held,

One rule the chief justice laid down was, that whenever notice is given for one particular business only, the body cannot go on to do other business, unless the whole body is met, and it is done by consent.

TEXT REFERENCE - FOOTNOTE 34

MACHELL v *NEVINSON*

(1724) 11 East 84

Facts

There was a by-law in the borough, by which the day of electing a mayor was fixed, but no certain day appeared to be settled for electing any other officer of the borough. The defendant summoned the members of the corporation to meet and elect a mayor. Nine of the common councilmen, which was a majority, sought to elect one J.S. into the office of common councilman and tendered a written proposal to the defendant, which he refused to accept. Upon the trial it was insisted for the defendant that the election of J.S. was void.

Held,

This is a void election.

Pratt Ch.J. cited the Carlisle case noting that the election was adjudged to be void, because the members were not assembled for that purpose.

Powis J. agreed.

Raymond J. agreed in all and said, if the members of a corporation are summoned to appear for one particular purpose, they cannot proceed to any other matter without the unanimous consent of the whole body. But if every member be present and consent, it is good; though they were not assembled for that very purpose.

TEXT REFERENCE - FOOTNOTE 35

In the matter of THE BRITISH SUGAR REFINING CO.

(1875) 3 K & J 408

Motions - Meetings - Calls - Validity

Facts

The 25th Section of the Joint Stock Companies Act 1856 enabling a shareholder whose name is without sufficient cause omitted to be entered into the company's register to apply by motion for an order that the register may be rectified, was not meant to give to every shareholder *ex debito justitiae* this summary remedy.

The object of that section was to enable the Court to avoid the inconvenience and injustice which occasionally arise from capricious or frivolous objections on the part of companies to complete the registration of their shareholders.

It was not intended by the Act that, in the event of there being a serious question to be tried, the matter should be disposed of summarily.

A resolution for a call may be good, though resolutions for calls for smaller sums had been previously negatived at the same meeting.

Whether, provided shareholders have had notice by means of circulars of a meeting for the purpose of making calls, a shareholder who has attended such meeting can object to calls made thereat, on the mere ground that the company omitted to advertise the meeting in any newspaper, as required by their deed of settlement — quaere.

But where a shareholder having so attended at such meeting had allowed others to pay their calls, and after lying by for six months assigned his shares:

Held,

The assignee could not, by motion under the 25th section of the Act, apply to have his name entered on the register, so long as the calls remained unpaid; and his motion was dismissed with costs.

TEXT REFERENCE - FOOTNOTE 40

NATIONAL DWELLING SOCIETY LTD v SYKES

(1894) 3 Ch 159

Company - General Meeting - Conduct And Power Of Chairman

Facts

The National Dwelling Society Ltd was incorporated under the Companies Act 1875. By its Articles of Association the business of the society was to be managed by a council, who were invested with all the usual powers of directors. The articles provided that a member of council should preside at every general meeting of the society; but if no such member should be present within 15 minutes after the time appointed for holding the meeting, the members present should choose one of their own number to preside at the meeting; that any ordinary meeting might, without any notice in that behalf, receive and or consider the accounts and the reports of the auditors and of council.

In April 1894, the council issued the accounts to the shareholders and a notice convening the annual general meeting for 12 April 1894. On the 4th of April a circular was sent out by a shareholder to all the other shareholders stating that a resolution would be proposed at the annual general meeting for the appointment of a committee of shareholders to investigate the affairs of the society, and asking for proxies.

When the annual meeting was held 35 shareholders attended. The chair was taken by the defendant Sykes, a member of council, who moved a resolution "that the report and accounts be received", and this was seconded by another member of council. An amendment to this resolution was moved and seconded by shareholders, that a committee of investigation be appointed to ascertain the position of the company. After some discussion the chairman ruled this amendment out of order, on the ground that no special notice had been given, and stated that on the advice of his solicitor he would refuse to put the amendment to the meeting. Ultimately the chairman put the original resolution, and took a show of hands upon it, and declared that there were 6 votes in favour of the motion, 28 votes against, and then said "I declare the resolution lost, and I dissolve the meeting", and left the chair and the room with his supporters, though the election of directors and auditors, which formed part of the business of the annual meeting, had not been disposed of.

The shareholders in the room afterwards unanimously elected another shareholder to be chairman, and unanimously passed certain resolutions.

Held,

It is the duty of a chairman to preserve order, conduct proceedings regularly, and take care that the sense of the meeting is properly ascertained with regard to any question before it; but he has no power to stop or adjourn a meeting at his own will; and if he purports to do so, it is competent for the meeting to resolve to go on with the business for which it has been convened, and to appoint another chairman for that object.

Per Chitty, J.: . . . The meeting is called for the particular purpose of the company. According to the constitution of the company, a certain officer has to preside. He presides with reference to the business which is there to be transacted. In my opinion, he cannot say, after the business has been opened, 'I will have no more to do with it; I will not let this meeting proceed; I will stop it; I declare the meeting dissolved, and I leave the chair.' In my opinion, that is not within his power. The meeting itself can resolve to go on with the business for which it has been convened, and appoint a chairman to conduct the business which the other chairman, forgetful of his duty or violating his duty, has tried to stop because the proceedings have taken a turn which he himself does not like.

TEXT REFERENCE - FOOTNOTE 48

SCOTT v *SCOTT*

(1942) 1 All ER 582

Companies - Directors - Powers - Financial Control Given To Directors By Articles - Attempted Control By Members In General Meeting - Resolution For Payment Of Instalments Of Preference Dividend Before Dividend Declared - Interim Dividend - Companies Act 1929

Facts

A private limited company by its Articles of Association incorporated under the Companies Act 1908. The plaintiffs were two members of the company and the defendants were the remaining members of the company. The plaintiffs contended that the following resolutions passed in general meeting were invalid:

(1) that a payment to be made to each preference shareholder of a weekly sum calculated on the paid up capital on the preference shares, by way of advance and without interest, until the payment of the dividend for the current year, the sums to be deducted from the dividend when declared and, if the dividend was insufficient, any deficiency was to be repaid to the company;

(2) that Messrs A.H. and Co. be instructed to investigate the financial affairs of the company for the last two financial years;

(3) that Messrs A.H. and Co. should be the auditors of the company for the ensuing year. On the supposition that this appointment was invalid, an application had been made to and granted by the Board of Trade for the appointment of auditors on the footing that the company had failed to appoint them. It was subsequently admitted by the plaintiffs that the appointment by the company was valid, and the defendants counterclaim for a declaration that the appointment by the Board of Trade was inoperative.

Held,

(1) The first and second resolutions were invalid as being attempts by the company in general meeting to usurp the powers of the financial direction of the company which under the articles rested solely in the hands of the directors.

(2) The defendants were entitled to a declaration that the auditors appointed by the company should be the sole auditors.

Case Editor's Note

Under the articles of this private company, as is the case with most such companies, the management of the business and the declaration of interim dividends were both assigned to the directors. That being so they were not subject to any control in that respect by the company in general meeting.

It is true that if the company in general meeting disapprove of the management or the declaration of an interim dividend, they could remove the directors, but the general meeting could not, as the articles stood, directly interfere by resolution with the management or the declaration of an interim dividend.

The division of authority is important even in the case of what may be called family companies; and having regard to the liability of directors as occupying a fiduciary position, it is necessary that it should be strictly observed.

TEXT REFERENCE - FOOTNOTES 49 & 74

Re HORBURY BRIDGE COAL, IRON, AND WAGGON CO.

(1879) 11 Ch D 109

Company - Voting - Show Of Hands - Poll

Facts

The articles of a company provided that at any general meeting, unless a poll was demanded by at least two members, a declaration by the chairman that the resolution was carried, and an entry to that effect in the minute book, should be sufficient evidence of the fact; that if a poll was demanded it should be taken in such manner as the chairman should direct; that at any general meeting the chairman should be entitled to a second or casting vote; and that every member should have one vote for every share.

At a meeting at which five members were present an extraordinary resolution to wind up the company was passed. K. was then proposed as liquidator, and an amendment was moved that M. should be appointed. Three of the five persons present voted for M., the other two holding a greater number of shares than the three, voted for K. A poll was not demanded:

Held by Bacon V.C., that K. was duly elected.

Held on appeal, that a poll not having been demanded, the voting was to be by show of hands, without counting shares, and that M., therefore, was duly elected.

TEXT REFERENCE - FOOTNOTE 51

QUIN & AXTEN LTD AND OTHERS
v
SALMON

(1909) AC 442

Company - Directors - Articles Of Association - Vesting Of Management In Directors - Control Of Management By Company In General Meeting

Facts

By the 75th article of association of a company the business of the company was to be managed by the directors, who might exercise all the powers of the company "subject to such regulations being not inconsistent with the provision of the articles as may be prescribed by the company in general meeting".

By the 80th article no resolution of a meeting of the directors having for its object the acquisition or letting of premises should be valid unless notice should have been given to each of the managing directors A. and B. and neither of them should have dissented therefrom.

The directors passed resolutions with the object of acquiring and letting premises, from which B. duly dissented, and resolutions to the same effect were passed at an extraordinary general meeting of the company by a simple majority of the shareholders:

Held

Upon the true construction of the articles, the resolutions of the company were inconsistent with the provisions of the articles and that the company must be restrained from acting upon them.

Lord Loreburn L.C. made the following observation:

"My Lords, I do not see any solid ground for complaint against the judgement of the Court of Appeal. The bargain made between shareholders is contained in Articles 75 and 80 of the Articles of Association, and it amounts for the purpose in hand to this, that the directors should manage the business; and the company, therefore, are not to manage the business unless there is provision to that effect."

TEXT REFERENCE - FOOTNOTE 52

Re IMPERIAL BANK OF CHINA INDIA, AND JAPAN

(1866) 1 Ch App 339

Company - Voluntary Winding Up - Amalgamation

Facts

At a general meeting of the shareholders of a banking company resolutions were passed for the voluntary winding up of the company, and appointment of liquidators and for confirming an agreement for the amalgamation of the company with the Bank of Hindustan upon certain terms therein specified. The liquidators proceeded to wind up the company upon the footing of the amalgamation. Two dissentient shareholders presented a petition impeaching the amalgamation on the grounds of the insufficiency of the notice convening the meeting and for other reasons; and praying

(1)   that the company might be wound up by an order of the Court;

(2)   that if not, the voluntary winding up might be considered under the supervision of the Court;

(3)   that the rights of the petitioners as against their co-contributories and the liquidators might be declared; or,

(4)   that they might be at liberty to use the names of the company and the liquidator in any proceedings they might be advised to take in reference to the winding up.

Order of the Master of the Rolls dismissing the petition discharged, and

Held

First, that in the absence of any distinct allegation in the petition of misconduct on the part of the liquidators, the Court would make no order for continuing the voluntary winding up under the supervision of the Court;

secondly that inasmuch as the voluntary winding up and the amalgamation were all one transaction, and the amalgamation could not be impeached in that jurisdiction, and in the absence of the Bank of Hindustan, the petition must stand over to permit the Petitioners to take proceedings to set aside the amalgamation; and

thirdly, that the Petitioners might be at liberty to use the names of the company and the liquidators in such proceedings, on giving an undertaking to abide by such order as to costs as this Court might make.

TEXT REFERENCE - FOOTNOTE 54

THOMPSON v HENDERSON'S TRANSVAAL ESTATES LTD

(1908) 1 CH 765

Company - Resolutions - Combination - Invalidity - Separate And Distinct - Invalidity Of One Not Affecting The Other

Facts

This action was brought by a shareholder in the defendant company, suing on behalf of himself and all other shareholders, for a declaration that a resolution passed at an extraordinary general meeting held on 24 January 1908, and confirmed at an extraordinary general meeting held on 6 March 1908, for the voluntary winding up of the company, and a resolution passed at the last minute meeting appointing the defendant J.D. Patullo liquidator of the company, were invalid and that the company was not in liquidation, and for an injunction restraining the defendant Patullo from acting as such liquidator and from dealing with the assets of the company. The defendant company in this action was the first-named defendant company in the action of Bisgood v Henderson's Transvaal Estates Ltd (1), and the object of this action was to determine the question whether the decision of the Court of Appeal in the preceding case, declaring the reconstruction scheme and the resolutions relating thereto invalid, affected the validity of the resolution of the voluntary winding up of the company.

The notice convening the meeting of 24 January 1908, was issued on January 16. It enclosed an outline of the scheme for reorganisation, and stated that the meeting was to be "held for the purpose of considering the enclosed reorganisation scheme and, if thought fit, passing the subjoined resolutions, with or without modification":

(1) "That the agreement proposed to be made between this company of the one part and Henderson's Transvaal Estates Limited (incorporated in Rhodesia) of the other part be and the same is hereby approved.

(2) "That the reorganisation scheme submitted to this meeting be and the same is hereby approved.

(3) "That it is desirable to wind up the company and accordingly that Henderson's Transvaal Estates Limited be wound up voluntarily.

(4) "That the liquidator of this company be and is hereby, as from the date of his appointment authorised and required to offer 1,770,386 of the shares of the new company of 10s. each (credited with 7s as paid up theron) receivable under the above agreement for sale referred to in the reorganisation scheme for distribution among the members of this company at the rate of one of such new shares for each share in the company held by such members.

(5) "That in the event of any of the said members not accepting their due proportion of such shares within a time to be limited in such offer (not less than 14 days), the liquidator be authorised and required to use his best endeavours to sell the shares not so accepted upon the best terms obtainable, and to hold any net proceeds of such sale upon trust to distribute the same among the non accepting members in proportion to the number of shares of this company held by them respectively."

The notice further stated that resolutions (4) and (5) would be submitted as extraordinary resolutions, and that resolution (3), if duly passed, would be submitted for confirmation as a special resolution at a subsequent extraordinary general meeting.

The first extraordinary general meeting referred to was held on 24 January but it was adjourned, first to 7 February and then 13 February with a view to the scheme being amended.

On the last mentioned date the resolutions mentioned in the notice were passed subject to certain modifications in the reorganisation scheme as shown in the preceding report; and at an extraordinary general meeting held on 6 March the winding up resolution was duly confirmed and the defendant Patullo was appointed liquidator.

The action came on 10 April 1908, upon motion for an injunction to restrain the defendant Patullo from acting as liquidator and from intermeddling with the assets of the company.

Held

The motion was refused and the plaintiff appealed. The appeal was heard on 11 April 1908

The appeal was dismissed.

Cozens-Hardy M.R.: . . . We have here an admitted fact that the resolution no. 3 was passed and confirmed by the requisite majority . . . It seems to me that there is no possible ground for impeaching that, subject to the question whether the notice to the shareholders was sufficient to cover such a transaction . . . On reading that notice it seems to me plain that the shareholders were told that five separate resolutions would be proposed at the meeting, any one of which they might pass without reference to any other of them, and that, in fact, it would not have been competent to the chairman, if nos. 1 and 2 had been rejected, to decline to put no. 3 to the meeting. In other words, I cannot bring myself to say that there is any ground for holding that these five resolutions are to be regarded as one, or as so interdependent that you cannot reject one and pass the others.

TEXT REFERENCE - FOOTNOTE 55

CLEVE v FINANCIAL CORPORATION

(1873) Lr 16 363

Company - Voluntary Winding Up For Purpose Of Invalid Amalgamation - Qualified Sanction - Compulsory Winding Up - Effect Upon Previous Voluntary Liquidation

Facts

Plaintiffs contracted to purchase shares in a company, and shortly afterwards the directors (with the plaintiffs' knowledge) agreed to amalgamate with another company. Resolutions (the validity of which were disputed on the grounds of insufficient notice) were passed and confirmed at two successive meetings, for amalgamation, and that "for enabling the said agreement and the amalgamation thereby agreed on to be carried into effect", the company should be wound up voluntarily.

Immediately before the confirmation meeting one of the plaintiffs agreed to sell his shares; and the other plaintiff having purchased as agent merely, transfers from the two plaintiffs, one to his principal the other to his purchaser were executed; but, upon the transfers being presented for registration, the liquidators refused to register, except on the terms of the plaintiffs executing deeds poll, whereby they should agree to guarantee to the liquidators payment by the transferees of all calls. Plaintiffs accordingly executed the deeds.

Afterwards the company were ordered to be wound up compulsorily; and by a decree of the Court, the agreement for amalgamation and consequent resolutions were held to be *ultra vires* and not binding on any dissentient member of the company.

Actions having been commenced by the official liquidators against the plaintiff upon the guarantee deeds, bills were filed alleging that the liquidation was invalid, and that the deeds were obtained without consideration, and by misrepresentation and concealment, and were null and void, and ought to be cancelled:

Held,

The liquidation resolution was valid, and that the charges of want of consideration, misrepresentation, and concealment failed; and bills dismissed with costs.

Observations on the powers of voluntary liquidators, and on the effect of proceedings under a voluntary winding up, when followed by a compulsory order were then made.

TEXT REFERENCE - FOOTNOTE 56

Re NOWICH YARN Co. Ex Parte BIGNOLD

(1856) 22 Beavan 143

Facts

This case came before the court on appeal from the Master's certificate, regulating the rights as between the directors of the company and their co-proprietors.

One of the issues which required determination arose from an allegation of the proprietors that full disclosure of the state and circumstances of the company was not made to the proprietors generally or to any general meeting . . . and that even if such disclosure had been made, it lay not within the competency of a general meeting to bind the absent proprietors in such matters: that all the proprietors of the company were bound by the provisions of the deed, that they relied upon the contract thereby entered into, and that no majority could bind a minority in such matters.

Held

On the point in question: Absent members of a company are affected by the information furnished by the directors at a general meeting, and bound by the proceedings, as to matters within its competence.

TEXT REFERENCE - FOOTNOTES 57 & 100

BETTS & CO. LTD v MacNAGHTEN

(1910) 1 Ch 430

Company - General Meeting - Special Business - Minutes - Notice - Sufficiency - Resolutions - Alterations Or Amendments

Facts

The notice of the annual general meeting of a company stated that such meeting was for the purpose of considering and, if thought fit, passing certain resolutions, "with such amendments and alterations as shall be determined upon at such meeting". One of such resolutions was that three named gentlemen should be appointed directors. According to the minutes of the general meeting the minutes were taken as read, and the three named gentlemen were proposed as directors.

An amendment was, however, carried that in addition to these three gentlemen, two additional named directors should be appointed.

Under the Articles of Association of the company it was provided: (54) that the notice of an ordinary general meeting at which special business was to be transacted should specify the general nature of such special business; (69) that the number of directors should be no more than seven or less than three; (62) that the signed minutes of the proceedings at a general meeting should be conclusive evidence that the proceedings were regular.

Upon motion by the company for an injunction to restrain the two additional directors from acting:

Held,

That the Court was entitled to look at the notice convening the meeting as part of the *res gestae*, to see if the proceedings were regular.

Held, further, that having regard to the terms of the Articles of Association, the business transacted at the meeting was within the scope of the special notice indicated in the notice.

TEXT REFERENCE - FOOTNOTE 58

In Re MOORGATE MERCANTILE HOLDINGS LTD

(1980) 1 Wlr 227

Company - Meeting - Special Resolution - Purported Amendment At Extraordinary General Meeting - Whether Special Resolution Validly Passed

Facts

Until 12 March 1979, the company's share premium account had stood at 1,356,579.31 pounds sterling reflecting premiums received on the issue of shares as consideration for the acquisition of subsidiaries prior to 1973, less a scrip issue in 1973 and certain issues expenses.

On 12 March 1979, a small issue of shares was made upon the acquisition of the outstanding minority interests in a subsidiary which resulted in increasing the amount of share premium account by 321.17 pounds sterling.

The company's articles of association empowered the company to reduce its share premium account and on the basis that the share premium account had been lost, notices, accompanied by an explanatory circular, were sent out to members, convening an extraordinary meeting for 26 April 1979, at which a special resolution was to be proposed: "that the share premium account of the company amounting to 1,356,900.48 pounds sterling be cancelled". The draftsman of the resolution was unaware of the recent issue which had resulted in the share premium of 321.17 pounds sterling. At the extraordinary general meeting, the chairman of the company, having received advice that the 321.71 pounds sterling from the recent share issue could not be regarded as having been lost, proposed "that the share premium account of the company amounting to 1,356,900.48 pounds sterling be reduced to 321.17 pounds sterling". That amended version of the resolution was passed on a show of hands and no poll was demanded.On the company's petition for an order confirming the reduction of the share premium account:

Held,

That for a special resolution to be valid under 141 (2) of the Companies Act 1948, the notice of the meeting had to specify either the entire text or the entire substance of the resolution which was intended to be proposed as a special resolution; that the resolution as passed be the same resolution as that identified in the notice circulated to members, although grammatical or clerical errors might be corrected provided that there was no departure from the substance of the proposed resolution; that the resolution passed at the extraordinary general meeting of 26 April 1979 was not the same either in form or in substance as the text that had been circulated to shareholders, and, accordingly, it was not validly passed and the court had no jurisdiction to confirm the reduction of the share premium account.

TEXT REFERENCE - FOOTNOTE 64

NORTH-WEST TRANSPORTATION CO. v BEATTY

(1887) 12 App Las 589

(Privy Council)

Sale By Director To Company - Ratification At General Meeting - Vendor's Right To Vote As Shareholder

Facts

This was an appeal from the Supreme Court of Canada reversing a decree of the Court of Appeal, Ontario and affirming a decree of the Ontario Chancery Division which set aside the sale in question by the appellant Beatty to the company.

The main question in the case was whether a shareholder in a company is entitled to vote at a meeting of the company on a question in which he is personally interested.

The judgement of the first court was to the effect:

"All suspicions of fraud or unfair dealings may be discarded and the question resolves itself into one of purely equitable law, that is, whether the purchase from the director having been submitted to the body of the shareholders and adopted by a majority of votes it is open for the dissident plaintiff to undo the sale by the intervention of the court. One important element to be considered is that the majority was secured by reason of the votes upon the shares held by the vendor without which the result would have been adverse to the purchase." The judgement proceeded "upon the ground that the vendor's fiduciary position incapacitates him from coercing the minority by means of a majority secured by his own vote in his own favour, without regard to the fairness or unfairness of the transaction. There has been no valid ratification by the company."

The Court of Appeal, agreed with the court below in holding that the case was free from imputation of fraud or collusion and unanimously reversed the decree. They held in effect that there was no principle of equity to prevent the defendant Beatty exercising his right as a shareholder and voting as a shareholder in favour of the purchase, although he held a personal interest in such purchase.

The Supreme Court of Canada unanimously reversed this decree and restored that of the first court.

The Chief Justice held that the defendant Beatty by reason of his position as a director of the company could not vote at the shareholders' meeting for the confirmation of the by-law authorising a sale from himself to the company.

Held,

That the vendor was entitled to exercise his voting power as a shareholder in general meeting to ratify such contract; his doing so could not be deemed oppressive by reason of his individually possessing a majority of votes, acquired in a manner authorised by the constitution of the company.

Sir Richard Baggallay: Unless some provision to the contrary is to be found in the charter or other instrument by which the company is incorporated, the resolution of a majority of the shareholders, duly convened, upon any question with which the company is legally competent to deal, is binding upon the minority, and consequently upon the company, and every shareholder has a perfect right to vote upon any such question, although he may have a personal interest in the subject matter opposed to, or different from, the general or particular interest of the company.

On the other hand a director of a company is precluded from dealing, on behalf of the company, with himself, and from entering into engagements in which he has a personal interest conflicting, or which possibly may conflict, with the interest of those whom he is bound by fiduciary duty to protect; and this rule is as applicable to the case of one of several directors as to a managing or sole director. Any such dealing or engagement may however be affirmed or adopted by the company, provided such affirmance or adoption is not brought about by unfair or improper means, and is not illegal or fraudulent or oppressive towards those shareholders who oppose it.

The material facts of the case were not in dispute.

Their Lordships allowed the appeal and discharged the order of the Supreme Court of Canada.

TEXT REFERENCE - FOOTNOTE 65

EAST PANT MINING CO. v *MERRYWEATHER*

(1864) 2 H & M 254

Facts

The question at issue was whether the voting at the meeting was proper. The majority of the persons present negatived the amendment, but upon a poll being demanded upon the said amendment, proxies were admitted and there was a majority for the amendment if Merryweather's votes were counted, but not otherwise. The issue therefore resolved itself into whether Merryweather's claim to vote on the question was valid; Merryweather being a director of the company who wanted to sell his interest in a lease to the company.

Held,

A prohibition in a company's articles against a director's voting in respect of any matter in which he has an interest does not preclude him from voting as a shareholder at a general meeting in respect of any such matter.

TEXT REFERENCE - FOOTNOTE 68

McLAREN v *THOMPSON*

(1917) 2 Ch 261

Company - Meeting - Voting By Proxy - Proxies To Be Lodged Two Days Before Meeting - Adjourned Meeting - Proxies Lodged After Date Of Original Meeting But Before Adjourned Meeting - Invalidity

Facts

The question in this case was whether certain instruments of proxy which had been given and lodged with the City of Chicago Brewing and Malting Co. Ltd, at a later date than that originally fixed for the general meeting of the company, and at which that meeting was commenced, but before the date to which the meeting was adjourned, were duly lodged within the meaning of the company's articles so as to entitle the persons named in the instruments of proxy to vote at the adjourned meeting. Astbury J. held that the proxies were invalid. From this decision the plaintiffs appealed.

Held

Where the articles of a company provide that "The instruments appointing a proxy shall be deposited at the registered office of the company not less than two clear days before the day for holding the meeting at which the person named in such instrument proposes to vote." Proxies lodged after the date of an original meeting, but more than two days before the day fixed for an adjournment thereof, cannot be used for the purpose of voting at the adjourned meeting.

TEXT REFERENCE - FOOTNOTE 69

SHAW v *TATI CONCESSIONS LTD*

(1913) 1 Ch 292

Company - Meeting - Poll - Adjournment - Proxies To Be Lodged Forty-Eight Hours Before Meeting Or Adjourned Meeting - Poll Fixed For Future Date - No Adjournment Of Meeting - Validity Of Proxies Lodged Forty-Eight Hours Before Poll

Facts

A poll demanded at a company meeting was directed to be taken at a future date, but the meeting itself was not adjourned:

Held

That the mere postponement of the poll was not an adjournment ad hoc of the meeting within the meaning of an article allowing the lodgement of proxies 48 hours before a meeting "or adjourned meeting", but the original meeting continued for the purpose of the poll, and no fresh proxies could be lodged.

TEXT REFERENCE - FOOTNOTE 71

COUSINS v INTERNATIONAL BRICK CO. LTD

(1931) 2 Ch 90

Company - Shareholder - Voting - Proxy Given Not Properly Revoked - Right Of Shareholder To Attend Meeting And Vote In Person - Companies Act 1929

Facts

A company's Articles of Association provided (Art. 74), that votes might be given personally or by proxy; (Art. 75) that the instrument appointing a proxy should be deposited at the office not less than forty-eight hours before the time of holding the meeting at which it was to be used; and (Art. 76) that "a vote given in accordance with the terms of an instrument of proxy will be valid notwithstanding the previous . . . revocation of the proxy . . . provided no intimation in writing of the . . . revocation . . . shall have been received at the office before the meeting".

Held,

That in a case where a proxy had not been validly revoked in accordance with Art. 76, the shareholder who had given the proxy was free to attend at the meeting and vote personally; and that, when he had done this, the vote tendered by the proxy was properly rejected.

Motion,

The International Brick Co. Ltd., was incorporated under the Companies Acts in February, 1928 . . .

The Articles of Association (so far as material) provided as follows:-

"71. Every member shall upon a show of hands have one vote and upon a poll one vote in respect of each preferred ordinary share and one vote in respect of each five deferred shares held by him."

"74. Votes may be given personally or by proxy . . ."

"75. The instrument appointing a proxy, together with the power of attorney (if any) under which it is signed, shall be deposited at the office not less than forty-eight hours before the time for holding the meeting at which the person named in such instrument proposes to vote."

"76. A vote given in accordance with the terms of an instrument of proxy will be valid notwithstanding the previous death of the principal or revocation of the proxy or transfer of the share in respect of which the vote is given, provided no intimation in writing of the death, revocation or transfer shall have been received at the office before the meeting."

On October 10, 1930, the report of the company and its audited accounts were issued, together with a notice convening the second annual general meeting of the company for October 20, 1930. The report of the directors stated that under the articles of association the defendant C. W. R. Pantlin, the chairman of the company, retired and being eligible offered himself for re-election. The plaintiff Henry Cousins being desirous that Mr. Pantlin should not be re-elected but that the plaintiff Henry George Talbot Carr should be elected a director in his stead, secured proxies in favour of the plaintiff Carr, representing 102,138 votes, and these proxies were duly lodged at the registered office of the company as required by Art 75 . . . The resolution to re-elect the defendant Pantlin was then put to the meeting and declared carried on a show of hands. A poll was thereupon demanded and the meeting was adjourned till November 3.

. . . At the meeting Mr. Hopkins, another director, took the chair, and on the taking of the poll, Mr. Cousins, besides his own votes, which numbered 900, tendered the 102,198 votes for which he held proxies. Shareholders who were present and voted against the resolution represented 96,604 votes . . . The chairman announced that the number of votes cast for an amendment was 52,081 and against 96,604, and that the amendment was therefore defeated. The defendant Pantlin was then elected to be a director on a show of hands. The explanation of the chairman's announcement was that shareholders whose votes amounted to 11,396 had purported by notice in writing to revoke the proxies given to Mr

Cousins, and had voted personally against the amendment; that shareholders whose votes amounted to 96,991 had purported by notice in writing to revoke the proxies given to Mr Cousins; and that shareholders whose votes amounted to 3,700 had without giving notice to revoke their proxies voted personally at the meeting against the amendment. The proxies given by all the shareholders had therefore been rejected, and where shareholders who had given proxies had voted personally their personal votes were accepted. It was admitted that the notices purporting to withdraw proxies were all given between October 20 and November 3.

On November 6, 1930, the plaintiffs issued a writ claiming a declaration that upon the poll of the shareholders held upon November 3, 1930, votes tendered by the plaintiff Cousins as proxy had been wrongfully disallowed and that the plaintiff Carr was elected as a director in the place of the defendant Pantlin; and injunction restraining the defendant company and the defendants from preventing or interfering with the plaintiff Carr's acting or attending as a director of the defendant company. On the same day notice of motion was issued claiming interim injunctions in the above terms.

Luxmoore J. The sole question to be determined on the motion and in the action is whether certain votes were properly rejected or improperly accepted on the taking of the poll referred to in the writ. There is no dispute with regard to the material facts. [His Lordship then stated the facts.] The plaintiff Cousins claims that the admission of the 11,396 votes as voting against the amendment, and the rejection of the proxies in respect of these 11,396 votes as well as those for the 36,991 votes, were respectively invalid and improper, and he further claims that if no improper admission or rejection had been made, the amendment would in fact have been carried. The answer to the question whether his claims are correct or not depends on the construction of the material articles contained in the company's articles of association. The material articles to consider are those which relate to the giving of proxies, and the user and revocation thereof, for it is admitted that the right to vote by proxy is a contractual right depending entirely on the terms of the contract conferring that right.

The articles relating to proxies are articles 74, 75 and 76. The first part of article 74 confers on the members the right to vote either personally or by proxy. The rest of that article deals with the form of proxy and the personality of the person who may be appointed. Nothing turns on this, for it is admitted that the proxies originally given to the plaintiff Cousins are unimpeachable in form. [His Lordship then read articles 75 and 76]. Now it is said that a proxy once given for a particular meeting cannot be revoked except by a notice in writing which is received at the office before the meeting; that the meeting of November 3 was an adjourned meeting, and therefore in law a continuation of the meeting of October 20, and that as none of the proxies given to the plaintiff Cousins were in fact revoked before the meeting of October 20, the plaintiff Cousins was entitled to use all of the proxies given to him, even if the members who had given such proxies attended the adjourned meeting and tendered their votes in person.

. . . The proxy is merely the agent of the shareholder who appoints him/her. As between himself and the proxy he can determine the agency and the agent is not entitled to vote if the agency is in fact determined.

Shareholders, as between him/herself and the company, has the option of voting in person or by proxy. If shareeholders vote in person quite obviously cannot also vote by proxy. As between himself and the company if he allows the proxy to vote, and the company accepts that vote, he cannot afterwards claim to vote personally. But this is not what happened in the present cast. The shareholders in question and their proxies tendered votes in respect of the same shares, and it was not until the votes came to be considered that the company had to determine which of the votes had to be accepted. A company finding votes cast in respect of the same shares is bound to consider which votes are to be accepted and where the votes of a shareholder are cast by that shareholder himself in a manner justified by the articles, I think the company is, in the absence of any particular circumstances, bound to accept those votes, notwithstanding that a person who has been validly appointed as proxy in respect of the same shares has also purported to vote.

The right of the shareholder to vote in person must, in my judgment, and in the absence of any special contract between himself and the company expressly precluding the right to vote in person where a proxy has been validly given, be paramount to the right of the proxy to vote in respect of the shares in question.

There is, in my judgment, no contract binding the shareholder vis-à-vis the company to exercise the option to vote either in person or by proxy at any time before the actual moment when the vote is to be given. The giving of the proxy may obviously, as between the shareholder and his proxy, be conditional on the shareholder being prevented from attending the meeting and voting at it in person.

I must accordingly refuse the relief sought in the motion.

The plaintiffs appealed. The appeal was heard on January 12, 1931.

Lord Hanworth M.R. In this case we have to determine a point as to voting in a company. It is a point arising under the articles of association of the company. Luxmoore J. has stated the facts fully and sufficiently and I do not desire to make any alteration or add to his statement. The question we have to determine is whether at the adjourned meeting of the company on November 3, 1930, the chairman was right in counting 11,396 votes as cast against an amendment then put or whether they should be counted on the other side in view of the proxies that had been given.

. . . But the point we have to determine is whether a shareholder who has given a proxy is bound by it, when it has been given some days before and not been determined in accordance with the articles, so as to prevent his giving a valid vote at the meeting when he attends personally. Has he or has he not instituted a system under which his vote must be given by proxy?

. . . In the present case due steps were taken to give valid proxies to be effective at the meeting of October 20 and any adjournment thereof and there was no effective attempt to revoke them in accordance with article 76. Therefore at the date of the adjourned meeting there were in the hands of the proxy the 11,396 votes in question, which in the ordinary case would have been valid and counted when tendered. But the persons who had given those proxies were present, and instead of allowing their proxy to hand in the votes, they determined to exercise their alternative right and vote personally, and the votes cast by them personally were in a contrary sense to what they would have been if the proxies had been accepted.

It is said that by giving proxies they were prevented from attending personally and voting, that having set in motion the proxy provisions they had disabled themselves from voting personally. The articles might be so drawn as to produce that result, but when I examine these three articles I find no such exclusion of the personal right of the shareholder to vote . . . It follows that the personal right to vote is not taken away and, indeed, it would be strange if a person in the position of an agent could say to his principal: "You have entrusted to me a power which I will not allow to pass back to you, although you demand the right to exercise it."

In the absence of clear words taking away the shareholder's personal right to vote after he has put in force the proxy system, that personal right remains and the shareholder is able to attend and give his own vote according to his own volition and the proxy has no right to prevent it.

For these reasons, in addition to those given in the clear judgment of Luxmoore J., with which I agree, the appeal must be dismissed.

Lawrence L. J. In my judgment that article does not prevent the shareholder from exercising his right to vote in person. Every proxy is subject to an implied condition that it should only be used if the shareholder is unable or finds it inconvenient to attend the meeting. The proxy is merely the agent of the shareholder, and as between himself and his principal is not entitled to act contrary to the instructions of the latter.

Romer L. J. I am of the same opinion. The decision of Luxmoore J. seems to me to be summed up in these four lines of his judgment: "There is, in my judgment, no contract binding the shareholder vis-à-vis the company to exercise the option to vote either in person or by proxy at any time before the actual moment when the vote is to be given." With that sentence I find myself in complete accord . . . A proxy is always subject to an understanding that the shareholder giving it does not elect to give his vote in person and when he in fact gives a vote in person he is not revoking the proxy but taking a step which obviates the necessity of the proxy being used at all.

For these reasons I agree that the appeal must be dismissed.

TEXT REFERENCE - FOOTNOTE 72

KNIGHT v *BULKELEY*

(1859) 5 Jur. (N.S.) 817

Principal May Be Restricted From Revoking Authority

Facts

The defendant, a retired officer in the army, having received a pension assigned same to the plaintiff to secure an annuity for him. He also executed a power of attorney in the form employed by the War Office, empowering the plaintiff to receive the pension and pay himself the annuity.

After two payments of the pension the defendant revoked the power personally going to the office and receiving the pension.

Judgment

The defendant was ordered to execute a proper power of attorney to enable plaintiff to receive the pension, and an injunction was granted against the defendant's revoking the power or doing any act whereby the plaintiff's right might be interfered with.

Annotations *Constd Dent* v *Dent* (1867) LR 1 P&D 366; *Apld Willoek* v *Terrell* (1878) 3 Ex D 323; *Crowe* v *Price* (1889) 58 LJQB 215.

Author's note:

This case lends authority to the view that in certain circumstances a proxy may not be revoked. In my opinion the determining factor would be the issue of valid consideration and written evidence of the contract.

In respect of a sale of shares a proxy given by a transferor to a transferee may fall within this category, if the proxy was given as part of the consideration for the sale and purchase of the shares so as to enable such transferee to attend a meeting of shareholders before such shares were registered in the name of the transferee. However, enforcement of any right or claim would remain a matter between the transferor and the transferee, the company not being party thereto.

The company should therefore treat such 'irrevocable proxies' in the same manner as all other proxies and should even permit the revocation of such proxies, unless it had received therewith a copy of a court order or an injunction providing otherwise.

TEXT REFERENCE - FOOTNOTE 78

REGINA v THE WIMBLEDON LOCAL BOARD

(1882) 8 Qbd 459

Meeting Of Ratepayers - Poll

Facts

A meeting of ratepayers was summoned for the purpose of determining whether the provisions of the Public Libraries Acts should be adopted in the defendants' district. A chairman having been chosen, the resolution to adopt the Acts was carried upon a show of hands; a poll was demanded, but the chairman refused to grant it. The defendants declined to put in force the Acts:

Held

That the right to demand a poll existed by the common law, and had not been taken away by any of the provisions contained in the Public Libraries Acts, and that the defendants could not be compelled by mandamus to carry out the Acts.

TEXT REFERENCE - FOOTNOTE 79

REGINA v *LAMBETH*

(1838) 8 A & E 356

Facts

On 17 April 1838, being Tuesday in Easter Week, a vestry meeting of the parishioners was held at the Boys School House, Lambeth Green, pursuant to notice, for the purpose among others specified in the notice, of appointing churchwardens. One churchwarden having been appointed on the part of the rector, according to custom, certain persons were proposed to the parishioners to be the three other churchwardens, it being the custom to have three nominated and appointed in addition to the rector's warden.

Six appearing as candidates, and a shew of hands being taken, Saunders, Hunt and Barton were declared to be elected, whereupon two rated inhabitants handed the following notice in writing to the chairman (who was appointed in the rector's absence, according to stat. 58 G. 3, c. 69, s. 2): "We demand a poll of the whole parish, on behalf of, Ex. (the unsuccessful candidates) proposed as churchwardens." Some of the ratepayers then required that the poll should be confined to the vestrymen present; others insisted that a poll of the inhabitants at large should be taken.

The chairman took a shew of hands (though protested against by many of the ratepayers) on this question; the majority was in favour of polling (as was stated on affidavit) "the inhabitants ratepayers then present only"; and such mode of polling only was allowed by the chairman to take place, two of the ratepayers, however, giving in a written protest against it in the following terms: "We protest against the polling of the inhabitants assembled vestry only on the election of churchwardens, and require the poll to be taken of the whole parish."

Saunders, Hunt and Barton again had the majority, and were declared to be elected.

During the poll, the doors of the vestry room were closed by order of the chairman. One of the parties making affidavit stated that while the doors were closed he saw several persons assembled against them on the outside, three or four of whom he knew to be inhabitants, and among them an aged gentleman, a ratepayer, who knocked repeatedly, but could not gain admittance until the poll was over; and that the time during which the said person remained excluded was half an hour.

Held,

In the election of churchwardens, if a poll be demanded, the votes are to be given by the qualified inhabitants present; but all qualified inhabitants (whether they were present or not at the shew of hands) have a right to be admitted into the vestryroom and vote during such poll — although the qualified inhabitants present at the time of granting the poll resolve that the poll shall be confined to those then present.

It is not a sufficient ground for impeaching such election (on motion for a mandamus to elect) that the poll was taken with closed doors, unless it be expressly sworn that some qualified person who meant to vote was thereby prevented from doing so.

Semble, per Lord Denman C.J. that, if such an instance were shewn, the Court would grant a mandamus, without inquiring strictly whether the number of persons excluded was in fact such as to affect the result of the election.

TEXT REFERENCE - FOOTNOTE 80

REGINA v *MAYOR OF DOVER*

(1903) 1 KB 668

Municipal Corporation - Resolution Of Owners And Ratepayers - Demand Of Poll, What Amounts To

Facts

By Sched. III., R. 6 of the Public Health Act, 1875, which schedule contains the rules as to resolutions of owners and ratepayers under the Act, it is provided that the chairman shall propose the resolution, and the meeting shall decide for or against its adoption, "provided, that if any owner or ratepayer demands that such question be decided by a poll of owners and ratepayers", the poll is to be taken in the manner therein provided.

A resolution having been declared carried at a meeting of owners and ratepayers, one of the ratepayers present demanded a poll, and another rose and seconded it, "if necessary"; the latter was told by the town clerk that it was unnecessary to second the demand, which had been acceded to; the meeting then separated.

Subsequently the original demand for a poll was withdrawn by its proposer, and the mayor refused to treat the action of the seconder as a demand of a poll by him. Upon an application by the second ratepayer for a mandamus to the mayor:

Held,

That the action of the applicant was in substance a demand of a poll by him within the meaning of rule 6 of the schedule.

Quaere, whether the original demand for a poll could be withdrawn after the close of the meeting.

Lord Alverstone C.J.: . . . This rule must be made absolute . . . The rule must be construed with reference to the subject matter to which it is applied. The owners and ratepayers hear the demand made, and leave the meeting thinking that a poll will be held. It is unnecessary to decide when the demand, if made by one person only, may be withdrawn. It is clear that in the present case this gentleman went to the meeting with the intention of demanding a poll, and that, when it was demanded by another ratepayer, he said that he would second it: this ought to be treated as a second demand . . . I am by no means clear that a demand for a poll can be withdrawn after the meeting has separated, but I express no opinion on this point.

Ridley J.: I agree.

Darling J.: I am of the same opinion. Although our decision proceeds upon the ground that a demand was made by a second person, it seems to me, if it were necessary to decide the other point, that the demand for a poll could not be withdrawn after the meeting had come to an end. After the demand had been made and the town clerk had said that a poll will be held, the other persons present would naturally remain quiet. To allow the demand to be withdrawn privately might lead to all manner of collusion, and the owners and ratepayers might be deprived of their statutory right to a poll. Personally I am inclined to think that the demand cannot be withdrawn after it has once been accepted.

TEXT REFERENCE - FOOTNOTE 81 & 87

McMILLAN v *LE' ROI MINING CO. LTD*

(1906) 1 Ch 331

Company - Voting - "Personally Or By Proxy" - Poll - Power Of Chairman To Direct Manner Of Taking - Polling Papers - Invalidity

Facts

The articles of a company provided in the ordinary way for votes being given either personally or by proxy, the appointment of proxies, etc., but that if a poll was demanded it should be taken "in such manner and at such time and place as the chairman of the meeting directs".

At a general meeting of the company, a resolution having been lost upon a show of hands, the chairman demanded a poll and directed that it should be taken by means of polling papers signed by members and delivered at the offices of the company on or before a fixed day and hour:

Held,

That, having regard to the terms of the articles, such a mode of taking the poll was unauthorised and invalid.

TEXT REFERENCE - FOOTNOTE 90

JOHN v REES AND OTHERS

(1969) 2 Wlr 1294

Meetings - Chairman - Powers - Adjournment - Attempt By Chairman To Put To Vote Resolution Not On Agenda Against Wish Of Majority Of Those Present - Resulting Disturbance - Purported Adjournment Sine Die By Chairman

Facts

On 27 March 1968, D., member of parliament for Pembrokeshire, was expelled from the Labour Party. On 6 April about 100 people, mostly delegates from local Labour Parties within the constituency, were present at the annual meeting of the Pembrokeshire Divisional Labour Party (PDLP), at which J., president of PDLP took the chair. The assistant national agent of the Labour Party addressed the meeting, reminding members of their obligations, referring to D.'s expulsion and suggesting that a resolution be passed to the effect that PDLP should continue to act in strict conformity with its constitution, and the rules and constitution of the Labour Party.

Although no such resolution was on the agenda, J. attempted to put to the vote a resolution to that effect, which had been moved and seconded by delegates from the floor, but disturbances broke out because the majority of those present were supporters of D., and favoured disaffiliation from the Labour Party. There was noise disorder and, in a few cases bodily contact, but no real violence, and none appeared to have been put in fear.

After some attempt to restore order, J. purported to adjourn the meeting sine die and then left the hall with other delegates. Those who remained carried on with the business of the meeting which included the election of officers. C. was elected president in place of J., L. was elected treasurer, while R., the secretary, remained secretary, since his office was not amongst those to be filled. The meeting also passed, by 69 votes to one, a resolution to disaffiliate from the Labour Party and a resolution to support D.

On 6 May J., claiming to represent all members of PDLP other than R., C. and L. (the first, second and third defendants, respectively), issued a writ challenging the validity of the continuation of the meeting and by notice of motion sought an injunction to restrain R., C. and L. from dealing in any way with the moneys or other property of PDLP.

By counter notice of motion the defendants sought to have the writ struck out or, alternatively, so much of it as claimed relief in a representative capacity. Meanwhile, on 24 April the National Executive Committee of the Labour Party (NEC) passed two resolutions, one suspending the activities of PDLP and the right of its officers to handle the party funds, the other authorising the "national agent" to take such steps as are necessary to complete the reorganisation of the PDLP.

Pursuant to those resolutions, the national agent resolved, inter alia, to convene a meeting of the Haverfordwest Local Labour Party, but before doing so he wrote to leading members of the dissident faction who supported D., informing them of the proposed reorganisation and requesting from them an undertaking to accept and conform to the constitution, programme, principles and policy of the Labour Party, that they neither belonged to nor were actively associated with any proscribed organisation and that they would cooperate in re-establishing PDLP in accordance with the rules and constitution of the Labour Party. Four members including M. and B.L.D., did not reply and four others, including R., sent replies which the national agent regarded as unsatisfactory. By reason of their failure to give the required undertakings, the eight members were deemed to be disqualified from membership of the Haverford Local Labour Party, and were neither informed of the reorganisation nor permitted to attend it. The meeting was held on 20 May. Officers were elected and delegates were chosen to represent the Haverfordwest Local Labour Party at a proposed reorganisation meeting of the PDLP.

M. and B.L.D. challenged the validity of the whole of that meeting in a writ issued on 12 June and by notice of motion of the same date sought to restrain the officers and delegates elected at the meeting of 20 May from dealing in any way with the moneys and other property of the Haverfordwest Local Labour Party and from acting as delegates for it. Despite the issue of the second writ the proposed reorganisation meeting of PDLP was held on 22 June and was attended by delegates purported to have been elected at the reorganisation meeting of 20

May and by delegates from other local Labour parties elected in a similar manner at similar meetings convened by NEC. At the meeting of 22 June those attending purported to re-elect J. as president of PDLP. The validity of the whole of the third meeting was challenged in a writ issued on July 5 by R. and C., and on the same day, by notice of motion R. and C. sought to restrain J. from dealing in any way with the moneys or other property PDLP.

On the hearing of the four motions in the three actions:

Held,

(1) That the rule as to representative actions laid down in RSC Ord. 15 r.12(1) was not a rigid matter of principle, but a rule of convenience in the administration of justice and what was important was to have before the Court either in person or by representation, all those who would be affected, so that all should be bound by the result; that all members of PDLP had a common interest in PDLP and that since the only objection suggested to J.'s being allowed to act in a representative capacity for all the members (other than the three defendants), namely, that J. would then be representing some who in fact, supported the defendants and did not wish to be represented by him, could be cured by adding such persons as defendants individually or by securing their representation by other defendants, there was no reason to strike out the writ either wholly or in so far as it claimed relief in a representative capacity.

(2) That when in contravention of the decision made by the standing orders committee immediately prior to the main meeting and in contravention of the standing orders of PDLP, J. attempted to put to the vote a resolution not on the agreed agenda, he was guilty of a deliberate and substantial breach of duly, which caused the disturbances to occur; that J. possessed no inherent power as chairman to put such a resolution to the meeting, and that while he did possess an inherent power to adjourn the meeting for disorder for such period as might be reasonably necessary in order to restore order, his action in purporting to adjourn sine die was invalid and ineffective to produce a valid adjournment of the meeting; and that, accordingly, C. and L. were validly elected and since R. remained secretary all three defendants were validly elected officers of PDLP and J.'s motion in the first action must be dismissed.

(3) That the maxim 'Omnia praesumuntur esse acta' was not limited in operation to cases where it was sought to apply it in favour of outsiders or non-members of

a club or association, and since there was some evidence that certain rules of the Labour Party had for many years been treated as the rules of PDLP, the maxim could in the absence of any direct evidence of formal adoption, be applied in favour of the adoption of the rules; that in any event there was no reason why a person joining a club or association should not be bound by whatever rules had become established by usage even if they had not been adopted formally and were not brought to his attention on joining; but while PDLP was not a mere branch of the Labour Party but remained a separate entity, nevertheless on the true construction of the rules "Set B", PDLP was bound to accept the constitution, programme, principles, and policy of the Labour Party, and that, therefore, the resolution to disaffiliate, which in any event was procedurally invalid since it was not upon the agenda, was also invalid because PDLP could not lawfully disaffiliate itself from the Labour Party unless the rules had first been altered.

(4) That despite the passing of the resolution to disaffiliate and in support of D., it would not be right to grant the injunction sought to restrain the defendants, who were the lawfully elected officers of PDLP, since there was no evidence of any improper use of the funds or of any threat to flout the law once the law was known and J.'s motion must therefore be dismissed.

(5) That although clause 8 (2) of the constitution of the Labour Party empowered the NEC to take "any action it deems necessary . . . whether by . . . disaffiliation of an organisation or expulsion of an individual or otherwise", there was nothing in the rules or constitution of the Labour Party which excluded the application of the principles of natural justice, even though what was here in issue was suspension and not expulsion and that, accordingly, the resolutions suspending the activities of PDLP and the rights of its officers to handle its funds and the other resolution authorising the national agent to reorganise it were nullities, since in both cases those who were suspended were given no opportunity to be heard in answer to charges and in case of the second resolution, no notice was given to certain members of the Haverfordwest Local Labour Party of the proposed reorganisation meeting of 20 May.

TEXT REFERENCE - FOOTNOTE 92

SHAW v *THOMPSON*

(1876) 3 Ch D 233

Advowson - Right Of Presentation Vested In Parishioners - Mode Of Exercising The Right - Law Of Public Meetings - Vote By Ballot

Facts

The advowson of a parish church being vested in trustees who were bound to present the nominee of the parishioners and inhabitants, a vacancy occurred, and at a meeting of parishioners convened by the churchwardens, and presided over by one of them, the 30th of August was fixed upon for a meeting "to proceed to the election of a vicar". Meanwhile, upon the requisition of certain inhabitants, a meeting of the 25th of August, summoned by the churchwardens, but at which they declined to preside, was held, at which resolutions were passed to the effect that the election should be by ballot, on one day only, and at several polling places, and that the poll should be open from 9 a.m to 9 p.m.

On the 30th of August the meeting resolved upon was held, candidates were nominated, a show of hands taken, and a poll demanded, and one of the churchwardens, who was in the chair, announced that the poll would be taken by open voting, on the following and two successive days, at one polling place only, and that the poll would be kept open from 8 to 8. Upon a parishioner rising to move amendments similar to those of the 25th of August, the chairman left the chair and declared the meeting at an end. After the churchwarden had left the chair, another chairman was chosen, and a series of resolutions, similar to those of the 25th of August, were moved and carried.

The poll having been taken in the way announced by the chairman of the 30th of August:

Held,

That the conduct of the churchwardens had been erroneous and illegal; but, there being no evidence of any voter having been deprived of an opportunity of voting, that the election could not be disturbed.

Semble, an election by ballot, if duly resolved upon, is not at the present day an illegal mode of election.

TEXT REFERENCE - FOOTNOTE 93

CATESBY v *BURNETT*

(1916) 2 Ch 325

Company - Articles Of Association - Construction - Election Of Directors - 'Day Of Election" Adjourned Meeting - Notice - Injunction

Facts

One of the articles of association of a limited company provided that a member should not be qualified to be elected a director unless written notice of the intention in that behalf were given to the company not less than 14 clear days before the 'day of election' of directors.

The ordinary general meeting of the company was held on 10 December 1915, at which meeting, according to the articles, the two defendant directors retired by rotation. The report of the directors was not adopted; there was no election of directors, but a committee of shareholders was appointed to investigate the affairs of the company and report to a general meeting, and the meeting stood adjourned to receive this report.

On 21 February 1916, written notice was given to the company, by a shareholder, stating that at the adjourned meeting he proposed to move the election of four named members as directors. The adjourned meeting was held on 10 March 1916, to consider the committee's report and to transact the unfinished business. The chairman ruled the shareholder's written notification of 21 February 1916, to be out of order, and after declaring the election of auditors, but without considering the matter of the election of directors, said there was no further business and left the chair. Subsequently the shareholders appointed a chairman and elected the four new directors. On motion by the shareholders for an interlocutory injunction to restrain the two retiring directors from acting:

Held,

That the day of election of directors within the meaning of the article was the date of the adjourned meeting on 10 March 1916; that the notice on 21 February 1916, was in compliance with that article; and that the first two persons elected as directors in lieu of the two who retired were duly elected. The injunction asked for must be granted.

REFERENCE - FOOTNOTE 94

SALISBURY GOLD MINING CO. v HATHORN

(1897) Ac 268

(Privy Council)

Construction Of Articles Of Association - Power Of Chairman To Refuse Adjournment Of A Meeting - Practice

Facts

At the hearing of an appeal it appeared doubtful whether the order appealed against was a final judgement or had the effect of a definitive sentence; but it also appeared that the questions in controversy on the face of the pleadings were of much importance, and a determination of them might put an end to further litigation. Accordingly special leave to appeal was granted.

An Article of Association provided that "the chairman may with the consent of the members present at any meeting adjourn the same", etc.

On behalf of the appellants it was argued that the power vested in the chairman is a power to adjourn or not to adjourn at his option, subject to this: that if he adjourns it must be with the consent of the members present; if he does not adjourn, he may dispense with that consent.

The respondent contended that the chairman was wrong in refusing to put the motion for adjournment, and that the respondents were entitled to have the same put to the meeting. It is the inherent power in every public meeting and of meetings of members of incorporated bodies to adjourn themselves, and the chairman's duty in the matter is merely ministerial. Art. 66 was not intended to give the absolute power claimed.

Held,

That, upon the true construction thereof, the chairman is not bound to adjourn a meeting, even though a majority of those present desire the adjournment; and that he can, after rejecting a motion for adjournment, declare a provisional agreement specified in the circular convening the meeting to be confirmed.

Semble. Such confirmation is not affected by any statement of the chairman as to its effect even if incorrect.

Their Lordships are of the opinion that . . . if the intention had been that the majority of the members present should have the right to adjourn the meeting whenever they pleased, their Lordships think that the article would have been differently worded. According to the terms of Art. 66 it is the 'chairman' who may adjourn the meeting: it is to be his act, not that of the meeting or of those present at it. He cannot, it is true, adjourn it of his own mere motion, but the terms in which the members present are given a controlling voice strengthens the view that the adjournment is to be the act of the chairman. It provides for the 'consent' of the members present, which implies that the act is not theirs but his.

REFERENCE - FOOTNOTE 95

BYNG v *LONDON LIFE ASSOCIATION AND ANOTHER*

(1988) Ca - 1990 Lrc 500

Company - Meeting - Adjournment - Powers Of Chairman - Location Notified For Meeting Proving Too Small To Accommodate All Members Wishing To Attend - Chairman Of Meeting Adjourning Meeting To Another Location In Afternoon Of Same Day - Whether Chairman Having Power To Adjourn Meeting Without Its Consent - Whether Power To Adjourn Validly Exercised - Test To Be Applied

Facts

Notice was duly given of an extraordinary general meeting of the company to be held at a specified location at 12 noon on 19 October 1988. There was an assembly of members of the company at that time and place, but the location proved too small to accommodate all those members wishing to be present. D., the president of the company and chairman of the meeting, purported to adjourn the meeting and direct that it be resumed in the afternoon of the same day at another location. The reconvened meeting passed the sole resolution of which notice had been given. The plaintiff, a shareholder of the company, brought an action claiming that D. had not validly adjourned the meeting in the morning and that accordingly all business conducted at the reconvened meeting in the afternoon had been invalidly conducted. The judge dismissed the plaintiff's claim. The plaintiff appealed to the Court of Appeal.

Article 18 of the company's Articles of Association provides: "The chairman may, with the consent of the meeting at which a quorum is present (and shall if so directed by the meeting) adjourn the meeting from time to time and from place to place" etc.

It was common ground between the parties that, in the circumstances obtaining at the Barbican Centre on the morning of 19 October, no business could have been validly conducted at that meeting. The issue between the parties is whether the chairman could and did validly adjourn anything which was 'a meeting' of London Life to the Cafe Royal. If there was no valid adjournment the business purported to be done at the alleged adjourned meeting would have been wholly invalid.

Held,

(1) There was no rule of law that a meeting from which members were wrongly excluded was a nullity notwithstanding the fact that it was incapable of conducting any business. On the true construction of the company's Articles of Association an inquorate meeting of the company incapable of conducting any business was nevertheless a 'meeting' of the company which was capable of being adjourned.

(2) Where there was a meeting at which the views of the majority could not be validly ascertained, the chairman had a residual common law power to adjourn the meeting without its consent in order to give all persons entitled a reasonable opportunity of voting and speaking at the meeting.

(3) The test to be applied in deciding whether the chairman's decision to adjourn was lawful was the same as that applicable on judicial review in accordance with accepted principles relating to unreasonableness. However since the chairman's power was only exercisable for the purpose of giving members a reasonable opportunity to debate and vote on the resolution, there had to be very special circumstances to justify a decision to adjourn a meeting to a time and place where, to the chairman's knowledge, a number of members who had attended the original meeting would not only be unable to attend but also be unable to lodge a proxy vote. Accordingly, although D. had acted in good faith, his decision to adjourn to another location on the same day was not valid, on the grounds either that he failed to take into account relevant factors or that the decision was unreasonable. The appeal would therefore be allowed.

TEXT REFERENCE - FOOTNOTE 96

In *Re PORTUGUESE CONSOLIDATED COPPER MINES LTD*

(1889) 42 Ch D 160

Company - Rectification Of Register Of Shareholders - Invalid Allotment Of Shares - Irregular Appointment Of Quorum Of Directors - Attempted Ratification After Repudiation By Allottee - Qualification Of Directors

Facts

The Articles of Association of a company excluded Table A to the Companies Act 1862. They provided that the shares should be allotted by the directors; that the qualification of a director should be the holding of at least 40 shares; that the directors should not be more than ten nor less than three in number; that the first directors should be appointed by the majority of the subscribers to the Memorandum of Association; and that the directors might determine the quorum necessary for the transaction of business. On the 22nd of October the seven subscribers to the memorandum met and unanimously appointed four persons directors. On the 24th of October, S. applied for 100 shares. On the same day the first meeting of directors was held, at which two only of the four directors were present. No sufficient notice of this meeting had been given to all the directors. They resolved that two directors should form a quorum, and then proceeded to allot shares, including 100 to S. They adjourned the meeting till the next day. S. received notice of allotment on the 24th. At this time none of the directors had any shares, but at the adjourned meeting on the following day 40 shares were allotted to each of them. On the 25th S. gave notice to the company that he withdrew his application. On the 25th the meeting was further adjourned to the 26th. On the 26th three directors were present, and one of them, which had been absent on the 24th, expressed in writing his approval of the resolution as to a quorum. At this meeting the former allotments were confirmed. The other absent director on the same day wrote an approval of the resolution as to a quorum, and it was received by the company on the 27th. On application by S. to have his name removed from the register:

Held by North, J.,

That the two directors had no power to appoint themselves a quorum, and that, consequently, the allotment of shares to S. was invalid and that it could not be ratified after S. had withdrawn his application for shares, but that the allotment, if it had been made by all four directors, would not have been invalid merely because they had not previously acquired qualification by the holding of shares.

Held by the Court of Appeal,

That assuming every other point to be decided in favour of the company, the allotment was invalid on the ground that notice of the meeting of the 24th had not been given to all the directors, that this meeting was therefore irregular, and the adjourned meeting of the 26th was therefore equally irregular.

TEXT REFERENCE - FOOTNOTE 97

SMITH v *PARINGA MINES LTD*

(1906) 2 Ch 193

Company - Directors - Powers - Postponement Of General Meeting

Facts

The Paringa Mines Ltd was incorporated under the Companies Acts 1862 to 1900 on 17 April 1902.

In February 1906, there were only two directors of the company, Mr Blair, chairman, and Mr Smith. Blair proposed to Smith that a Mr Foulkes should be appointed as a third director to fill up a casual vacancy, and on 18 February Smith received a notice calling a board meeting for 21 February at the company's offices. Smith did not attend the board meeting, but intimated by telephone that he would see Blair at his (Smith's) office at 2:30. Blair accordingly went there and saw Smith outside the door of his private room. He explained to Smith the necessity of appointing a director in the place of a director who had retired, and pointed out that he had nominated Foulkes and that there was no other nomination, and asked him if he objected. Smith said that he did, and Blair replied that by his casting vote he declared Foulkes duly elected, and the board meeting closed. The records were duly entered up and signed by Blair as chairman.

On 28 March 1906 Smith received a notice calling the annual ordinary meeting of shareholders for 5 April 1906 for the purpose of receiving the annual report and statement of accounts and of electing directors.

On the same 28 March Smith on behalf of himself and all others the shareholders of the company commenced an action against the company, Blair and Foulkes, for a declaration that an agreement entered into by the company for the purchase of certain mines in Australia was void, and an injunction to restrain the defendants from carrying it into effect, and also for a declaration that the appointment of

Foulkes as a director was illegal and an injunction to restrain him from acting as a director, and served a notice of motion on the defendants for injunctions in the terms of the writ.

On 4 April 1906 Smith received from the secretary of the company a notice purporting to postpone the meeting of 5 April. The notice was dated 3 April. On the same day, 4 April Smith wrote to the secretary notifying him that as he had been advised that the attempted postponement was illegal the meeting would be proceeded with, and required him to be present at the meeting with all necessary papers, and he also caused a notice to sent to the public press that the ordinary general meeting would be held.

Smith attended the meeting, at which there were about 50 shareholders present. After waiting for quarter of an hour, the time fixed by the articles, for the arrival of the chairman of the company, Smith being the only director present, explained that he did not wish to take the chair, and the chair was taken by a Mr Parker.

The meeting then unanimously passed resolutions re-electing Smith as a director, rejecting Foulkes as a director, and electing a Mr Boyle and Mr Parker as directors, and the meeting was then adjourned until 26 April the same day to which the secretary had purported to postpone the meeting by the notice of 3 April.

The Articles of Association of the company contained no provision for the postponement of a general meeting.

Held,

The directors of a limited company, in the absence of express authority in the Articles of Association, have no power to postpone a general meeting of the company properly convened.

TEXT REFERENCE - FOOTNOTE 101

KERR v JOHN MOTTRAM LTD

(1940) 1 Ch 657

Company - Articles Of Association - Minutes Of Meeting - Bona Fide Record - Whether Conclusive Evidence Of Facts Stated

Facts

A shareholder in a company, the Articles of Association of which provided that the minutes of any meeting if purporting to be signed by the chairman should "be conclusive evidence without any further proof of the facts therein stated", brought an action against the company for specific performance of an alleged contract and proposed to call evidence inconsistent with the signed minutes of an extraordinary general meeting:

Held

That the words 'conclusive evidence' meant evidence which was not to be displaced and was conclusive as between the parties bound by the minutes and that, accordingly, the evidence tendered by the plaintiff was inadmissible.

TEXT REFERENCE - FOOTNOTE 107 & 122

GREAT EASTERN RAILWAY CO v *TURNER*

(1872) Lr 8 Ch 149

Trustee - Illegal Trust - Bankrupt - Order And Disposition

Facts

This case centres around the incident of the chairman of a company, who with the assent of the company, held in his name shares in another company, which had been purchased with the money of the first-named company. The chairman became bankrupt.

In the month of June 1863, *Horatio Love,* then chairman of the board of directors of the *Great Eastern Railway Co.*, on behalf of the company, and by their direction (as alleged by the bill), and with their money, purchased 102 shares in the *Lynn and Hunstanton Railway Co.*, which shares were duly transferred to *Horatio Love* as a trustee for the company; the *Lynn and Hunstanton Railway Co.*, having notice of the facts. In August 1863, Horatio Love ceased to be chairman, and *J. Goodson* succeeded him, whereupon the above mentioned shares were afterwards converted into £1,020 (sterling) stock, which was registered in the name of *J. Goodson.* In February 1866, *J. Goodson* ceased to be chairman, and *C.H. Turner* succeeded him, whereupon the £1,020 (sterling) stock was transferred to *C.H. Turner* as a trustee for the *Great Eastern Railway Co.* The stock certificate was sent to the *Great Eastern Railway Co*, and remained in their possession. In September 1869, *C.H. Turner* was duly adjudicated a bankrupt, and *J. Field* and *E.C. Foreman* were appointed assignees under the bankruptcy.

Field and *Foreman* refused to transfer the shares to new trustees for the *Great Eastern Railway Co.*, and the company thereupon filed the bill in this suit containing the statements above mentioned, and praying that the assignees might be ordered to transfer the shares as the *Great Eastern Railway Co.* shall direct.

C.H. Turner, who was made a defendant, stated that he was willing to make the transfer but was advised that he could not safely do so, as *Field* and *Foreman,* his assignees in bankruptcy, objected.

Field and *Foreman* alleged that the purchase of the shares out of the money of the company and the transfer of the stock were illegal transactions, and that vesting the same in the successive chairmen and the trust of the stock were not effectual, and that it remained in the order and disposition of *C.H. Turner* at his bankruptcy, and as such passed to his assignees, who claimed the same accordingly.

The Master of the Rolls dismissed the bill with costs as against all the defendants (1).

The plaintiff appealed.

Held,

(Reversing the decree of the Master of the Rolls), that, though the purchase by one company of shares in another company was illegal, the shares were not within the order and disposition of the bankrupt so as to pass to his assignees, and that he must transfer them as the company should direct.

Per Lord Selborne, L.C.: "I am sorry that I am unable, in this case, to follow the view of his Lordship the Master of the Rolls.

As I see the facts, the legal conclusion to be drawn from them is not difficult. Supposing that there had been an authority by law to invest the funds of the Company in the purchase of shares in the *Lynn and Hunstanton Railway Co.* in the name of the Chairman for the time being, then I take it to be clear, beyond controversy, that, even without any notice to the company, the principle of *Joy* v *Campbell* (1), and the other case of that class, would have prevented the application of the order and disposition clause of the Bankruptcy Act, and that the shares would not have passed to the assignees of the chairman.

The difference between the case which I have supposed and the present case is just this: that there was no authority to purchase either in the name of the company or in the name of the chairman, or in any other name.

The company is a mere abstraction of law. All that it does, all that the law imputes to it as its act, must be that which can be legally done within the powers vested in it by law. Consequently, a thing which is *ultra vires* and unauthorised is not an act of the company in such a sense as that the consent of the company to that act can be placed.

The directors are the mere trustees or agents of the company — trustees of the company's money and property — agents in the transactions which they enter into on behalf of the company. In this case, without legal authority, and therefore without the consent of the corporation, whose trustees and agents they were, the directors took a part of the company's money, and therewith purchased a property which this contest proves to be of some value — shares in the *Lynn and Hunstanton Railway Co.* Those shares so bought — not a farthing of any other person's money having contributed to the purchase — were placed in the names of three successive chairmen of the company, and were uniformly dealt with as that which they were, the property of the company.

True, it is that the investment was an unauthorised investment; but I entirely assent to what was said by *Sir Richard Baggallay,* that there is no difference between an unauthorised investment of the money of a public company by its trustees, and an unauthorised investment of the moneys belonging to any other trust by the trustees of that trust.

It would be monstrous — it would be extravagant to the very last degree — to say, that because the money of *cestuis que trust* has been laid out in an unauthorised manner, that therefore they are not to have the benefit of whatever value there is in the property bought with their money.

It is clear that the chairman, although this was an unauthorised investment, was a trustee of the shares bought with the money of the company; but if the shares had become burthensome, the burthen could not have been thrown upon the company. That is a proposition quite consistent with the other."

TEXT REFERENCE - FOOTNOTE 109

RAMA CORPORATION LTD v PROVED TIN

AND

GENERAL INVESTMENTS LTD

(1952) 2 QB 147

Company - Director - Authority - Articles Of Association - Power Of Board Of Directors To Delegate Their Powers To Single Director - No Delegation - Contract Made With Firm By Single Director - Repudiation By Company - Firm's Ignorance Of Power To Delegate - No Ostensible Or Apparent Authority - Company Not Liable

Facts

On 21 March 1949, one Wedderburn, the principal director of the plaintiff company, and George Eric Titley, an active director of the defendant company, each purported on behalf of his company to enter into a certain transaction. The defendant company had agreed to buy at a discount invoices of RBK Products Ltd in connection with sales of a telephone directory holder. The defendant company was expending 5,000 pounds sterling and the plaintiff company was invited to participate with them in a joint venture, the plaintiff company contributing 2,000 pounds sterling and the defendant company having the management of the venture and collecting the money and accounting to the plaintiffs for it. Wedderburn, who had known Titley for a long time, had never heard of the defendant company before 21 March 1949, and he made no inquiries about it.

After agreeing to the joint venture he was asked for and gave a cheque on behalf of the plaintiff company in favour of Titley. Titley shortly afterwards confirmed the agreement which had been reached between him and Wedderburn in a letter written on his own writing paper and referring to the defendant company. Titley never at any time disclosed to his fellow members of the board of the defendant company anything about the transaction which he had purported to make on its behalf with Wedderburn on behalf of the plaintiff company.

The transaction of 21 March 1949, was intra vires the defendant company, and by article 119 of the defendant company's Articles of Association: "The directors may delegate any of their powers, other than the power to borrow and make calls, to committees consisting of such members of their body as they think fit." The board had not in fact, however, delegated any of their powers, and neither the plaintiff company nor Wedderburn had at any time inspected the defendant company's file to satisfy themselves of the defendant company's power to delegate. The defendant company repudiated the agreement.

The plaintiff company claimed from the defendant company an account of moneys alleged to have been paid to the defendant company under the terms of the agreement of 21 March 1949. They claimed in the alternative 1,000 pounds sterling with interest under section 3 of the Law Reform (Miscellaneous Provisions) Act 1934, being the balance of the moneys which they alleged they had paid to the defendant company; and in the further alternative damages for the alleged fraud of the defendant company's agent. They contended that they had been induced to enter into the agreement and to pay moneys to the defendants by the fraud of Titley, acting within the scope of his authority as a director of the defendant company, in fraudulently holding himself out to the plaintiff company as having been duly authorised by the defendant company to enter into the agreement and to receive the moneys on their behalf.

The defendant company denied that they entered into the agreement as alleged or that Titley had any authority, express, implied or apparent, to enter into it, and they denied that Titley acted as their agent to receive moneys from or to pay moneys to the plaintiff company. They did not admit that the plaintiff company was induced to enter into the agreement by the fraud of Titley, and denied that he was acting within the scope of his authority as a director in the fraudulent holding out which the plaintiff company had alleged.

The plaintiff company submitted that the defendant company was estopped from denying that Titley was authorised to enter into the agreements on their behalf because, amongst other things, their Memorandum and Aticles of Association showed that he was capable of being so authorised.

Held,

A person who at the time of entering into a contract with a company, registered under the Companies Acts, has no knowledge of the company's Articles of Association, cannot rely on those articles as conferring ostensible or apparent authority on the agent of the company with whom he dealt. The doctrine of constructive notice of a company's registered documents is a purely negative one which does not operate against a company but only in its favour.

TEXT REFERENCE - FOOTNOTE 110

HOUGHTON AND CO.
v
NORTHARD, LOWE AND WILLS LIMITED

(1927) 1 KB 247 C A

Company - Contract Made By Director On Behalf Of - Ostensible Authority Of Director - Articles Of Association - Power Of Board To Delegate Powers   To Single Director - Presumption Of Delegation - Constructive Notice - Limits Of Doctrine.

Facts

The doctrine of constructive notice operates adversely to a person who neglects to inquire; it does not entitle such a person to claim for his own advantage to be treated as having knowledge of the facts which inquiry would have disclosed.

The plaintiff were a firm of fruit brokers. The defendants and the P. Co. were two companies engaged in the fruit trade. One M.L. was a director of both companies. By Art. 28 of the Articles of Association of the defendant company the directors were empowered to "delegate to any managing director, local board, head manager, manager, attorney or agent any of the powers . . . for the time being vested in the directors". The Articles of Association also incorporated table A, by Art. 91 of which the board of directors "may delegate any of their powers to committees consisting of such member or members of their bodies as they think fit".

M.L. purported to make on behalf of the defendants an agreement with the plaintiffs that in consideration of the plaintiffs advancing a sum of money to the P. Co., the plaintiffs should have the rights to sell on commission all the fruit imported both by the defendants and the P. Co., and that the plaintiffs should be entitled to retain the proceeds of sale of the defendants' fruit as well as of that of the P. Co. as security for the advance. M.L. had, in fact, no authority from the defendants to make such a contract.

The plaintiffs, with a view of securing themselves against any such want of authority in M.L., required confirmation of the agreement by the defendant company itself. The secretary of the defendants accordingly wrote the plaintiffs a letter purporting to confirm the agreement on behalf of the defendants, and the plaintiffs, treating that as a sufficient confirmation, made the advance. The secretary had no authority to give such confirmation. The defendants subsequently repudiated the agreement as made without their authority. In an action for breach of that agreement, the plaintiff claimed that M.L. or the secretary had ostensible authority, inasmuch as such an agreement might have been made by the board, and the plaintiffs were entitled to assume that the board had delegated their powers in that behalf to M.L. or to the secretary, under the Articles of Association. At the time they made the advance the plaintiffs had no knowledge of the terms of the defendants' article of association or that they incorporated Table A.

Held,

That, whether the agreement was to be treated as having been made by M.L. as an ordinary 'director' of the defendant company, or by the secretary as 'agent', or by the two combined, the plaintiffs were not entitled to assume that any authority to make it had been delegated to them by the board, and for the following reasons:

(1) Although a person who contracts with an individual director or servant of a company, knowing that the board of directors has power to delegate its authority to such an individual, may under certain circumstances assume that that power of delegation has been exercised and that he may safely deal with the individual in question as representing the company, he cannot rely on the supposed exercise of such power if he did not know of the existence of the power at the time that he made the contract.

(2) There was something so unusual in an agreement to apply the money of one company in payment of the debt of another that the plaintiffs were put upon inquiry to ascertain whether the person or persons making the contract had any authority in fact to make it.

(3) Per Sargant L.J. (in whose judgement Atkin L.J. concurred). Even if the plaintiffs had known of the existence of the express power of delegation they would not have been entitled to assume that it had been exercised in favour of M.L or the secretary to any greater extent than was to be inferred from the positions which M.L. and the secretary respectively occupied or were held out by the company as occupying.

TEXT REFERENCE - FOOTNOTE 111

KREDITBANK CASSEL GMBH v *SCHENKERS LTD*

(1927) 1 KB 826 CA

Company - Liability On Bills Of Exchange - Bills Wrongfully Drawn - Forgery - Ostensible Authority

Facts

The defendant company by its memorandum, had power to sign, draw, accept and endorse bills of exchange, and by its Articles of Association the directors were empowered "to determine who shall be entitled to sign and make, draw, accept, and endorse on the company's behalf bills . . . acceptances, endorsements". The defendants, whose business was that of forwarding agents, had a branch at Manchester under a branch manager S.C., who, without having received any authority from the defendants, and acting in fraud of them drew seven bills purporting to do so on the company's behalf, "S.C. Manchester Manager".

The bills were drawn to the order of the company, accepted by C. & W. Ltd, a company in which S.C. was interested, and indorsed on behalf of the defendants "S.C. Manchester Manager." The bills having been dishonoured by the acceptors, the plaintiffs, who were holders in due course, sued the defendants as drawers:

Held,

(1) applying *Houghton & Co* v *Nothard, Lowe & Wills Ltd*, that as it did not appear that the plaintiffs knew of the existence of the power of delegation contained in the defendants' Articles of Association they were not entitled to rely upon its supposed exercise;

(2) that the bills of exchange were forgeries and therefore, applying *Ruben* v *Great Fingall Consolidated* (1906) AC 439, that the plaintiffs could not in any event invoke the principle that they were not bound to inquire into the indoor management of the defendant company;

(3) that even if the plaintiffs had known of the power of delegation they were not entitled to assume that a person in the position of a provincial manager like S.C. had ostensible authority to draw and indorse bills on behalf of the defendants;

(4) that the defendants had done nothing to preclude themselves from setting up the forgery of the bills or the want of authority of S.C.; and therefore;

(5) that the defendants were not liable on the bills.

TEXT REFERENCE - FOOTNOTE 112

BARRON v POTTER
POTTER v BERRY

(1914) Ch 895

Company - Additional Directors - Appointment By Board Of Directors Informal Meeting Unable Or Unwilling To Act - Power Of Company In General Meeting

Facts

The British Seagumite Co. Ltd, was incorporated under the Companies (Consolidation) Act 1908 as a private company in 1912. Art. 21 of the Articles of Association provided that the number of directors should not be less than two nor more than ten. Art. 26 provided that unless otherwise fixed by the directors a quorum shall be two. The articles also provided that the directors shall have power from time to time to appoint a person as an additional director who shall retire from office at the next ordinary general meeting but shall be eligible for re-election. The articles also gave the chairman a second or casting vote in case of equality.

In the commencement of the year 1914 there were two directors only. Mr Potter, who was chairman and managing director and Cannon Barron. The conduct of the company's business was at a standstill as Cannon Barron refused to attend any board meeting with Mr Potter. On 9 February Cannon Barron, pursuant to the provisions of section 66 of the Act sent out a notice convening an extraordinary general meeting for 24 February at the registered office of the company for the purpose of passing a resolution terminating the appointment of Mr Potter as managing director of the company, and a resolution that one Charles Berry should be appointed an additional director.

On 21 February Mr Potter sent through the post to Cannon Barron a notice requesting him to attend a board meeting at the company's office on 24 February at 2:40 p.m. This notice was not received by Cannon Barron, who lived in the country, until a later date. Cannon Barron arrived at Paddington station on 23 February and on his arrival was met on the platform by Mr Potter, who there purported under the circumstances stated to hold a board meeting and by his casting vote to appoint three persons as additional directors of the company.

Cannon Barron came to the company's office on 24 February with the intention of attending not a board meeting but the extraordinary meeting of the company. Mr Potter met him in the office before the meeting and under the circumstances stated, again proposed the appointment of additional directors. Cannon Barron disregarded the proposal, whereupon Mr Potter purported to vote and declare them elected.

The extraordinary meeting of the company was then held, at which the first resolution was put to the meeting and carried on a show of hands. Mr Potter then demanded a poll, stating that he would fix a place and time. In default of the chairman, Cannon Barron put the second resolution to the meeting, which together with an amendment adding two more persons as additional directors, he declared to be carried. Mr Potter however ruled it to be illegal, as the power lay with the directors and not with the company.

Held,

A board meeting of directors can be held under informal circumstances, but the casual meeting of two directors even at the office of the company cannot be treated as a board meeting, at the option of one against the will and intention of the other, and it makes no difference that a notice convening a board meeting has been sent by the one to the other if such notice has not in fact been received by the other.

Smith v *Paringa Mines* (1906) 2 Ch 193, *distinguished*

Where the Articles of Association of a company incorporated under the Companies (Consolidation) Act 1908 give to the board of directors the power of appointing an additional director, and owing to differences between the directors no board meeting can be held for the purpose, the company retains power to appoint additional directors in general meeting.

TEXT REFERENCE - FOOTNOTE 113

BENTLEY - STEVENS v *JONES AND OTHERS*

(1974) 1 Wlr 638

Company - Director - Removal - Irregularities - Parent Company's Board Procuring Extraordinary General Meeting Of Subsidiary Company - Plaintiff Learning Of Board Meeting Too Late To Attend - Extraordinary General Meeting Of Subsidiary Company Convened Without That Board Meeting - Meeting Passing Resolution To Remove Plaintiff As Director - Whether Subsidiary Company To Be Restrained From Acting On Resolution

Facts

The plaintiff and the first two defendants were directors of both H. Ltd. and the third defendant company which was a wholly owned subsidiary of H. Ltd.

On 28 January 1974, following disputes between the plaintiff and the two defendants, the first two defendants held a meeting of the board of H. Ltd. A notice of the meeting was sent to the plaintiff but he, being away, did not receive it in time. At the meeting the first defendant was authorised to give special notice to the defendant company for removing the plaintiff from its board and H. Ltd requisitioned an extraordinary general meeting of the defendant company. The first defendant, as a director of the defendant company, purporting to act by order of its board although no board meeting was held, convened an extraordinary general meeting of that company for 26 February. At that meeting it was resolved to remove the plaintiff from the defendant company's board. On the same day the plaintiff issued a writ seeking certain reliefs. On his motion for an interlocutory injunction to restrain the defendants from acting on the resolution on the ground that due to irregularities the resolution was a nullity:

Held,

Dismissing the motion, that, even if the plaintiff's complaint of irregularities was correct, the irregularities could be cured by going through the proper processes and, since the ultimate result would be the same, the court would not interfere.

TEXT REFERENCE - FOOTNOTE 120

FERGUSON v *WILSON*

(1866) Lr 2 Ch 77

Company - Specific Performance Of Contract To Allot Shares - Damages - Sir H. Cairns Act (21 & 22 Vict. C. 27) - Liability Of Directors - Evidence - Oral Examination At The Hearing- 15 & 16 Vict. C. 86, S. 39.

Facts

The plaintiff by his bill prayed the specific performance of a resolution passed by the board of directors of a railway company, under which he alleged that he was entitled to have a certain number of shares allotted to him; and he also prayed that if it should appear that all the shares had been allotted to other shareholders, the directors might indemnify him out of their own shares, or might be charged with damages. All the shares had been allotted before the filing of the bill:

Held,

That as no relief by way of specific performance was possible, the plaintiff's claim for damages under Sir H. Cairns' Act (21 & 22 Vict. C. 27) failed also.

Decree of *Stuart* v *C.*, affirmed.

In such a case the plaintiff's claim against the directors to be indemnified out of their shares was only a claim for damages in another form .

Per Cairns, L.J.: Directors are agents of the company, and their personal liability in a suit, upon a contract made by them, must be governed by the ordinary law of principal and agent. But a shareholder may sustain a bill against directors personally, where he charges them as trustees, and seeks redress against them for a breach of duty to the company of which he is a member.

In a case where, under the old practice, the Court would have directed at the hearing of an inquiry or issue on a doubtful question of fact, the Court may now examine a party or a witness viva voce at the hearing, under the 39th section of the 15 & 16 Vict. C. 86.

Whether that section applies to a person not a party who has not been a witness in a stage of the proceedings — Quaere.

TEXT REFERENCE - FOOTNOTE 121

YORK AND *NORTH MIDLAND RAILWAY* v *HUDSON*

(1853) 16 Beavan 485

Facts and Decision

A general meeting of a railway company placed 12,050 shares in a projected extension line at the disposal of the directors.

The chairman of the railway company appropriated various unallotted shares to the use of various persons, whose names he did not mention, in order to secure or reward services which he declined to state, but which it was insinuated was in the nature of "secret service money".

The chairman of the railway company also allotted a number of the unappropriated shares to his nominees; they were sold at a premium, and the produce received by him.

Held, that, as trustee, he was bound to the company for the profit made.

Held, that the disposal was merely as trustees for the company, and not for their own benefit; and Hudson, who was the chairman and exercised uncontrolled authority in the conduct of the concerns of the company, having sold a considerable part of such shares at a premium, was held liable to account to the company for their produce, with interest at 5 percent.

Held, also, that he could not retain the profits, either as a large landowner on the line, or as remuneration for his great services, or on the ground of the acquiescence of the shareholders, to be inferred from a presumed knowledge of the sharebook.

Held,

That if the defendant had applied the property of the company in a manner which would not bear the light, he must suffer the consequences; and that being charged with the receipt of the money, he could not discharge himself by the suggestion of such an application.

TEXT REFERENCE - FOOTNOTE 124

AIR CANADA v *M & L TRAVEL LTD*

(1993) 3 LRC 510

Commercial Law - Breach Of Trust - Constructive Trustee - Companies - Whether Relationship Between Parties That Of Trustee And Beneficiary - Whether Appellant Company Director Personally Liable For Breach Of Trust

Facts

The appellant and M. were sole directors in a travel company, but the appellant was not closely involved in the day to day running of the business. The company made an agreement signed by both directors, with the respondent for the sale of the respondent's tickets on the basis that the sale proceeds would be held in trust and be remitted to the respondent twice monthly less commissions on the sales. M. set up trust accounts on behalf of the company for the ticket proceeds, but these accounts were never used.

The company obtained a bank loan, guaranteed personally by both directors, and repayable on demand from the company's general account. All transactions, including ticket proceeds went through the general account. Following a dispute between M. and the appellant, the appellant instructed the bank to stop payment of all cheques. For a period of ten days business was closed and during that time both M. and the appellant attempted to pay the respondent money owing or to transfer the respondent's money to a trust account, but because of the dispute the bank refused to act.

The bank, having served a demand notice, withdrew money owing to it from the general account. The respondent obtained judgement against the company for breach of trust, but the trial judge dismissed the claim against M. and the appellant for personal liability.

On appeal by the respondent, judgement was also entered against M. and the appellant on the grounds that they had both been parties to the conversion of trust funds and should be held personally liable. The appellant appealed to the Supreme Court.

Held,

Appeal dismissed.

(1) The nature of the relationship between the parties was a matter of intention and there was clear evidence of the intention to create a trust in the agreement between the company and the respondent despite the absence of any prohibition on the commingling of funds.

(2) Where a breach of trust had occurred, the basic rule was that personal liability would only be imposed on a stranger to a trust if the stranger's conscience was sufficiently affected to justify such imposition. In the present case personal liability would only be imposed if the appellant, as a stranger to the trust, was shown to have become a constructive trustee by knowingly participating in a fraudulent and dishonest breach of trust. It was unnecessary to show that the appellant himself acted dishonestly but because the trustee was a corporation there was difficulty in conceptualising its actions as dishonest and fraudulent as it could only act through the same human agents whose liability was in issue.

Regardless of the type of trustee, the most relevant description of fraud was the taking of a risk to the prejudice of another's rights, which risk was known to be one which there was no right to take.

In the present case it was known to the company that the air ticket proceeds were held on trust for the respondent . . . It was also known that any assets in the company's general account were subject to the bank's demand. By placing the trust money in the general account the company prejudiced the rights of the beneficiary and the breach of trust by the company was dishonest and fraudulent from an equitable standpoint.

Notwithstanding the appellant's lack of involvement in the day to day running of the business, he was fixed with actual knowledge of the breach of trust by having signed the agreement with the respondent and by his knowledge that the trust funds were deposited into the general account of the company which was subject to the demand loan from the bank; furthermore he benefited from the breach in that his personal liability to the bank was thereby extinguished.

The appellant knowingly and directly participated in the breach of trust and the appeal would therefore be dismissed.

Per curiam. Per McLachin J. In cases of breach of trust English courts have required subjective knowledge of the breach, i.e. actual knowledge or wilful blindness and recklessness. Canadian cases, however, suggested that a stranger to the trust may be liable when he should reasonably have known that the trust was being breached by his actions. Some Canadian authorities also differed from the English in taking the view that it was not necessary to establish that the breach was dishonest and fraudulent. It was not necessary to resolve these differences in this case which met the higher English standards on both points. Personal benefit had been held to be a circumstance in favour in imposing liability on a stranger to the trust in some Canadian cases and in a future case it might be necessary to decide whether liability should be imposed in the absence of personal benefit but it was not necessary to address the question in this case.

TEXT REFERENCE - FOOTNOTE 125

In *Re CITY EQUITABLE FIRE INSURANCE CO. LTD*

(1925) C 407

Company - Winding Up - Misfeasance - Directors And Auditors - Duties - Investments Loans - Signing Cheques - Inspection And Safe Custody Of Securities - Declaration Of Dividends - Fraud Of Managing Director - Clause In Articles Exempting Directors And Auditors From Liability - "Wlful Neglect Or Default" - Companies (Consolidation) Act, 1908.

Facts

In the winding up by the court of the above mentioned company an investigation of its affairs disclosed a shortage of the funds, of which the company should have been possessed, of over 1,200,000 *l*, due in part to the depreciation of investments, but mainly to the instrumentality of the managing director and largely to his deliberate fraud, for which he had been convicted and sentenced.

Art. 150 of the company's Articles of Association provided (inter alia) that none of the directors, auditors, secretary or other officers for the time being of the company should be answerable for the acts, receipt, neglects or defaults of the others or other of them, or for any bankers or other persons with whom any moneys or effects belonging to the company should or might be lodged or deposited for safe custody or for insufficiency or deficiency of any security upon which any moneys or effects belonging to the company should be placed out or invested, or for any other loss, misfortune, or damage which might happen in the execution of their respective offices or trusts, or in relation thereto, unless the same should happen by or through their own wilful neglect or default respectively.

On a misfeasance summons under section 215 of the Companies (Consolidation) Act 1908, the Official Receiver as liquidator sought to make the respondent directors, all of whom (except the managing director) had admittedly acted honestly throughout, liable for negligence in respect of losses occasioned by investments and loans, and of payment of dividends out of capital.

In determining the questions of the liability of the respondent directors raised by the summons, Romer J. enunciated and adopted the following principles relative to the duties of directors and to the meaning to be attached to the words "wilful neglect or default" in Art. 150.

Duties of Directors. The manner in which the work of a company is to be distributed between the board of directors and the staff is a business matter to be decided on business lines. The larger the business carried on by the company the more numerous and the more important the matters that must be of necessity be left to the managers, the accountants, and the rest of the staff.

In ascertaining the duties of a director of a company, it is necessary to consider the nature of the company's business and the manner in which the work of the company is, reasonably in the circumstances and consistently with the Articles of Association, distributed between the directors and the other officials of the company. In discharging those duties a director:

(a) must act honestly; and

(b) must exercise such degree of skill and diligence as would amount to the reasonable care which an ordinary man might be expected to take, in the circumstances, on his own behalf; but

(c) he need not exhibit in the performance of his duties a greater degree of skill than may reasonably be expected from a person of his knowledge and experience; in other words he is not liable for mere errors of judgement;

(d) he is not bound to give continuous attention to the affairs of his company; his duties are of an intermittent nature to be performed at periodical board meetings, and at meetings of any committee to which he is appointed and though not bound to attend all such meetings he ought to attend them when reasonably able to do so; and

(e) in respect of all duties which having regard to the exigencies of business and the Articles of Association may properly be left to some other official, he is, in the absence of grounds for suspicion, justified in trusting that official to perform such duties honestly.

A director who signs a cheque that appears to be drawn for a legitimate purpose is not responsible for seeing that the money is in fact required for that purpose, or that it is subsequently applied for that purpose, assuming, of course, that the cheque comes before him for signature in the regular way, having regard to the usual practice of the company.

A director must of necessity trust to the officials of the company to perform properly and honestly the duties allocated to them. Before any director signs a cheque, or parts with a cheque signed by him, he should satisfy himself that a resolution has been passed by the board (as the case may be), authorising the signature of the cheque; and where a cheque has to be signed between meetings, he should obtain the confirmation of the board subsequently to his signature.

The authority given by the board or committee should not be for the signing of numerous cheques to an aggregate amount, but a proper list of the individual cheques, mentioning the payee and the amount of each, should be read out at the board or committee meeting and subsequently transcribed into the minutes of the meeting.

Joint Stock Discount Co. v *Brown* (1869) LR 8 Eq 381 *distinguished*

It is the duty of each director to see that the company's moneys are from time to time in a proper state of investment, except so far as the articles may justify him in delegating that duty to others.

Before presenting their annual report and balance sheet to their shareholders and before recommending a dividend, directors should have a complete and detailed list of the company's assets and investments prepared for their own use and information, and ought not to be satisfied as to the value of their company's assets merely by the assurance of their chairman, however apparently distinguished and honourable, nor with the expression of the belief of their auditors, however competent and trustworthy. It is not the duty of a director of a big insurance company to supervise personally the safe custody of the securities of the company. It would be impractical, on every purchase of securities, for every delivery thereof to be made to the directors, or on every sale, for the delivery to the brokers of the securities sold to await a meeting of the board or of a committee of directors. The duty of seeing that the securities are in safe custody must of necessity be left to some official of the company in daily attendance at the office of the company, such as the manager, accountant, or secretary.

A director is not responsible for declaring a dividend unwisely. He is liable if he pays it out of capital, but the onus of proving that he has done so lies upon the liquidator who alleges it.

Wilful Neglect or Default: An act, or an admission to do an act, is wilful where the person who acts, or omits to act, knows what he is doing and intends to do what he is doing, but if that act or omission amounts to a breach of that person's duty, and therefore to negligence, he is not guilty of wilful neglect or default unless he knows that he is committing, and intends to commit, a breach of his duty, or is recklessly careless in the sense of not caring whether his act or omission is or is not a breach of his duty.

(This statement of the meaning of "wilful neglect and default" was subsequently approved by Warrington and Sargant L.J. in the Court of Appeal on the Official Receiver's appeal against Romer J.'s decision exonerating the auditors:)

Held,

(1) Following *Re Brazilian Rubber Plantations and Estates Ltd* (1911) 1 Ch 425, that the immunity afforded by Art. 150 was one of the terms upon which the directors held office in the company, and availed them as much on a misfeasance summons by the Official Receiver under section 215, as it would have done in an action by the company against them for negligence; and

(2) Upon the evidence and in accordance with the principles enunciated above, that none of the respondent directors (other than the managing director) was liable for the losses covered by the points of claim, and that in those instances in which all or some of the directors had been guilty of negligence, such negligence was not wilful and Art. 150 applied to exonerate them from liability.

On the same misfeasance summons the Official Receiver sought to make the respondent auditors liable for negligence and breach of duty with respect to the audit by them of the balance sheets for the three years immediately previous to the winding up. In determining the question of liability of the respondent auditors raised by the summons, Romer J. applied the principles enunciated by Lindley

L.J. in Re *London and General Bank* (No 2) (1895) 2 Ch 673 and also the following further principles relative to the duties of auditors.

An auditor is not ever justified in omitting to make personal inspection of the securities that are in the custody of a person or company with whom it is not proper that they should be left, whenever such personal inspection is practicable. A company's stockbrokers, however respectable and responsible they may be, are not proper persons to have custody of its securities except on such occasions, when, for short periods, securities must of necessity be left with them; but immediately such necessity ceases the securities should be lodged in the company's strong room or with its bank, or placed in other proper and usual safe keeping.

Whenever an auditor discovers that securities of the company are not in proper custody, it is his duty to require that the matter be put right at once, or if his requirement is not complied with, to report the fact to the shareholders, and this whether he can or cannot make a personal inspection:

Held,

On the evidence and in accordance with the principles enunciated above:

(1) That the auditors were not guilty of any breach of duty as auditors:

(a)   In describing, after a full investigation in which they were misled and deceived, and their reports to the board suppressed, by the chairman of the company, large sums of money left in the hands of the company's stockbrokers and lent to the general manager of the company as "Loans at call or short notice", "loans" or "cash at hand and in bank";

or

(b)   In failing to discover that the company's stockbrokers, in order to reduce their indebtedness to the company for the purposes of the audit, made purchases, on behalf of the company, immediately before the close of the company's financial year, of treasury bills which in fact never came into the possession of the company and were sold immediately the new financial year had opened.

(2) That the auditors committed a breach of duty in not personally inspecting the securities of the company in the hands of the stockbrokers of the company, and in not either insisting upon those securities being put in proper custody, or in reporting the matter to the shareholders; but that inasmuch as throughout the audit the auditors honestly and carefully discharged what they conceived to be the whole of their duty to the company, such negligence was not wilful, and Art. 150 applied to exonerate them from liability.

On the appeal of the Official Receiver from the above decision so far only as it affected the respondent auditors, the Court (Pollock M.R. Warrington and Sargant L.JJ.), in affirming as a whole the decision of Romer J.:

Held,

(1) That section 215 was a procedure section only and created no new or additional liability.

(2) That the measure of the auditors responsibility depends upon the terms of his engagement. There may be a special contract defining the duties and liabilities of the auditors. If there is, then that contract governs the question. The articles will however be looked at if there is no special agreement, because the auditors will presumably have taken their duties upon the terms (among others) set out in the articles. That is not to say that auditors can set aside a statutory obligation. No agreement or article of association can remove an imperative or statutory duty.

(3) Section 113 does not lay down a rigid code. The duty imposed on the auditors by it is not absolute, but depends upon the information given and explanations furnished to them, so that there is abundant scope for discretion. Art. 150 is not in conflict with the section. The onus lies upon the auditors, who would not be excused for total omission to comply with any of the requirements of the section, or for any consequences of deliberate or reckless indifferent failure to ask for information on matters which call for further explanation.

(4) Auditors should not be content with a certificate that securities are in possession of a particular company, firm or person unless the company, etc., is trustworthy, or, as it is sometimes put, respectable, and further is one that in the ordinary course of business keeps securities for its customers. In all these cases the auditor must use his judgement. The definition of 'wilful conduct' by Lord Alverstone C.J. in *Forder* v *Great Western Railway Co.* (1905) 2 KB 532, 536,

adopted by Pollock M.R. Quaere, whether in the particular circumstances of the case, apart from Art.150, there was negligence on the part of the auditors (as held by Romer J.) in not personally inspecting the securities which were in the possession of the company's stockbrokers and accepting their certificate instead.

TEXT REFERENCE - FOOTNOTE 128

HOGG v CRAMPHORN LTD, AND OTHERS

(1967) 1 Ch 254

Company - Directors - Fiduciary Duty To Company Use Of Powers To Issue Shares And Lend Money In Order To Retain Control Of Company - Bona Fide Belief That Transaction In Best Interests Of Company - Whether Ultra Vires - Ratification By General Meeting

Company Shares - Articles Of Association - Power For Directors To Issue Shares "With A Special Or Without Any Right of Voting" - Provision That In Case of A Poll "Every Member Shall Have One Vote For Every Share Held By Him" - Whether Directors Empowered To Issue Shares Carrying 10 Votes Each On A Poll

Facts

Article 10 of the articles of the defendant company provided that "the shares shall be under the control of the directors who may allot or otherwise dispose of the same . . . on such terms and conditions . . . as the directors think fit . . ." Article 13 provided that ". . . new shares shall be issued upon such terms and conditions and with such rights and privileges annexed thereto . . . as the directors determine . . . and with a special or without any right of voting . . ." Article 75 provided: "On a show of hands every member shall have one vote only. In case of a poll every member shall have one vote for every share . . . held by him".

The directors of the company and their supporters held some 37,000 of the 126,181 issued shares in March 1963. On 29 March 1963 B offered to buy the whole of the issued share capital at 25s, for each preference share and 50s for each ordinary share.

The directors, acting in good faith and believing that the establishment of a trust and avoidance of the acquisition of control by B. would benefit the company, devised a scheme, the primary purpose of which was to ensure control of the company by the directors.

By a deed dated 18 April 1963, the company established a trust for the acquisition of shares in the company to be held by the trustees, the individual defendants, for the benefit of the company's employees. On the same date the trustees applied for 5,707 un-issued preference shares on condition that there should be attached to them 10 votes per share on a poll. The directors allotted those shares to the trustees at par with such special voting rights, and made a loan to the trustees out of the company's funds of £5,707 free of interest and not to be repaid until the termination of the trust. The trustees used that loan to pay for the shares. The effect or purported effect of those transactions was that the directors could rely on the support of more than half the total votes. On the same date B. was informed that the directors did not propose to place his offer before the shareholders.

On 9 May the plaintiff became the registered shareholder of 50 ordinary shares. On 14 May the Board resolved to advance £28,293 to the trustees on similar terms to enable them to buy further preference shares at 25s, per share, and on 13 and 15 May the board circularised the shareholders informing them of B.'s offer and inviting them to sell their preference shares to the trustees at 25s per share.

On the questions first, whether the resolution attaching the right on a poll to 10 votes per share to the 5,707 preference shares was *ultra vires*, secondly, whether the allotment and issue of such shares to the trustees was *ultra vires*, and thirdly, whether the trustees held the sum of £28,293 as trustees of the trust deed or in trust for the company absolutely:

Held,

(1) that on the true construction of the articles, any special right of voting attached to any share under Article 13 must be one that was consistent with Article 75 and so could not confer more than one vote in respect of that share; accordingly, the directors had no power to attach the special voting rights to the 5,707 preference shares; but that the plaintiff, whether suing on his own behalf or in a representative capacity, was not competent to procure the allotment to be set aside, although it might be open to the trustees to do so.

(2)   that the power to issue shares was a fiduciary power, and if exercised for an improper motive the issue was liable to be set aside, it being immaterial that the issue was made in the bona fide belief that it was in the interests of the company.

Punt v *Symons & Co. Ltd.* [1903] 2 Ch 506 and *Piercy* v *S Mills & Co. Ltd* [1920] 1 Ch 77; 35 TLR 703 applied.

(3)   That, the loan of £28,293 was not made with the single-minded purpose of benefiting the company otherwise than by securing control for the directors, and formed part of one scheme for this purpose; accordingly, the issue of the shares, the execution of the deed and the loan were all *ultra vires* the directors and invalid unless ratified by the company in general meeting.

(4) that the plaintiff was justified in suing in a representative capacity in respect of the loan of the company's money.

TEXT REFERENCE - FOOTNOTE 129

HOWARD SMITH LTD
v
AMPOL PETROLEUM LTD, AND OTHERS

(1974) Ac 821

(Privy Council)

Company - Director - Fiduciary Duty - Allotment Of Shares - Australian Company In Need Of Capital - Primary Object Of Directors To Alter Majority Shareholding Of Issued Shares - No Personal Advantage To Directors - Whether Power To Allot Shares Validly Exercised By Directors.

Facts

Two companies A and B, held 55 percent of the issued shares of Company M, which required more capital. A made an offer for all the issued shares of M. and another company. H. announced an intention to make a higher offer for those shares. M's directors considered A's offer too low and decided to recommend that the offer be rejected. A and B then stated that they intended to act jointly in the future operations of M and would reject any offer for their shares. H then applied to M for an allotment of 4½ million ordinary shares; M's directors decided by a majority to make the allotment and immediately issued capital; A and B's shareholding was reduced to 36.6 percent of the issued shares and H was in a position to make an effective take-over offer. A challenged the validity of the issue of the shares to H and sought an order in the Supreme Court for the rectification of the share register by the removal of H as a member of M in respect of the allotted shares. M's directors contended that the primary reason for the issue of the shares to H was to obtain more capital.

Street J. found that M's directors had not been motivated by any purpose of personal gain or advantage or by a desire to retain their position on the board, that M needed capital, but that the primary purpose of the allotment was to reduce the proportionate shareholding of A and B so that H could proceed with its take-over offer. The judge held that in those circumstances the directors had improperly exercised their powers and he ordered that the allotment of shares be set aside and the share register rectified.

On appeal by H to the Judicial Committee:

Held, dismissing the appeal, that, although the directors had acted honestly and had power to make the allotment, to alter a majority shareholding was to interfere with that element of the company's constitution which was separate from and set against the directors' powers and, accordingly, it was unconstitutional for the directors; to use their fiduciary powers over the shares in the company for the purpose of destroying an existing majority or creating a new majority; and that, since the directors' primary object for the allotment of shares was to alter the majority shareholding, the directors had improperly exercised their powers and the allotment was invalid.

Mills v *Mills* (1938) 60 C.L.R. 150 considered.

Per Curiam. A matter such as the raising of finance is one of management, within the responsibility of the directors. It would be wrong for a court to question the correctness of the management's decision if bona fide arrived at. But, when a dispute arises whether the directors of a company made a particular decision for one purpose or for another, or whether there being more than one purpose, one or another purpose was the substantial or primary purpose, the court is entitled to look at the situation objectively in order to estimate how critical or pressing or substantial an alleged requirement may have been. If it finds that a particular requirement, though real, was not urgent or critical at the relevant time, it may have reason to doubt or discount the assertions of individuals that they acted solely in order to deal with the matter.

Judgement of the Supreme Court of New South Wales affirmed.

TEXT REFERENCE - FOOTNOTE 130

MACAINE (LONDON) LTD v COOK & WATTS LTD

(1967) CLY 482

Take over - Avoidance - Purchase of share capital

Facts

The defendant company entered into a contract to purchase the share capital of GB Co. at a time when ML Co. was making a take-over bid for the defendant company.

The effect of this transaction was to ward off the take-over bid. ML Co. and certain shareholders of the defendant company sought an interlocutory injunction to restrain the execution of the proposed contract.

They contended that the negotiations had been conducted with indecent haste and that the agreement had not been made with an eye to the best interests of the defendant company.

Held,

That on the evidence before the court the primary purpose of the proposed contract was not that contended for by the plaintiffs and no injunction would be granted.

TEXT REFERENCE - FOOTNOTE 132

LAGUNAS NITRATE COMPANY v *LAGUNAS NITRATE SYNDICATE*

(1899) 2 Ch D 392

Company - Memorandum And Articles Of Association - Promoters - Directors, Duties Of - Fiduciary Relation - Appointment Of Directors Of One Company As Directors Of The Other - Contract - Sale By Directors In One Contract To Themselves In Another - Dual Relation - Independent Board - Contract By Company With Its Directors - Agency - Prospectus - Concealment From Shareholders Of Material Facts - Misrepresentation - Misfeasance - Breach Of Trust - Vendor And Purchaser - Voidable Contract - Rescission - Damages - Delay - Change Of Position.

Facts

The L. Co. was promoted and formed by the directors of L. Syndicate for the purpose of purchasing part of the property of the syndicate, consisting of nitrate works. The directors of the syndicate prepared and signed the Memorandum and Articles of Association of the company, the articles nominating them as directors and stating specifically that they were also the directors of the syndicate. They also prepared the company's prospectus and purchase contract, and affixed the seals of the syndicate and of the company to the latter. The company's solicitors and secretary were also the same as those of the syndicate.

Two years after the date of the contract and the completion of the purchase the shareholders of the company, believing that their property had been purchased at an overvalue and that there had been misrepresentations in the contract and prospectus, appointed an independent board of directors who, after investigating the facts and with the sanction of a general meeting of the shareholders, brought an action against the syndicate and the directors for rescission of the contract and damages on the ground of misrepresentation, misfeasance, breach of trust, and concealment of the material facts, but not alleging fraud. From the date of the contract and down to and also since the commencement of the action the company had, first by its original directors and afterwards by its independent board, carried on business and worked the property the subject of the contract.

On appeal by the company:

Held, by Lindley M.R., and Collins L.J., that the company was not entitled to rescission or damages, for

(1) at the date of the contract the company had, by its memorandum and articles, notice that its directors were also the vendors or agents of the vendor syndicate, and the mere fact that its directors did not constitute an independent board was not a sufficient ground for setting aside the contract;

(2) there had been no misrepresentation made to, or any material fact concealed from, any of the persons who were members of the company at the date of the contract, those persons being directors themselves;

(3) although the contract and prospectus were, on the evidence, misleading in certain particulars which would have entitled the company at the time to repudiate the contract, yet through the subsequent alteration of the property consequent on its being worked by the company, the position of the parties had been so changed that they could not be restored to their original position; and

(4) the defendants, the directors had not been guilty of such negligence or breach of trust as to render them liable in damages in law for the loss occasioned to the company, or in equity to make good the loss.

But held, by Rigby L.J. (1) that, in the promotion of the company, the preparation and sealing of the contract, and the preparation and issue of the prospectus, the original directors had, while acting as sole agents for the vendor syndicate, constituted themselves sole fiduciary agents for the purchasing company, and that the company was therefore entitled to rescission (but accounting for the profit of its working) on the principal that no fiduciary agent can bind his principal by a sale to him of such agent's property, where the principal had purchased without independent advice; and that the notice in the memorandum and articles of the company of the double relation of its directors was ineffectual to discharge them from the obligations involved in that principle; and (2) that the company had not lost its right to rescission either (a) through delay — for time did not run during the domination of the original directors and the non-disclosure by them of material facts or (b) through alteration of the property, the alteration having been in effect the act of the vendor syndicate by its directors.

> *Erlanger* v. *New Sombrero Phosphate Co.* (1878) 3 App. Cass. 1218
> and *Salomon* v. *Salomon & Co.,* (1897) A.C. 22, *discussed*

Statement of the principles as to (1) the fiduciary relationship between the promoters of a company and its shareholders; (2) the validity of contracts between a company and its directors as promoters; (3) the non-liability of directors for losses when acting *intra vires* and honestly; (4) the voidability of a contract for misrepresentation; and (5) the impossibility of rescinding a contract after change of position.

TEXT REFERENCE - FOOTNOTE 133

Re WHITE and OSMOND (PARKSTONE) LTD

1960

Background

This is an unreported case, judgement on which was delivered on 30 June 1960 and referred to in *Palmer's Company Law* (23rd edition, 1982) Volume 1, para 84-85 wherein is to be found a passage from the decision of Buckley J. already mentioned in this text.

The case was cited in R. v Grantham (1984) BCLC 270 at pages 274-75.

Buckley J. eventually decided in favour of the trader on the basis that, although he may have been guilty of insufficient care and supervision of his business, he could not be said (in the words of Maugham J.) to have been guilty of real moral blame so as to justify the judge in saying that he ought to be liable for the debts of the company without limit. In other words he acquitted the trader of dishonesty — an essential ingredient to personal liability.

APPENDIX IV

Typical shareholders' questions

Acknowledgement

The following shareholders' questions were extracted and/or adapted from a publication by Coopers & Lybrand (USA) entitled Annual Meetings Questions from Shareholders.

Introduction

Annual Meetings: Questions from shareholders offers a cross-section of the types of questions that may be asked at annual shareholder meetings. Its purpose is to give management an opportunity to prepare informed responses to issues that may be raised. We trust that directors and officers will find these questions useful in preparing for the annual meeting.

Directors and Management

The responsibilities, compensation and performance of the board of directors and management are always of great interest to shareholders, especially when earnings and dividends are disappointing. Shareholders are also concerned about their representation on the board, as well as the make-up of the board's membership in general.

Board of Directors

1. Why doesn't the company have more outside directors? Does it plan to add more outside directors?

2. Does the company have a committee for nominating candidates for board membership? What qualifications are required for prospective board members? How does the committee ensure that those nominated represent shareholders' interests?

3. What is the company doing to attract qualified women and minority shareholders for board membership? Have employees or their union representatives been considered for board membership?

4. Why does the chairman of the board, who is responsible for policy, also serve as chief operating officer responsible for day-to-day activities?

5. How often did the board of directors meet this year? Last year? What is the attendance record of individual members at board meetings?

6. Does any director on the board have a potential conflict of interest because of membership on another board? Does the company require the board of directors and officers to submit conflict of interest statements?

7. Has the board approved any transactions with related parties? Why? Are any members of the board or management involved in a related party transaction?

8. Is there a mandatory retirement age for directors? Why isn't there cumulative voting for directors?

9. Do directors receive their fees if they are absent? Do they receive additional fees for serving on board committees? Are directors reimbursed for travel expenses? Are directors who are also employees paid additional fees for attending directors' meetings? Does the company provide pension benefits or life insurance for its directors?

10. Are all directors also shareholders? Why aren't directors required to own a minimum number of shares? Have any directors sold company stock during the year? Why?

11. Do all directors vote on appointments and promotions of senior officers?

12. Has the board of directors formed a social responsibility committee? An ethics committee? An audit committee?

13. Has any officer or director resigned or declined to stand for re-election? Why?

14. Does the company carry liability insurance for the directors? Have premiums for directors' liability insurance gone up significantly during the past year? Are insurance limits adequate in light of court decisions holding directors personally liable for amounts over the limits? If not, will coverage be increased so the company can continue to attract qualified candidates?

Executive Compensation and Benefits

1. How does the company explain the trend in executive compensation compared to the trend in earnings? Why was executive compensation increased when the company is cutting costs or not increasing dividends (or not paying dividends)? What factors determined management salary increases or bonuses?

2. Do any officers have employment contracts? Do they exceed five years? Are the terms similar to those of other companies in this industry? What do the contracts provide in the event of a take-over of the company? Do any retired officers have consulting agreements?

3. What perquisites do executives receive? How are personal benefits valued? Do executives reimburse the company for the fair value of personal benefits received?

4. Are executive perquisites checked by the internal auditors and reported to the audit committee (compensation committee)?

5. Will there be any new executive compensation plans (e.g. stock purchase, profit sharing, incentive bonus) or changes in existing plans?

6. Is shareholder approval required for new executive incentive plans? Are plans structured to emphasise the company's long-term objectives rather than short-term goals?

7. What stock options have been granted to officers? Why aren't all employees eligible? Does the board (compensation committee) evaluate option plans periodically? Is there a ceiling on the number of options that may be granted to an individual? How much potential dilution of common stock could occur as a result of the stock option plan?

8. Is there a ceiling on executives' retirement benefits?

9.   What is the company's policy on loans to officers and directors? What is the total dollar amount of all loans to officers and directors? What were these loans for? Have any loans been made to officers to exercise stock options? Do interest rates on loans reflect current borrowing rates?

Audit Committees, Internal Auditors, and Independent Accountants

Audit committees provide a means of overseeing internal controls, financial reporting practices, and internal and external audit functions.   The internal auditors' role is to reliably record and objectively analyse data, both financial and operations related, while the independent accountants' role is to provide assurance about the fairness of presentation of the company's financial statements. Shareholders are concerned about the audit committee's effectiveness in performing its duties and the nature of its relationship with the internal and external auditors. They are also concerned about the objectivity and competence of the internal and external auditors.

Audit Committee

1.   How frequently does the audit committee meet? How often do they report to the full board of directors?

2.   How often do the internal auditors and independent accountants each meet with the audit committee? Does the audit committee review the scope of both internal and external audit activities in advance? Does it meet with the independent accountants at the conclusion of the audit? Does the committee follow up on the recommendations of both the independent accountants and the internal auditors?

3.   Are corporate and division controllers given confidential access to the audit committee?

4.   Does the audit committee receive the same comments on internal control from the independent accountants and internal auditors as management?

5. Does the audit committee review all financial press releases and earnings reports before their release to the public?

6. How are audit committee members appointed? Are inside directors prohibited from serving on the committee? Do outside directors constitute a majority of audit committee members? What are the backgrounds of the members?

Internal Auditors

1. Does the company have an internal audit department? If not, why?

2. How many internal auditors does the company have? Do they report to a sufficiently high level of management? Do they have ready access to the audit committee?

3. Does the company have internal auditors who specialise in reviewing Electronic Data Processing (EDP) controls?

4. Do the internal auditors review all transactions with related parties?

5. How often do internal auditors visit each operating location? Do they cover foreign operations?

6. Have the standards and performance of the internal audit department been evaluated by an external review?

7. How does the internal audit department encourage its personnel to obtain relevant professional accreditation?

8. Do the internal auditors have full, unrestricted access to all company functions, records, property and personnel?

9. Does the internal audit department engage in operational (management) audits? How much of its time is spent on operational audits compared to financial audits?

Independent Accountants

1. What fees were paid to the independent accountants last year? How do these compare with the previous year?

2. Have the independent accountants undergone a peer review?

3. Does the company use different auditing firms for some of its subsidiaries? Are all company operations audited? Was the auditors' report on any subsidiary's financial statements qualified? If so, why doesn't the principal auditor's report disclose this?

4. Do the independent accountants investigate and report on all acquisitions?

5. Has the company engaged the independent accountants to perform a limited review of its quarterly or half yearly financial statements before they are issued?

Internal Control

Because companies' accounting systems have become increasingly more sophisticated, shareholders are very concerned about the adequacy of the system of internal control, especially in the area of security and integrity of EDP operations. Instances of questionable accounting practices, computer fraud, and authorised transactions are topics of shareholder interest.

1. Are the company's internal accounting controls adequate to identify errors, irregularities, or illegal acts?

2. Do the controls identify unauthorised transactions?

3. What safeguards does the company have to prevent managers from 'cooking the books' or otherwise abusing generally accepted accounting principles?

4. Are steps being taken to make sure that neither employees nor outsiders can use the company's computer system to gain confidential information, disrupt operations, or commit fraud? Are there adequate safeguards over improper access? What steps has the company taken to ensure that computer security keeps pace with rapidly evolving technology?

5. Does the company have a plan to make sure that business operations would not be disrupted if there were a disaster at a data centre or a failure of the data communications network?

6. Did the independent accountants report any material weakness in internal control? What has been done about it ?

7. How often does the internal audit department review the system of internal control? Were any significant weaknesses in internal control reported by the internal audit department? If so, what has been done about them?

8. Have the independent accountants issued a report on the company's internal accounting controls?

9. Who is responsible for corporate security? Are there adequate controls to protect the company's technology, trade secrets, and other sensitive records?

10. Have employees been caught in apparently fraudulent activities? Were they prosecuted?

Operations

Shareholders want to know about the effects of current economic and political environments on the company. Shareholders are concerned with how changes in interest rates, foreign markets, capital availability, tax laws, and new products and competitors may affect the company's operations.

Economic Environment

1. What are the sales and earnings forecast for the coming year? How do they compare with last year? How do the results from the first quarter of this year compare with what was anticipated? With the last quarter of last year? First quarter of last year? What is the current backlog of orders? How does it compare with last year?

2. How much do fluctuations in the stock market affect the company? Last year, did they affect the company's earnings? Ability to raise capital? How is management addressing this issue?

3. How did the cost of incentive plans (i.e. profit sharing, bonuses, etc.) compare with the previous year?

4. How much of the change in sales and earnings was due to volume? Product mix?

5. Who are the company's major customers? Will the take-over of a particular major customer affect the company's sales and earnings?

6. Who are the company's major competitors? Why haven't the company's sales and earnings increased as much as our competitors?

7. Has the company closed any plants, branches or divisions this year? Are these shutdowns temporary or permanent? Will a loss result from a plant closing? Will the laid off employees be rehired, retrained, or relocated? How does the company justify these closures when they appear to be profitable?

8. Are there plans to phase out any products? Does the company plan to sell any of its divisions, branches or subsidiaries? Is any sale or liquidation of such being postponed to avoid recording a loss? At what capacity are the plants, branches or subsidiaries operating?

9. Is anything being done to improve worker productivity? Is there resistance to these efforts? Does improved productivity depend on significant investment in new plant and equipment? If so, what plans have been made, and what will it cost the company?

10. How much variable rate debt does the company have? What hedging strategy is the company using in case interest rates fluctuate widely?

11. Has management ensured that the company's attorneys are instructed to report any possible violations of laws or regulations? Have any been reported? What actions have been taken as a result?

12. What litigation is the company currently involved in? What are the potential costs? What litigation has been settled during the current year? What did it cost the company? Have there been any changes in the status of litigation since the annual report was published? What about 'hidden' litigation, where the company might be vulnerable to future product or worker liability claims?

13. Is the company involved in any patent or trademark disputes?

14. Are the company's products properly labelled to cover, where applicable, hazards and safe handling procedures? Is product packaging tamper resistant?

15. Has the company had difficulty getting insurance? What types of business risks are self-insured? How much product liability coverage is there? Have deductibles increased? How much? Does the company have insurance consultants regularly assess all its coverage?

16. Is there sufficient cash flow after dividends to pay for replacing plant and equipment?

17. What were the total fees paid to outside consultants?

Political Environment and Taxes

1. What percentage of current business is supported by governmental grants or contracts? Has the government questioned any amounts we billed them? How would it affect the company if governmental contracts were reduced or cancelled?

2. How much has it cost the company to comply with governmental directives and regulations?

3. Are any products currently being investigated by the government for alleged violations of regulations?

4. Has the company complied with all applicable trade regulations?

5. Do you anticipate any tax legislation in the coming year that will be significant for the company? How will earnings be affected? What is management doing to lessen any potentially adverse impact?

6. Have there been any recent political or economic developments in foreign countries that will affect the company's overall tax liabilities?

Mergers and Acquisitions

1. Does the company have plans for acquisitions or new ventures? How will they be financed? What criteria are used to identify potential acquisitions? Will they dilute present shareholders' equity?

2. Has management received any offers or inquiries from companies seeking to acquire it? Has the company solicited any take-over offers?

3. Is there a strategy for warding off or thwarting a take-over? Does it involve a 'poison pill' technique, which would be contrary to shareholders' best interests? Does it involve a leveraged employee stock ownership plan (ESOP)? What about placing a large block of stock with a friendly investor as a take-over defence? Does the company monitor changes in

stock ownership to anticipate take-over attempts? Has the company paid more than fair value to repurchase any of its shares?

Operating Units and Product Lines

1.   Are any divisions or product lines currently losing money? What are the plans for them? What divisions or product lines are expected to be stronger/weaker performers this year?

2.   Do any of the company's subsidiaries or divisions operate in a high technology environment? What's being done to manage growth and technological development and ensure effective management in such a rapidly changing environment?

3.   What is the company's share of this market? Is the market increasing or decreasing? Why? Is the company's share increasing or decreasing? Why? What are the principal marketing methods used? What special skills or advantages will enable the company to maintain its market position? Are competitors' operations more profitable? How do competitors' pricing strategies compare with ours?

4.   How much was spent for advertising and other promotion this year? Will these budgets be increased or decreased next year?

5.   How much was spent on product research and development? What new products or product improvements have recently evolved from the research and development programme? Have any of these new products been patented? What new products does the company plan to introduce in the near future? Does the company participate in any research and development joint ventures?

Foreign Operations

1.   What percentage of the company's earnings or total revenues is generated from foreign markets? What are our major foreign markets? Are there plans to enter any new foreign markets?

2. Have changes in the value of the dollar affected the company's ability to compete in foreign markets?

3. Has a joint venture with any foreign company been considered?

4. Does the company get raw materials from or operate in any countries that deny basic human rights? Has the company considered discontinuing operations or investments in those countries?

5. Have the recent economic problems in a particular country adversely affected the company's profitability? What is the outlook?

6. Have terrorist acts or political unrest (in general or in a particular country) had any effect on the company? Are company personnel or property in danger? What safety measures are being taken?

7. Has the company considered hiring a consulting firm to assess the risks of operating in foreign countries?

8. Is there a threat of nationalisation in a foreign country where we have operations? What steps have been taken to protect our assets from foreign expropriation?

9. What was the effect of foreign currency translation on earnings?

10. Do we have any safeguards against losses from foreign currency fluctuations? How much of the company's debt is payable in foreign currencies? What is the company's policy on forward exchange contracts?

11. Does the company have operations in countries with highly inflationary economies? Will operations be continued or expanded in these countries? How will this affect earnings?

Liquidity and Capital Resources

1.   How does the company evaluate the risks associated with holding cash and cash equivalents and investing in securities?

2.   How much money will be spent on capital projects? How will this impact on cash flow and liquidity? How do our cash flow and liquidity compare with competitors'?

3.   Are there sufficient lines of credit available?

4.   What new financing arrangements are planned? Do these plans include a re-entry into the long-term debt market, or will financing continue to be based on short-term debt? Are any changes expected in the company's debt ratio of earnings to fixed charges? Can future debt maturities be met without significant new borrowings?

5.   Does the company plan to extinguish or refinance any debt? How will this affect the financial statements? Has the company considered issuing convertible adjustable preferred stock? 'Deep discount' or 'zero coupon' bonds? Bonds through a special-purpose corporation?

6.   Are any outdated plants scheduled for renovation? What financing has been arranged?

7.   Is the company planning to pay or raise cash dividends, issue a stock dividend, or split the stock?

Financial Reporting Matters

The annual report is the shareholders' primary source of information about the company's financial affairs and overall strength. Shareholders are concerned about the company's accounting policies, compliance with authoritative pronouncements and changes in account balances from year to year.

1. What amount does the company consider material for financial reporting purposes?

2. Are the financial statements prepared in accordance with international accounting standards as well as generally accepted accounting principles?

3. Why are financial statements and footnotes in the annual report not simplified so that a non-accountant can more easily understand them?

4. Why is the independent accountant's report qualified? What are the latest developments on a particular issue for which the independent accountants qualified their opinion?

5. What is the company doing about   (problem) disclosed in the annual report?

6. Were any accounting policies changed during the year? If so, why? What was the impact on profits?

7. Why are there major differences in accounting policies between the company and a major competitor?

8. Has the company engaged in any off balance sheet financing? What is the nature and amount of such financing?

9. Does the company issue financial forecasts, projections, or other 'forward-looking' data? Who receives this information? Will it be reported on by independent accountants?

10. What was the total amount of bad debts written off last year? How does it compare with other companies in the industry? What were the largest debts written off last year? How much money is due from bankrupt companies?

11. Has the company considered revaluing any assets?

12.   Why are there large fourth-quarter adjustments? Do they indicate that the system of internal control is not functioning properly?

Corporate Social Responsibility

Because corporate decisions have a great impact on society and the environment, shareholders are concerned about how the company's actions will affect them. In particular, shareholders want to know about the company's policies regarding safety regulations, hazardous waste disposal, employee benefits and labour contracts, and political matters.

General

1.   What is the company's plant safety record? Are there active programs to promote safety, accident prevention, etc? How does the company ensure that its subcontractors adhere to the safety programmes?

2.   Is the company actively involved in community affairs?

3.   What charitable contributions did the company make? Were any officers or directors associated with organisations that received contributions? Is there a list published of the organisations to which the company gives charitable, educational, or other grants?

4.   Why did the company contribute to   (organisation)?

5.   Why does the company not reduce charitable contributions and increase dividends so that shareholders can give to the charities of their choice?

6.   Has the company made any contributions or loans or given other support to any political candidate or organisation, including lobbies? If so, to whom? How much was spent? What was the business reason for doing this?

7. Does the company have any officers or other employees on loan to governmental, political, educational or other organisations while drawing full salaries from the company?

8. Has the company hired any former governmental employees in executive positions or retained their services as lobbyists, consultants, or counsel?

9. How is the company fostering its image within the investment community?

Employee Relations

1. What is the status of labour contracts? Which contracts will expire in the coming year? What was (is) the effect of the recent (current) strike?

3. Does the company plan to offer early retirement incentives as a means of reducing the workforce? What will it cost the company? Does it expose the company to allegations of age discrimination? Is there a pre-retirement counselling programme?

4. What plans are there for increased automation? What effect will this have on labour costs or labour relations?

5. Does the company allow participants in employee profit sharing plans to vote their shares?

6. Did company employees suffer any serious injuries during the year? If so, what were the circumstances?

Employee Benefits

1. Was the pension plan changed during the year? Are changes anticipated? Have pension benefits to retirees kept pace with inflation?

2. Is the pension plan overfunded? If so, why has not the company used one of the techniques currently available to reacquire the excess assets?

3.   Did the auditors express a clean opinion on the pension plan's financial statements? Why not?

4.   What percent of pension plan assets are invested in stocks, bonds, money market securities, etc? What was the return on the plan's assets last year?

5.   Are company securities held by the pension plan? How are they voted?

6.   Has the company considered starting an ESOP? Why not?

Environmental and Consumer Matters

1.   How much has been spent on environment projects? How much will be spent in the future? When?

2.   Does the company use any hazardous materials in its production processes? What safeguards are in effect to protect employees and the public, both on-site and in transit?

3.   What is the company doing to recycle waste? How are dangerous waste materials disposed of? If the materials are disposed of by a contractor, how does the company ensure that the disposal is done properly?

4.   Has the company been fined or warned for violating environmental laws? What corrective action has been taken?

5.   How does the company ensure quality customer service? Is there a way customers can file complaints against the company?

6.   Has the level of product complaints, product returns, warranty costs etc., risen? What action has management taken to reduce or prevent these problems? Are any suits pending on the company's products?

7.   Have any consumer groups recently criticised the company? If so, how were the matters resolved?

Shareholder Matters

Shareholders demand to be kept abreast of current information about the company. In particular, they are interested in protecting their direct interests and want information about stock prices, dividends, voting, and other proxy matters.

Shareholder Interests

1. What is being done to safeguard against insider trading of company stock?

2. What causes the unusual fluctuations in the price of company stock? Why does the company have an unusually high (low) price-earnings ratio compared with its competitors? Why is the company's book value so much greater than market value?

3. Is the company planning to repurchase outstanding preferred or common shares? Why? Were any treasury shares purchased from officers or directors in the past year? Private sources? How did these purchases affect earnings per share?

4. Why are various classes of stock, with different rights, issued?

5. Why are shareholders not granted pre-emptive rights for new stock issues?

6. Have shareholders approved all stock option and employee stock ownership plans? Why aren't actions that would significantly increase the cost of employee benefit plans subject to shareholder approval?

7. Has a dividend reinvestment program been considered? How many shareholders are enrolled in the program? Who votes the shares held in trust?

8. What percent of the company's shares are held by directors, officers, or employees? Does the company monitor trading by board members,

officers, and others in management? What percent of the company's shares are held in nominee or street name or by foreign investors?

9.   How much of the company's stock is owned by institutional investors? Does the company try to identify beneficial owners of securities held in 'street' names?

10.   Have the company's by-laws changed? If so, what are the changes? Why isn't shareholder approval required?

Shareholder Relations

1.   Does the company have shareholder relations personnel that answer proxy-related questions?

2.   Why does the company not take action to determine the proper addresses of shareholders whose dividend checks or proxy material are returned as undeliverable (for example, by contacting the shareholder's last known bank or stockbroker)?

3.   Does the company provide information to financial analysts or institutional investors that it does not give to other shareholders?

Annual Reports, Annual Meetings and Proxy Matters

1.   Why are all the directors, officers, and independent accountants not at this meeting?

2.   Why is a ballot not used in shareholder voting? Why isn't the number of votes for and against each director and each proposal disclosed?

3.   Why does the company not issue a post-meeting report summarising annual and special meetings, including the question-and-answer session? Why isn't the report more detailed?

4. Are proxy votes tabulated by optical scanners? If so, are they checked for shareholder comments?

5. Why don't the proxies indicate the number of shares owned?

6. What proposals were submitted by shareholders but not included in the proxy statement? Why were they excluded?

7. Why does the ballot not provide space to vote for a director other than those nominated by management? Why aren't nominations accepted from the floor? Why aren't nomination proposals supported by shareholders owning a certain percentage of shares included in the proxy statement?

APPENDIX V

Selection
of questions
for students

CHAPTER 1

1. What do you understand by the term:
    (a) sole trader or proprietor
    (b) partnership
2. Define a company.
3. "The property of the company belongs to its shareholders." True or false? Discuss.
4. What do you understand by the term *ultra vires?*
5. How is a company formed?

CHAPTER 2

1. What is the purpose of a meeting?
2. In what ways does a discussion differ from:
    (a) A debate
    (b) A conversation
    (c) An argument
3. What are the essential characteristics of a good discussion?
4. Is discussion important at company meetings? If so, why? If not, why not?
5. "Discussion is an integral part of a meeting". True or false? If true, how and when does it take place?

CHAPTER 3

1. Define the term "corporate resolve".
2. "Companies are constitutionally democratic but they are not egalitarian." Discuss the statement.
3. What do you understand by the statement "a company is a creature of statute"?
4. What do you understand by the term "a meeting of shareholders"?
5. Explain what is meant by the statement "the company in general meeting is the repository of the ultimate authority of the company." Give an example.

CHAPTER 4

1. Where is the law of company meetings to be found?
2. What is meant by the term "the company's corporate instruments"?
3. Define the three basic rules which are applicable to the conduct of company meetings.
4. What do you understand to be the rule emanating from the case *Foss* v *Harbottle*?
5. "Under the provisions of older company law, the extent of a company's powers was set out in its memorandum". Discuss this statement and give an example as to how such powers were set out in the memorandum.

CHAPTER 5

1. What is meant by the statement "a company has no mind of its own"?
2. List three types of company meetings and briefly describe their function.
3. What is a resolution in lieu of meeting?
4. What is a requisitioned shareholders' meeting? Explain the process for convening such a meeting.
5. What is the prescribed business to be transacted at the annual meeting?
6. Can special business be dealt with at annual meetings? If so, what are the procedural prerequisites?

CHAPTER 6

1. A representative of a deceased member is entitled to attend and vote at annual meetings of the company. True or false? Discuss.
2. Define the functions of a trustee in bankruptcy.
3. What is a proxy and what are the rights of a proxy holder?
4. Discuss the statement "All joint holders are members of the company."
5. What do you understand by the term "a corporate representative"?

CHAPTER 7

1.   You are asked to plan the company's annual meeting. What considerations would you take into account in selecting the venue?
2.   What is the purpose of the pre-AGM board meeting?
3.   What are the prescribed contents of the annual report to shareholders?
4.   The annual meeting presents an opportunity for directors to foster and enhance the goodwill between management and members of the company. How may this be achieved?
5.   What is a class meeting and under what circumstances are class meetings held?

CHAPTER 8

1.   What are the requirements of a valid notice?
2.   Who is entitled to receive a notice of meetings?
3.   What is the purpose of a record date?
4.   Can a transferee who was unregistered at the record date attend the annual meeting? Discuss.
5.   The Act provides that shareholders entitled to attend a meeting may waive notice of the meeting, yet it has been held that shareholders attending a meeting cannot waive the right to adequate notice on behalf of those not in attendance. Discuss.
6.   Notice of a meeting of directors need not detail the matters to be discussed. True or false? Discuss.
7.   What is meant by "special business" and how must notice be given in respect of such business?
8.   What documents are required to be sent with the notice for an annual meeting of members?
9.   What are management proxy circulars and how do they differ from proxies?
10. Prepare a notice for an annual meeting of shareholders.

CHAPTER 9

1. What are the functions of:
   (a) Stewards
   (b) Scrutineers
2. Define what is meant by a quorum.
3. How would you summarise the functions, duties and powers of a chairman?
4. By what authority does the chairman of the board of directors preside over shareholders' meetings?
5. You are secretary to ABC Ltd whose annual meeting has been properly summoned but on the date specified a quorum is not present at the beginning of the meeting. The chairman has asked your advice as to what should be done in the circumstances. Please advise.

CHAPTERS 10 & 11

1. What are the rules applicable to procedural motions?
2. What is the priority of a motion to adjourn and in what manner, if any, may it be amended?
3. What is the purpose of a motion to close nomination?
4. What is an amendment and what effect does a motion of amendment have on the substantive motion being debated?
5. What are the rules applicable to withdrawal of motions?
6. Why must motions generally be framed in positive terms? Are there any exceptions to the rule?
7. What is the preferred method of dealing with several amendments to a single motion?
8. What is the difference between a motion and a resolution?
9. What are the general rules which apply to discussion at company meetings?
10. How may discussion be terminated?
11. It is the duty of the chairman and the company secretary to ensure that persons nominated for the office of director are properly qualified as required by the Act and the company's corporate instruments. What matters would you take into consideration in your process of evaluating the nominee?

CHAPTER 12

1.   Who is entitled to vote at company meetings?
2.   A matter has been brought before the board for consideration. Mr A, a director and shareholder of the company voted in favour of the proposition at the directors' meeting. It was subsequently decided that the issue should be referred to the shareholders. At the shareholders' meeting Mr A voted against the proposition. The chairman has asked for your advice as to whether Mr A's actions are legal. Discuss.
3.   Shares of a class which have no voting rights are nevertheless entitled to a vote under the Act. True or false? Discuss.
4.   Define a nominee.
5.   What are bearer shares?
6.   Is a proxy holder entitled to speak at company meetings?
7.   Describe the principal voting methods used at company meetings.
8.   Voting by ballot is always a secret vote. True or false? Discuss.
9.   What is a poll and how is it conducted?
10.   What do you understand by cumulative voting? Give an example.
11.   List the sequence of events and the process of planning and conducting a poll.
12.   The chairman has asked you to advise him whether he has a casting vote. How would you determine the matter?
13.   Briefly describe a voting trust agreement.

CHAPTER 13

1.   What are the characteristics of postal voting?
2.   What is the difference between a proxy and a postal vote?

CHAPTER 14

1.   If the meeting becomes unruly the chairman can adjourn the meeting and leave. Discuss.
2.   What care should be exercised in the expulsion of a member from the meeting?
3.   How would you cope with disorder at a meeting?
4.   Define defamation.

5. Should the ejection of a person from a meeting be minuted? Give reasons for your answer.

CHAPTER 15

1. Under what circumstances may a meeting be adjourned?
2. At an adjourned meeting additional items not on the agenda may be discussed. True or false? Discuss.
3. It is often convenient to postpone meetings if it is suspected that a quorum will not be present. True or false? Discuss.
4. What is the difference between adjournment and dissolution?
5. A motion to adjourn does not require a seconder. True or false? Discuss.

CHAPTER 16

1. Minutes are a narrative and report of the proceedings. True or false? Discuss.
2. What are the essential characteristics of good minutes?
3. Discuss the following statement: "The Secretary should always record reasons for decisions in the minute."
4. How may an individual shareholder enforce his rights?
5. Draft a set of minutes of a medium size private company covering the normal business of an annual meeting.

CHAPTER 17

1. Discuss the statement "Shareholders have rights but they have no duties."
2. List some of the rights which shareholders enjoy.
3. Shareholders may examine the minutes of directors' during normal business hours. True or false? Discuss.
4. Define the concept embodied in the term "good corporate governance".
5. A shareholder may ask as many questions as he wishes at company meetings. True or false?
6. Do you believe that shareholders have duties towards their companies? If so, list some of the duties.

CHAPTER 18

1. In whom is the management of a company vested?
2. What is a unanimous shareholders agreement? How does it affect the powers of management, if any?
3. Discuss the statement "Directors exercise their power and authority as individuals."
4. What are the purposes of by-laws?
5. Discuss the statement "A director who disagrees with a resolution passed by the board of directors is not bound by it."
6. A director is not bound by a resolution passed by the board in his absence. True or false? Discuss.
7. What is the purpose of board papers?
8. What formal business is usually conducted at the first board meeting?
9. Who is entitled to inspect minutes of a board meeting?
10. How are the first directors of a company appointed?

CHAPTER 19

1. Who is an officer in relation to a company?
2. Discuss the statement "Directors owe a duty of care to shareholders and employees of the company."
3. In what sense are directors agents of the company?
4. What do you understand by the statement "Directors stand in a fiduciary relationship to the company"?
5. What is the level of care, diligence and skill expected of directors in the exercise of their duty?
6 Are directors personally liable for mistakes or errors of judgement? Discuss.
7. What do you understand by the term "fraudulent trading"?
8. How may directors reach a formal decision without physically meeting as a board?
9. How is the chairman of the board of directors appointed?
10. Directors cannot delegate their authority. Discuss.

CHAPTER 20

1. Is the secretary an officer of the company?
2. Are there any requirements in the Act relative to the appointment of a company secretary to a public company?
3. The statement has been made that the secretary is the conscience of the board. Explain.
4. Is confidentiality an essential quality of a good corporate secretary? If so, why? If not, why not?
5. Which of the following statements is true or false? Explain.
    (a) The secretary determines corporate policy.
    (b) The secretary oversees the implementation of corporate policy as determined by the board.
6. If you say the secretary is an officer of the company, how can he/she then be described as a servant? Explain.
7. What are the general functions and duties of a company secretary?
8. What steps should a secretary take to ensure that matters awaiting consideration at the next meeting of the board are not overlooked?
9. Prepare a chairman's agenda for an annual meeting.
10. Describe the normal seating arrangements at a large shareholders' meeting.

GLOSSARY

Every profession, discipline or organised group has its own peculiar jargon. Corporate practitioners are no exception to this rule. This short glossary gives an interpretation of some of the more commonly used words or terms in company matters.

accept
To agree or concur. A factual matter is accepted, e.g. to accept the report.

adjourn
To defer to another day or time (but see *recess*).

adjourned meeting
The continuation of the meeting. An adjourned meeting is not a new meeting.

adopt
Such as to adopt recommendations or resolutions.

agenda
The order of business to be transacted.

amend
To change by adding, deleting or substituting words.

amendment
A motion to vary the motion under discussion.

approve
To adopt or to ratify. (See also *ratify*.)

ballot	A paper used by a voter to cast his vote especially at a poll.
chair/chairman	The chairman or presiding officer of the meeting. (If the presiding officer is female the term "Madam Chairman" should be used.)
committee	A group to whom a matter is referred for study action or recommendation.
conclude the meeting	To bring to an end after completion of its business.
confirm	To ratify or sanction a matter.
convene	To open a meeting.
debate	Discussion on a motion or proposition.
declaration	A decision or enunciation by the chairman.
have the floor	A person who has the floor has the right to speak.
lay on the table/table a matter	To open a matter for discussion. (In some institutions or jurisdictions it may mean to shelve the matter.)
majority	The largest number of those voting. Questions are usually decided by a majority of those voting for the resolution. This is termed a 'simple' majority, meaning that the motion was passed by the fact that more votes were cast for than against. Some motions may require passing by a 'special' majority, e.g. a two-thirds majority or a majority of say 75 percent of those voting, or of those present and voting, or of the membership. (Consult the corporate instruments.)

meeting	The assembly of eligible persons to transact business.
minority	The lesser number of those voting.
minutes	The official record of a meeting.
motion/main motion	A proposal put to the meeting for discussion and decision. (See also *substantive motion.*)
nominate	A procedural motion to propose someone for election to office.
per curiam	A phrase used, usually in the Court of Appeal, to distinguish the opinion of the whole Court from the opinion of any one judge.
poll	A method of voting. (The value of the vote being usually determined by the number of shares held.)
proposition	A suggestion usually not fully or formally phrased as a motion.
proxy	The agent or attorney of a shareholder. Also a signed document authorising someone (who may or may not be a shareholder depending on statute or the by-laws) to act on behalf of a shareholder at a meeting.
putting the question	Putting the motion to a vote. Sometimes a motion to vote immediately, usually proposed as follows: "That the question be now put".
quaere	It is a question, or, is open to inquiry.
question	The subject matter of a motion or discussion.
quorum	The minimum number of persons required to validly convene a meeting.

rank	A method to settle the precedence or priority of motions.
ratify	To confirm or make valid.
recess	A short interruption of a meeting — not an adjournment.
recognise	The chairman on recognising a person desirous of speaking gives him the floor, i.e. the right to speak.
reconsider	To review or reopen a matter previously dealt with.
repeal/rescind	To cancel or nullify a resolution.
resolution	A motion that has been properly passed by a meeting.
scrutineer	A clerk or teller appointed to assist in counting votes.
second the motion	A procedural motion to approve discussion of a proposition or motion by the meeting.
session/sitting	A sitting or session of a meeting. A lengthy meeting may be divided into two or more sessions.
shelve	To suspend any further discussion of a matter.
show of hands	A method of voting.
silent assent	General concurrence — no objection voiced.
sine die	Without a date being fixed.
special resolution	A resolution requiring more than a simple majority for passing.

state the question	A method by which the chair states and clarifies the motion before voting.
substantive motion	A concrete matter of business or a motion which was the subject of amendment.
table	See *lay on the table*.
terminate the meeting	See *conclude the meeting*.
unanimous	To pass with no dissenting vote.
unfinished business	Any matter left over from a previous meeting or session.
yield	A motion must yield to another of a higher rank. A speaker who has the floor must yield to another at the request of the chairman.

REFERENCES

We thank the authors, publishers and organisations listed below for their permission to reproduce excerpts from the publications so listed. Every effort was made on behalf of the author to obtain written permissions. Should any error or omission be brought to the attention of the author or publisher, appropriate steps will be taken to give proper credit.

Administrator (The Journal of the Institute of the Chartered Secretaries and Administrators). London: Institute of the Chartered Secretaries and Administrators.

Annual Meetings: Questions from Shareholders. U.S.A.: Coopers & Lybrand, 1988.

Bosh, Henry, *Corporate Practice and Conduct.* 2d ed. Melbourne: Australian Printing Group, 1993.

Butterworths' Company Precedents. 2d ed. London: Butterworths, 1967.

Canadian Corporate Secretary's Guide. Toronto, Canada: CCH, 1991.

Canadian Corporation Precedents. 3d ed. Toronto: Carswell, 1987.

CCH Directors' Manual. Ontario: CCH Canadian Limited, 1994.

Chant, James W, *Any Other Business: A Paper for Chairmen, Directors, Secretaries and Others.* Corporation of Secretaries. England.

Company Law by Robert Pennington. 2d ed. London: Butterworths, 1967.

Company Secretarial Practice. 19th supplement. London: ICSA Publishing, 1993.

Curry, T. P. E., and J. Richard Sykes, *The Conduct of Meetings.* 12th ed. London: Jordan & Sons, 1966.

Gore Browne on Companies. 42d ed. London: Jordon & Sons, 1972.

Hayton and Marshall Cases and Commentary on the Law of Trust. 9th ed. London: Sweet & Maxwell, 1991.

Head, F. D., F. P. Fausset, and H. A. R. Wilson, *The Corporation of Secretaries Manual of Secretarial Practice.* 7th ed. London: MacDonald & Evans, 1965.

In Touch Newsletter. (The Insurance Brokers Association of Ontario).

Kerr, M. K., and H. W. King *Procedures for Meetings and Organisations.* Toronto: Carswell, 1984.

Knepper, William E., *Liability of Corporate Officers and Directors.* 3rd ed., Indiana, U.S.A: The Allen Smith Company.

Maudsley & Burn's Trust & Trustees Cases & Material. 4th ed. London: Butterworths, 1990.

Palmer's Company Law. 23d ed. London: Stevensons and Sons, 1982.

Rajak, Harry, *Source Book of Company Law.* Bristol, London: Jordan & Sons, 1989.

Roberts, Dennis, *The Administration of Company Meetings.* London: ICSA Publishing, 1986.

Robert's Rules of Order, 9th ed. USA, Canada: Scott Foresman (division of Harper Collins), 1990.

Seitz, Steven Thomas, *Bureaucracy, Policy and the Public*. St Louis: C. V. Mostly, 1978.

Shaw, Sebag, and Dennis E. Smith, *The Law of Meetings*. 3d ed. London: MacDonald and Evans, 1956.

Shearman, Ian, S*hackleton on the Law and Practice of Meetings*. 7th ed. London: Sweet & Maxwell, 1983.

Stickler, Alan D., *Canada Business Corporations Act: An Accountant's Review of the Highlights*. 2d ed. Toronto: Butterworths, 1981.

Underhill and Hayton Law of Trust and Trustees. 15th ed. London: Butterworths, 1995.

Wainberg, J. M., *Company Meetings Including Rules of Order*. Toronto, Canada: Canada Law Book, 1969.

Wegenast, F. W., *The Law of Canadian Companies*. Toronto: Carswell, 1979.

Welling, Bruce, *Corporate Law in Canada*. Toronto: Butterworths, 1984.

INDEX

Numerical references are to numbered paragraphs of the main text

YOUR FEEDBACK

In this book I have shared with you some of the more fundamental ideas and the principles which govern the administration and conduct of corporate meetings.

The text was written with directors, shareholders, students and the corporate practitioner in mind.

I hope that in reading the text you have found useful nuggets of information. Please share your experience and your views with me. Write and tell me:

- What you like about the book.

- In what areas you would like to see the book expanded.

- What benefits you have derived from reading or using this book.

Your correspondence should be addressed to the author, c/o P.O. Box 618C, Bridgetown, Barbados, West Indies.

Thank You

G.W.P

www.ingramcontent.com/pod-product-compliance
Lightning Source LLC
Chambersburg PA
CBHW060425220326
41598CB00021BA/2296